William B. Philpot

England that is to be

And divers other Discourses served up with sundry Epiphoremata

William B. Philpot

England that is to be
And divers other Discourses served up with sundry Epiphoremata

ISBN/EAN: 9783743305793

Manufactured in Europe, USA, Canada, Australia, Japa

Cover: Foto ©ninafisch / pixelio.de

Manufactured and distributed by brebook publishing software (www.brebook.com)

William B. Philpot

England that is to be

ENGLAND THAT IS TO BE.

ENGLAND THAT IS TO BE.

AND DIVERS OTHER DISCOURSES, SERVED UP
WITH SUNDRY *EPIPHOREMATA.*

BY

WILLIAM B. PHILPOT, M.A., OXON.,

VICAR OF SOUTH BERSTED, BY BOGNOR, IN THE
COUNTY OF SUSSEX.

(*Author of "A Pocket of Pebbles, with a few Shells" (2nd
edition), "Pickings" from ditto in Bryce's Golden Series,
with Introduction by Dr. Grosart.—Essay on
Spenser in the Grosart Edition —Rhymes for
the Times, new and enlarged edition in
the press.*)

——◆——

[*The Sermons are reprinted from the "Church of
England Pulpit."*]

——◆——

LONDON :
MARSHALL BROTHERS,
3, AMEN CORNER, E.C.
AND
"CHURCH OF ENGLAND PULPIT" OFFICE,
160, FLEET STREET, E.C.

A.D. MDCCCLXXXVI.
All Rights Reserved.

HUMBLY DEDICATED
TO
OUR VICTORIAN DEMOCRACY.

"HOWBEIT WHEN HE, THE SPIRIT OF TRUTH, IS COME, HE SHALL GUIDE YOU INTO ALL THE TRUTH; FOR HE SHALL NOT SPEAK FROM HIMSELF; BUT WHATSOEVER THINGS HE SHALL HEAR, *THESE* SHALL HE SPEAK: AND HE SHALL DECLARE UNTO YOU THE THINGS THAT ARE TO COME."

CHRIST.

CONTENTS.

England that is to be.
The Times of England in the Hand of God.
Law the Forerunner of the Gospel.
The Witness of John.
The Name which is above every Name.
The Great Authority.
The Stiller of Tempests.
No part dark.
On the death of babes.
In *re* Rome *v.* England.
The Fast which God hath chosen.
The Goodwood Week.
On a Mission Week.
The Last Message of the President.
A Lesson from Archbishop Tait.
All Saints' Day.
Hymn for All Saints' Day.
The Wafer-God.
Substance of an Address at the Berlin Conference (Evangelical).
Part of an Address to a Literary Institute.
Claudia.
An Unspoken Speech.
Education and Permissive Bills.
Funeral Oration on Professor George Long.
Part of a Funeral Sermon on the late Earl of Beaconsfield.
Some Reflections at Election Time.

PREFACE.

Containing the Sketch of a Mode of preserving a State-Christianity without the violation of freedom in Religion.

As some of old time were wont to make a double-headed preface, first to the "noble," and then to the others, I will take a leaf out of their book. I will, however, reverse their order, and say first what I have to say to those of the caste of Thessalonica.

Into this glass none such will purposely look with a view to personal reflection. To them my word will be a βέλος ἠλίθιον. If any care not for the advance of himself, so neither can he truly care for the growth of his kind. If any man knows so little of himself and his defects, so little of the standard of morals, as to be careless of the Christ-nature—my soul hath no pleasure in him, nor his in anything he will find here. Any solicitude which I feel for him he would resent as an impertinence. So all I have to say to him is this:—I should feel heartily obliged to him if he would peruse this volume, in order by his strictures, if he be a scholar, to further my study of our mother-tongue, for which I confess with him a most filial regard. I should be further indebted to him if, being of a logical turn, he would take the kindly trouble to clear me of any fallacy in any argument which I have herein used; or if he would detect for me anything disproportionate, self-contradictory, or the like. This should be within his compass, except indeed the lower strata of his mind be also too deeply disordered by those convulsions whereby his spirit has, by hypothesis, been laid so desolate. I fear there is nothing more that he can do for me. As to the great truths themselves on which I have loved to dilate—the unwise do not consider these. " Ye fools, when will ye understand ? " " Behold, ye despisers, and wonder and perish." If any such, however, not yet having done to death their spiritual element, are still open to a preacher's warning; or if they take any interest whatever in morals, and in the destinies of this pleasing, anxious humanity, let them give ear to our Master's words —" Come unto Me, learn of Me, and I will give you rest." These I would beg them to turn over in their minds, and to judge for themselves whether it be not a perilous risk to do despite to the Spirit of Grace, and to trample under foot that Guide in human affairs, who, as we have reason to believe, is most able, in the least costly way, to keep themselves and their nation from being trampled under the inevitable wheels of His Kingdom. I would in all humility submit to them the things here said about Jesus and His Faith— remaining, with affectionate regards, theirs ever faithfully, W. B. P.

To the children of that kingdom I have much that I would say—far more than I can say here, or anywhere. Ye beloved fraternal and sisterly souls, though you may find here some views of our inheritance which may be new—what harm, tell me, need there be in that? If you do not want them for your own soul's health—if it be only round the *lower* regions of your life that the old superstitions hang with their distorting hazes, while the eternal sunshine settles on your head—why then, unless you love light to be all round you from base to crown of your being, you can safely wait, as far as I know, to have your visual ray purged by the Father of Lights. All your wood, hay, and stubble will soon be burnt away, and you will rub your blessed hands with untold delight as you watch the blaze. But meanwhile, I beseech you, yield me kindly credit, as we have a common wish to rule our conduct by the same plummet and to live on the square, for desiring to help, in some humble way, to the building up of our Church in her most holy faith ; and so, pray add your hopes to mine, that these few bricks of ours may be found not to be very irregular, but blameless, tetragonal, and meet for the Master's use.

These discourses, these thoughts, these ways of stating truth, having been already judged profitable for instruction in behaviour by our homiletic Doctor who has carried *The Church of England Pulpit* to its majority, it was "borne in upon me" to ask him of his grace to allow a few hundred more copies thereof to be struck off before the type was distributed, so that collected they might form this little volume, and be spread like a compost of dead leaves over a few more garden-beds of the time.

The short arms of this book do not profess to embrace the whole body of Christian doctrine ; nor is my glass arranged so as even to catch the contemplation of any set field of heavenly truth. Each sower of the seed of the new life has, I suppose, his special ways of carrying out the great work entrusted to him, and it is my hope that some of this seed may be suited to this land and this season.

Does any reader imagine that anyone who possesses, combined with the folly of publishing what he has written, the sense to write (I mean in the mere way of arranging articulate words in his vernacular)—does any reader think that such an

individual can contemplate a contingency so
remote as that of paying his printer's angel with
the proceeds? Why there is hardly any greater
triumph to be witnessed in the spiritual world than
this :—that the desire of utterance, so human, sometimes so pure, goes on its way in spite of the fact,
so well known to writers, that generally speaking,
nothing fingerable, nothing circulative, no stamped
guarantee, no imaged and superscribed metallic
bullion ever will come of it, except to those busy
much-exercised fellow-mammals who truck and
barter for his brains. And I for one certainly wish
all health and happiness to those laborious persons
who have interpreted my signs, and recomposed
my proofs, if they can accomplish the further feat
of making an honest penny out of W. P. Joy be
with them if by any money-gathering they can
turn into the channel of their own domestic comfort the honey-gathering of such shining hours as
Providence grants me, before I step up, pray
God, into the land where all things not worthy of
remembrance are happily forgotten. With most
of us it is of course *at nos non nobis*, and in return
for helping me to say my say in black and white,
that kindly and skilful angel aforesaid (to raise him
with my euphemism) is heartily welcome to far more
than from me at least he is ever like to gain. But
something too much of this *dulce desipere*.

There can be nothing *very* arrogant in that man
setting forth his teaching, who forty years ago was
commissioned by his Bishop, his Sovereign, and the
Head of the Church, to the cure of souls, to the
healing as well as to the care of them. Let me,
however, here break off with a sigh. Ah me!
What are men saying of our new Democracy?
Their first servant of the Crown should in due course
fulfil his highest function, and should, as now and
aforetime, prayerfully lay hands on, and carefully

pick from the choicest gentlemen of all ranks of England, men who are learned, tried, popular, and skilled to bless us. These again in their turn should examine, choose, and lay their hands on a kindly, cultured band of self-devoting officers, to be ministers in things spiritual to the whole people, without a shilling of salary coming out of the pockets of the poor. Alas, and thrice alas, to think that it can be felt by any to be within the bounds of possibility that the Commons of England are ready to deliver to the winds, to cast into the English Channel, this finest, this holiest patrimony in all the world—to wit, this patronage by which in God's name they now commission me and my 20,000 fellow-labourers in the Saviour's vineyard to help them, each and all, so to pass through things temporal that they finally lose not the things eternal! But I, for my part, will not believe that our old rural scholars, now our dearest neighbours and friends, will thus lift up their heel against us—*if they know it.* Aye, there's the rub. *Oh fortunati agricolæ—sua si bona nôrint.* I will rather believe that this steady current of strong country air, which always brings fresh revival to the body and soul of the nation, will only bosom out the white sails of our good old Ship, which, as the country-people know better than any, has done and is doing all it well can to bear them with good cheer to the Haven where they would be. So let that sigh, which I broke off to sough, rest in this hope.

I am well aware, as I was about to say, that the Press teems with our clerical forthflowings; and that the shelves, especially of publishers, run over with books, more voluminous than luminous, which some of their authors had reason, far more than I here can have, to hope would be acceptable. Oh, pitiful hallucination!

Your author feels his whole soul alive with truth; he feels certain parts of truth come freshly to himself; he is perhaps generous and unselfish, not caring to devour alone the morsels which may have been foraged for him by the ravens of his solitude. The warnings of the masters of the market either do not touch him at all, or are at any rate lost upon him.—He is like a certain little preacher whom I knew of some years ago. It was the habit of that excellent man to go on and on, with his head in the air. His eyes he was wont to close; and once the hour grew dark and late. The pigs wanted feeding, and first one and then another hearer slipped out, till none "sat under him" save his strapping Highland housekeeper. She also, wanting her tea, at length went up the pulpit stairs, and plucked him by his gown. She did not "share the good man's smile"; for the indignant prophet turned upon her, as though she were an emissary of the hour and power of darkness, and shouted in her ear, his eyes still closed, "Woman, I must prache whether they will hearre or whether they will forrbairre." To which she replied "But, ma gude sair, there's naebodie to hearre, and naebodie to forrbairre either"; and forthwith tucking him beneath her stalwart arm, she bore him off down the pulpit stairs, locked the church door, and took him home to tea. Well; so it is with some of the rest of us. We print, and print, and close our eyes to the fact that there are none to read us;—and here I am giving you another instance of delusion and fatuity—I hope you will not add incoherency.

Yet I would persuade myself and any readers whom I may find, that this volume puts forth some ideas of its own, and some of the old ideas in a form somewhat new.

It is with me a small matter as to the priority

or posteriority, with respect to other people, of the γένεσις of any of my own concepts; but for the sake of the date of the main idea here put forth, rather than of its channel, I take leave to say that, to whomsoever else it may secretly or in any form have come, it never struck along *my* mind till 10.35 p.m., on Feb. 9th, Anno Domini 1873. I sat preparing a sermon on the religious aspects of geology. In reading with that view Hugh Miller's " Footprints of the Creator," I came to the following words at p. 14, " There are however beliefs in no degree less important, etc., etc., which seem wholly incompatible with the development hypothesis." I sprang up and said, " So help me God—Christ Himself, in direct descent, is the development in Nature's history of the last type of Existence—the fulness of the Godhead, so far as He can be personally visible —in fact the final Flower of all Life and Being." And had not the hour been late, I verily felt as if I should have raised the house, or sent up a shout that should shiver to the tingling stars. I only held my breath to catch the full inflow of the idea.

From that time forth, I have viewed in my simple way theology and life in that light; I have found at every turn of my thoughts difficulties vanish right and left, as when the curtain of mist is rent and dissipated before the Alpine heights, which it had hidden; I have talked with many men of keen thought and of holy mind, and by none has it been gainsaid. Many according to their perception and candour have rejoiced with me.*

---

* If any psychological enquirer should care to note this incident—and as far as I know nothing is more interesting than to note, especially in children, the manner of the breaking of an idea into flower—I may further state that the 9th of February happened to be a date which fifteen years before had brought me face to face with the verities

Be that how it may, as my studies and the multitudinous wavelets of twelve years of reflection have

---

of the Eternal World more vividly than any occasion before or since, and it was naturally with me an anniversary of kindred insight. There is another thing connected with it, which, to me at least, seems not devoid of interest. Asking me to preach, my friend George Arbuthnot of Arundel said, "The lesson is from the 1st of Genesis." Mrs. Emberson, a lady of remarkable intellect and excellence, was present. She said, "*Remember geology.*" Now Mrs. Emberson had some years before been left a widow. A wife's occupations being gone, she had felt unusually lonely. She was sitting thus one day in utter distress, not knowing what to do with herself. She relates that at this juncture a voice from the unseen but not unheard world, said to her these two words, "*Study geology.*" She did not even know the import of the word, and she only learned it by taking down a dictionary. She was not disobedient to the heavenly order; and, as a simple matter of fact, soon found in that study a release from her mental despondency, and the quickening all round of her great powers; so that she has ever since been the clergyman's right-hand-woman in the Schools and in all good works. She has become the useful friend of men like Etheridge, Leo Grindon, and, going further afield, of Schliemann, calling her home "Troy House." She speaks of Andromache as an old acquaintance, and wears for a brooch one of Agamemnon's shirt buttons. I mention the above traits to show how sound and wide and pleasant this excellent lady is, and how little likely to be the victim of vague voices. *Quæ cum ita sint*, I have, in the light of the thought which in sequence came to myself, looked on her charge to "*remember geology*" as being an echo of the monition which had come to her. So that also from this point of view I reckon that there was something which came *divinitus* to me that night. If any light-minded reader regards the whole thing as nothing, or if any one regards nothing as anything, and if your psychologist sniffs at this narrative,— well, let it pass—for I don't press it, and perhaps I have cast what is of no price before those who are not porcine. Pray let my genial reader pardon this little piece of self-consciousness, which I find I have been here betraying. But the idea was, I assure you, to me so new and so delightful. Perhaps everybody has been familiar with it ! If so, how very unkind, that nobody has yet given us the benefit of it !

caught the illumination of the light which I saw, I have set down—after my own poor manner (which I cannot well help now), as in my little book "A Pocket of Pebbles"—the workings of my mind; and hundreds of these lie ready for arrangement, and, I hope, for offering abroad, as occasion may serve me for some sort of composition of them. It forms, however, the basis of many of these discourses, or gives them colouring. I once put it forth before "the Literary Institute at Chichester," on December 20th, 1876, in a lecture called "The place in Being filled by the New Man." But it fell stillborn in that city, and those good lads doubtless buried my ἔκτρωμα on the north side of the cathedral—though I have not observed the foundations in any way affected. I have not approached the subject through the same lines by which Dr. Henry Drummond has since done; but as soon as ever a fraternal soul, very much to be revered, and omnivorous of good books, told me, soon after the day of its issue, that that book had interested him more than almost any he had ever read, and that I should find in it what would please me, I read it with avidity, and found to my delight that, while I was lying in my impotence on the edge of this pool of printers' ink, yon priest of science had plunged in, and that his book was one whose special lines of inquiry my idea had in course comprised and necessitated. Indeed, I look for the genial labours both of many who are, and of many who as yet are not. I may add, by way of forestalling what I hope to say more fully, however inadequately, that my view will be seen to involve, not only a new commentary on all Scripture, but a rearrangement and structural enlargement of educational Legislation. And in this following out of my idea into its logical sequences I claim, by your leave, the fatherhood of a new policy.

As to the view itself, the late beloved Dean Stanley said that, in some general form, it was held more or less by most thoughtful persons. Of this there can be little doubt. But the nut of the matter is, that, when St. Paul spoke of the "New Man," he meant precisely what he said : — a man who, while a man, was a distinct and absolute novelty on the planet; a new kind, a new species—whose generation who could then declare? Jesus, I beg you to observe, was not an abnormal moral haze, not a mere bright exhalation, not a chance forth-playing of the wholly Unintelligible—but He was a natural, if also a supernatural, *PHENOMENON*. He came in the course of nature, though, like every lower species when freshly born, He was of a species thitherto unknown in Nature. He was in perfect order, and came forth from the Unseen in order to perfection. He was as new in the highest world of the spiritual life, as if, in the lower and already perfected conformation of the bodily life, some unexpected set of organs were to have come to us; were to have come, not by way of monstrosity or *lusus* (though your scientists, not having noted it in their experience, would at first have called it so), but as a new generation and a fresh departure, a further blossoming of the material *physique*. For take the greatest men that we have had, and it may be shown that, however remarkable the wisdom and goodness of Socrates and the rest, however wide the play of the imagination of a Shakespeare, however loudly, before or after contemporary or *post mortem* examination, men may have cried, "Ye are our heroes, ye are our demigods, ye are our gods," yet it has never occurred to any sane person to maintain that these good people were more than specimens of existing humanity, or that they were giving start to a new type of Being. Their virtues and their powers were no more than notable specimens of what men knew already. It may be shown, however, that the records about JESUS, while they betoken a MAN—betoken One specifically differenced. These records after all must be allowed, in the mere residuum of the most destructive criticism, to have referred to *some one*. And I am content here to claim from anthropologists, and from students of Being and of Man, a closer attention than, methinks, has hitherto been bestowed, to that particular Individual therein described. The consideration of that Man has hitherto been confined to those who love Him, or hate Him, for His own sake: but I should be thankful to be shown any writing wherein a serious thinker has set himself to make out *where, in the growth of Being, the Jesus comes*. If any competent persons, with open eyes, desiring Truth and loving Light, will bend themselves to this, they will find that those records, of what trusty people saw and heard, do but hold up to their gaze as natural historians the very Phenomenon which their studies must have led them to look for—namely the Omega and Bloom of Being. Those who see the beauty of the theory of development—if that can any longer be called a theory which at once commends itself to all who have a love of Order—will infallibly find the crown and consummation of Personal Nature in Jesus; nor will they need to remind themselves of the Stagirite and his dicta, when he says οὐδὲν εἰς ἄπειρον—"Nothing makes for the limitless"; ἡ φύσις οὐδὲν μάτην ποιεῖ—"Nature does nothing to no use or purpose." And when they come to *word* their discoveries, let them, if they can, find language more brilliant, and let them make, if they can, statements more brightly to the point, than those of the clear-minded, clear-hearted witnesses who looked in the face and clung to the side of this New Man.

As for leaps and bounds of growth—that is, whether that which now is, is what it is in virtue of, or after having passed through, grades, discernible or not by any eye, human or otherwise—all this does not in the smallest degree affect the heart of the business. That is to say, the essential dignity of the Christ-Flower can in no way be impaired if there *were*, or had been, any blessed eyes that could see, lips that could say, or pens that could write any series of infinitesimal shades, realised or not, phenomenal or merely theoretical, by which the *eozoon Canadense* has been creeping up until Being bloomed in Him. All this, however intensely interesting, in no way, I say, affects the fact that, when the Christ transpired, from anywhere you please—say, from the abysmal Bosom of the Personality which, as we take it, is immanent in the Universe—He was sufficiently new in this embryonic race of the first instalment of Man, to be called THE SECOND ADAM. The mind of Paul had never been enlightened, nor perplexed, by Darwin; while the Supreme Intelligence of the New Man Himself was bent on far other business than to question the modes by which the Father and the Ages had "only-begotten" Him. But it seems, as knowledge now stands, ere it vanish away, to be quite requisite for thinkers to divide and to define. While protesting, in his ironical manner, against there being any division in the nature of things, Aristotle himself finds it convenient to contemplate the human subject piecemeal. So there seems to be also here something more manageable for human uses, if—laying aside the idea, destructive of all scientific classification, of the possibility of first imagining and then proving all infinitesimal and unbroken *additamenta* in the course of Being—we regard the Master of Christendom on a broad view as a New Kind of Man—not a breach in the order of things, but as a marked advance and a healer of order that was being broken—broken by the constitution of the kind of man that came before Him, of that Adam, who, perfect in his own type, but not of the perfect type, could not in all things say "Thy will be done." The power of practically saying this was reserved to be the differential mark of that consummate species of humanity, which, in its first specimen, could say " I and my Father are one ; " and who could pray to His Father (John xvii. 9-11) to keep His new type from any admixture of the elements of the effete ; to keep them *one*, *even as He and the Father were one.* Christ, by whatever stages, grades, or shades (seen or unseen, known or unknown) His nature in the course of the ages may have reached this altitude, *is who He is* — an identical proposition for which there is authority — though faithless students from their *bassi lidi*, their low shores of common understanding, will not yet, with Coleridge, regard Him as " Reason, in its highest form of Self-affirmation." Christ, I say, in so far forth as to the purest of us He can as yet appear, is a historical and scientific Phenomenon, whatever more He is and may be found to be. It does not affect His knowable, exemplary, and generative Self, if, in the upright-growing, heaven-shooting line of Semitic manhood, or even in any of the side-shoots of the human family, this or that Prophet, as Moses and Elias (for whom He appears to have had close regard and distinct preference), or any other light of Europe, Asia, Africa or America, may have come more or less near to Him in nature, or evidenced any preliminary traits of His finished humanity. Indeed Christ learned to know who He Himself was, and what His mission was, by feeding on David, and the literature of His pre-destined nation. This race was

well called the chosen nation, a peculiar people.
How could Jesus ever have become what he was by
feeding on Homer, Æschylus, or Vergil? It could
only be with the sweet Psalmists of Israel that on
His Galilean heights He could "open His mouth
and draw in His breath," and find ecstatic world-
saving delight in coming to do, and in drawing all
humanity to know and do, *the Will of God.*
Besides, whatever may be said of the blessed
Buddha, or of any other great local preachers and
teachers, and however high, holy, and powerful they may have been, and however "the Desire
of all nations" may have budded in them, they
have none of them been such, none of them have
exhibited such all-embracing traits of perfect manhood, that cultured civilisations, all and singular
through all time and through the whole round
world, could have found in any of *them* their only
hope of escaping decadence and decay. There is
obviously in Christ that which will keep pace with,
or rather give pace to, all the progress of mankind.
As far as the east is from the west, so wide may be
His influence on "every man that cometh into the
world." Look at our Western Anglo-Saxon race.
What peoples could be more different in nature
and habits than we and the old populations of the
Levant? yet what difference does it make to the
good we are gaining from Him, that Christ was an
Oriental? Antique, He can never be antiquated.
So far from being effete, in what community, however narrow, have His principles, as Arthur
Stanley used to ask, come fully and fairly into
play? There doubtless has been, and is,
much in many national and popular religions and
codes of morals, which, like the Apocryphal books,
might be profitable and interesting even to Christian
peoples. But what teacher in all history had
that in him which could have saved the world?

while the New Man, if we knew no more of Him than His prayer, His last great "table-talk," and the scene on Calvary, brought to light a Nature which can renew every national and individual nature that will come and find lodgement and life in its branches. Verily He is the Sun of Righteousness that lights this planet, wherever there is growth of men and seed of heart and human life. It is clear that England and all other States can find, and therefore ought to find, their highest hopes realised in Christ, *if they set honest men upon the quest.*

Nor, let me add—to pursue what I was saying—would it affect the utility of Christ's survival, except from the aspect of delay, if it could be shown that a thousand Christs had been overlaid in their infancy. Good and great babes, children, youths, and men, both in the mental and spiritual region, have been lost to the world in the growth of this race; and Jesus Himself was early driven back into His bright ideal, though he had many things yet to say to us. So, there need be no oversetting shock to morals, sadder still though it were to think of, if we were to be told by any who could know, that the Christ some few centuries ago was only permitted by the Father's laws to effect His entrance and find a brief space for life and speech on this globe, after the failure of an infinite number of approximate organisms alike delicate and fragile. Till now all these questions have been regarded as forbidden and pertaining exclusively to what has been exclusively called theology; but now I suggest, from the standpoint of natural history, that those who reject the theological* approach,

---

* In his splendid speech at the Congress, Canon Westcott has just put forth the state of the case in the best manner from that standpoint. The voice of Wace, however, was sadly missed this time ; for, alas, he was sick. He also is a

shall at least come and contemplate the Christ from this other point of view. They cannot deny this to what they are bound to regard as a Phenomenon, and we require that they shall give an honest answer to His own question, " What think ye of Christ? Whose son is He?" Of what antecedents was He the Consequent? To what, in David's Son and Lord, has the long result of Time brought us? Those to whom I appeal say He was no more than a *man*. Good ; then let them be pleased to note, so far as outside His Faith they may and can, what manner of man He was. Why is the Christ not to have the same advantage of being studied in the way of analysis as other human natures? That Person surely is no less a Phenomenon, but more, who has made such and so great changes, clean against our debased wills, in the fortunes of our race. If the Christ has done so much to improve behaviour, to create personal comfort, and to better the condition of States, when all mankind—except a few resolute souls, faithful to Him even unto death, and going upon their inward and spiritual convictions—have taken His contrary part, how much more good, I ask, may not our nation gain from Christ for the advancing of our civilisation, nay, *the saving of our national Exchequer*, if something more be done ? What if, over and above all the enthusiastic, but in some sort unordered and unscientific (not to say sometimes superfluous) efforts of those who are inspired with the full assurance of their faith—advice, as to the wisest practicable modes of keeping Christian knowledge alive in our land, be taken of a chosen body of our best and highest students ? These, of course, must be students of anthropology, of morals,

---

guide from his high ground to them that sit in darkness, or wander in the mazes of their ignorance of divine order and law.

of the most advanced life, and also persons acquainted with the failures, difficulties, and needs of the State, and empowered to formulate and interpret statistics of the elements at work among the population for evil and for good. I would humbly implore that a body summoned for this very thing be gathered round the Sovereign Lady of our Democracy. Now that Her most religious and gracious Majesty finds Her Christ being ousted from Her Parliament, from the schools of Her sweet children, and from top to bottom of Her realm, it is time, methinks, that she call her best and wisest round her. To these she may well say: "My people owe much to that just Man. Ye must not lightly hang about my neck this millstone, and drown us all in the depth of that sea. While men fight about those mysteries of His nature which none can understand, all men understand and know that He is doing my poor sinners good, and would fain do us more, if we would let Him gather our children and our people together under His wing. Search, therefore, oh my wise men, and see what there is in the nature and teaching of Jesus, which all men may understand and agree to act upon, so that we may not thus offend our little ones." Then these wise men would of course speedily prove to the satisfaction of Her Majesty and of her Houses, what solid, unimagined, and unique benefits would necessarily accrue from the dibbling-in of this seed of the New Man. As for the mysteries of that most blessed Nature, these they would agree for the present to leave to the Church, the sects, and to all and any private students. Such agencies would always be working, not less but more fervently on their own lines. These would make ready, and hold ever open, the old highways for the constant advances of a people, who would all go under a sound, however partial, training. For under the recommendations of our wise men of the West, the Democracy, rendered less timid by time and use, and freed from all suspicions of priestcraft, would beyond doubt follow on to know more of a Guide so valuable and so economical. The common people hear Jesus gladly. Meanwhile the State would see its way to stamping on all children of England, gentle and simple, His principles of behaviour and His modes of making themselves and one another comfortable and harmless, right-minded and good—in a word—fellow-citizens growing to their heavenly perfection. If any one says all this is in the air, I only beg to say he does not know what he says, while I know what I say. If men in power decline this challenge, all honest men will say that they go upon a dishonest, illogical, and cowardly policy—or rather on no policy at all, for with them for our guides our πόλις will soon be ἄπολις.

Whatever, then, may be said as to the newness of the species of the Blessed Jesus, and whether this has ever by any been gone into or dwelt on before, I know not, nor care. To me at least the idea flashed with sudden newness, as I dare say many old ideas have done and may again, but as to this practical upshot of it, I believe, with all due and no undue diffidence—certainly with all gratitude to the Giver of all good—I hold it to be so far mine, that I hereby freely make a present of it to the Conservative or to any other non-destructive Democracy, if they can find a statesman fit to work it out. I once broached it to one of our foremost Liberal statesmen, and after having for the space of an hour, "over the walnuts and the wine," brought his greatest guns to bear on my position, said, when I asked him his final view of it, "We shall see this come about before we die." Yet he was neither so young nor so unwise that he could be taunted as "sanguine." I found a Tory politician, of great name, say much the same only the other day. My late lamented patron of Canterbury, a statesman wise, if any other, in a long summer afternoon in the woods of Addington, dwelt upon the idea with recurring interest, the only immediate difficulty with his Grace being the finding of the wise men. Such also was at one time the preliminary obstacle with a master in Christendom, the point of whose lash can still flick our foibles from his home across the Atlantic. But, as I urge, this difficulty falls before the very nature of my proposal. It were a strange thing, and a needless admission of national helplessness, if a plan which would nullify " the religious difficulty " be paralysed thereby on the outset. Such a difficulty need no more be found in the choice of the wise men than in acting upon their report. For, be it noted that, if the highest nature can be proved to go upon the lines of known, or knowable law — then there is not only no reason why the whole population should *not* be, but every reason, domestic, social, and political, why all the children of the State *should* be, taught at least the main part of the truth as it is in Jesus. This will get rid, at a stroke, as I have said, of all that old so-called "religious difficulty"; for the religion of Jesus will herein and hereby cease forthwith to be a matter simply for the battling of private consciences, from which the easy-going statesman can now stand aloof on the score of what is called "religious freedom;" and it will become far more evidently necessary that our children should learn the main truths which concern the highest welfare of the rational mammal, than that they should have their school walls hung with pictures of reptile and *fungus*.

The practical upshot, then, of what I propose is, I repeat, that a Royal Commission, sitting in permanence and always adding to its numbers, be appointed, to arrange the limits within which it may as yet be possible for this *scientia scientiarum* to play. The Churches and sects will of course all still go on upon their own special lines, as freedom of conscience and their sense of the ridiculous shall allow; but meanwhile our children will all henceforth be put in possession, irrespectively of their parents' "religious" views, of the highest laws of nature and the laws of the highest Nature. This scientific teaching will correct and co-ordinate, and by degrees eliminate all the private follies of mere religionists; will teach England and all other sincere and intelligent communities who may go and do likewise—without any of the confusing mysteries of dogma, or of *quasi*-dogma, whether false or true—all that is most necessary for *the regulation of conduct;* and probably in the end, as the freer conception of the Christ-nature shall grow to the measure of the stature of His fulness, will form the basis of the Church of the Future; and a very sane Church that will be—so far as it goes, and the farther probably the saner. Nor do I think that it will eventually differ very widely in eternal matters from that which all truly thoughtful members of all Churches would on reflection even now admit ; for it will obviously be based upon plain Christian records as well as upon the clearly ascertained and fairly formulated facts of life, and on the needs of humankind; the more so, because it will be found that the *cost* of crime varies inversely, and the welfare of the community directly, with the prevalence and dominance of the Christian type. Moreover if the State undertakes and carries out this, there will be a less devastating shock, and a less crucial disaster inflicted on the morals of this country, if eventually our beloved old Church, having done her grand part in saving Christianity up to this revivification of truth, shall then, but not till then, be vivisected from the body politic. *Tarda sit illa dies, et nostro senior ævo.* If any of your young statesmen be in search of a Radical policy for his new Conservatism, I, with kind regards, hereby present him with this; and if he wants to be instructed therein more perfectly and likes to ask me, I will help him out with it, feebly enough, but as best I may.

A word or two more on this, at the risk perhaps of repetition, though the little that I can say here is obviously but a preliminary canter over the course. Like every other science, so this most proper study of mankind has been pioneered by the intuitive. Perhaps it is right and natural that Theology in her majestic bearing and solemn paces should be the last to leave this field for any other. Nor will she in fact ever leave it. She will hold her own grounds of intuition also, into whatever fresh fields or new pastures she may invite her votaries to wander. It was not to be expected that she should too readily subject herself and her great Phenomenon to analysis—at least till the minds of men, practised on lower ground, should have learned how to approach that work, not only with reverence and godly fear, but with humble courage and tried skill. Paul said that God had in those last days spoken to man by His Son, whom He had made heir of all things; and so we may feel that only at this juncture of this last era are we able to gaze with steadier reason on Him through whom God speaks, to find *in what sense* He is Heir of all things, and to note how His Germ has lain all along in the Father's purpose, and has advanced with all advancing phenomena through the making and rounding off of the world and its inmates. It is now at length open for us, of course under vast limitations, to trace, by the processes of a more real knowledge, *in what manner* the unseen Father was to fulfil Himself in visible Being. In Jesus the wheel of phenomenal Personality has come full circle. When He said, "I have finished the work which Thou gavest Me to do"; "the things concerning Me have an end"; "I am no more in the world, but these are in the world, and I come to Thee;" when He exclaimed at the last, "It is finished,"—He meant, as we may with grateful awe and profoundest reverence interpret Him, "I have planted the seed of the New Man in the old humanity". Not, I pray you to mark, that men of the old type, of whom (to save *petitio principii*) my Commission must in part be formed, will be able to appreciate, admit, and recommend to our Sovereign for the use of the nation the complete Christ. Our beloved scientific friends must not expect that they will be able, with eyes bleared over their microscopes, and lost in open-mouthed wonder at things creeping innumerable, to contemplate unflinchingly the full beatific vision, and to exclaim with one voice, "This is God's beloved Son, this is the fulness of the Godhead bodily, hear ye Him." But I maintain that, short of this, a gathering of wise light-seeking men ought to be available, who will have the insight to note and the candour to record that these Christian principles are at least too economical to be neglected by any open-minded State. For I am ready to meet those who care for no higher object, and to stake the value of this proposal on the mere *saving of cost to the rate-payer and the tax-payer*. The Commission must be a standing one, and the probability is that they will eventually find themselves drawing closer to the intuitionists. These will, as I have said, maintain all their genuine, fuller, truths till the nation comes round to be ready for them. For instance, if our select body find reason to discover that the Christ has traits of a new kind of man, they may admit that it is possible and probable that He would come in a new way, do strange things, possess secrets of the highest nature, and close his fruitful career in a manner unprecedented. As with philosophy, so with theology. The Apostles said "Yes," science said "No.'" Now in turn science will be found to support the Apostolic affirmation.

But I have been led on further than I meant—away from my immediate work of endeavouring to claim a reading for this little volume.

This is an attempt to scatter some of the ripened seeds of that Flower of Humanity. I have named this collection of discourses after the subject of the first, because, though most of them have a personal and domestic bearing, yet it is the nation, the community, the State, made up as it is of families and persons, which we thus try to lead up to its ideal through the bettering of its component parts.

What we ministers aim at is, that the Christ lifted up and looked at by us all, flowering among us and shaking out His life-giving anemophilous seeds to all the Divine winds, blow they where they list, may cause all soils that catch them, and all souls that are coloured and made fragrant by His farina, to flower and bloom in all their varieties for the richness and beauty of the Master's garden. Our part is that of bees flitting about with this supernal meal whithersoever we may.

May the Spirit of God and of His beloved Son—Who was in the Alpha, and Who is the Omega of His design in Being, the last kind of Phenomenon which He has to show—that Heir of all things, Who

C

potentially and by design was in the beginning of the forthrolling of life—may that Spirit of the Universe, and herein especially of humanity, bless to all honest and good hearts any good seed which they may chance to catch from this seed-lip of mine.

As for our beloved Church in these realms, unto her, as to each of us, must surely be said this old proverb—"Know thyself." And upon this must follow for her, as for each of her members, "Know thy Master." These two sayings are correlatives. We can only know ourselves by knowing our Standard, and only change ourselves for the better by reaching up to our Model. It is obvious that if our Church would live in clear and wholesome unison with the nation, and not as a monstrous abstraction—(and it can only be a *quasi*-abstraction, for so long as the good conduct and well-being of the citizens is her *raison d'être*, the abstraction can only be nominal except in the matter of her endowments—and even in the case of her vivisection, it is the citizens, after all, who will have to find home, food, and raiment for their ministers, and this will always give a concrete form to her existence)—if, I say, the Church would live vigorously and healthily, the ancient chambers of her palatial dwelling must be overhauled, swept, ventilated, supplied with water from the purest wells, lit with the last electric lights, garnished suitably to this age, and for ever to be garnished again suitably to each progressive age, and made always as meet as may be for the Spirit of the new and growing life. In fact, that same Spirit is always tendering for this great contract. Nor is it enough—as indeed our clergy have begun to feel—to go on battling about postures and vestures. The whole matter must be gone into upon deeper issues. And this must be done by men of place, name, and weight, and not of mere theological colour. Solitary thinkers may say their say, and so they best deliver their own souls. Their words, where they have the luck to gain a hearing, may go far to form that public opinion which is necessary for English action. But this is slow work (as Blackley, alas, is finding in England, though happily no longer in Germany, with his splendid idea for "National Providence"); and the foundations of civil life are being thrown down in the interim. The steeds of the chariot of the Master are starving while the grass of national sentiment is growing. Both the priest-party, orthodoxically and methodically mad, and the sects, scoliodoxically bewildered, are all this while, too many of them, seeking, no doubt unconsciously, to palm off upon these poor sheep of the people all manner of follies, and, amidst all their excellence and energy, breaking multitudinous heads with their precious balms—sorry householders, bringing forth from their meagre treasuries superstitions new as well as old, while the old supply keynotes and directions for the new. Take only the rampant conceptions in vogue as to the Atonement and Sacraments—nay, the confusion of persons and false divisions of eternal entities. I do not say that holy men, however silly, are to be gagged and branded: it were "a consummation devoutly to be wished" that, however imbecile, there were more of them in the market-place; but what I mean is, that it is high time—as anyone must see who watches which way the currents are working—that the pillars of the Church, who seem to be somebodies, the high-standing Memnons, who ought to be catching the earliest lights, should chant clearly forth what the great reconciling truths mainly and really are. These they should pour in clear and unmistakable English into the ears of the people; so that it shall be the citizens' own fault, and not by default of their spiritual and mental ministers, who are appointed to prevent this very thing, if the multitudes still blunder and stumble on among the quagmires of the dark mountains of ignorance, under which are rolling the earthquakes of change. Men in high place will then at least save their own souls. Cambridge indeed seems to be making a timely effort for Reform, but I venture to doubt if her brave physicians yet contemplate, in what they have said, the depth to which they must cut, in order to reach the roots of the cancer.

The *Times* wisely, if vainly, warns the Spaniards to shift their cities and villages from the known course of the seismic commotions; and so the people of our nation should be moved away from all ground that can be shaken. Some leaders of thought and of religion sometimes indeed speak some of the truth, and now and then a great book comes forth full of special light and isolated wisdom; but rarely *ex cathedrâ*, and never with anything like union of authority. No doubt caution well becomes every seat of Moses, being its condition and *sine quâ non*, but not only is there a time to be silent, but there is also *a time to speak*, and *that time is now*. Let it be remembered that he who leaned on the bosom of Christ coupled the fearful with the abominable. When you talk with cultivated and reflective men of these things, some will tell you that the matter must be left, as aforetime, to the gradual inflow of random influences; but meanwhile, I repeat, the people are left as sheep without a shepherd, and the enemy has taken care that the voice of the Good Shepherd shall be lost in the confusion of His hirelings. The masses are left in trackless and hopeless aberrations under the Will o'-the-wisps of false impressions, which seem to flicker with authority over their "Sloughs of Despond." These being now masters of the situation, masters of all except themselves, are said to be about to wipe out the public recognition of the Master of their best humanity! So that it becomes obviously imperative that such part at least of His teaching as bears more directly on conduct be legally and by sovereign authority kept for us and for our children by some such policy as I have ventured to foreshadow.

This, with my kindest regards, with my best wishes, with my most earnest prayers, I now commend to thee—oh Victorian Demos. It is our highest hope that you will be found ready to help the New Man to make all things new. If you cast the best Son of Man out of your vineyard, and, though you know so much more about Him than the old Jews did, virtually crucify Him afresh —lo! He forewarns you, with His strong crying and tears, of what must speedily be your fate. Instead of being heirs to an inheritance, of which, by the provision of your fathers, you have hitherto so largely partaken, the King of nature and of men, the Guide of all growth, in whose Fatherly Hand mysteriously lie the states of all souls and the souls of all States, will swiftly and surely come down upon you. With Natural Law as His Commander-in-Chief, and the black banner of Destiny floating over His van, He will come with His armies of sorrows, and miserably destroy your wicked and ridiculous polity. You and your country will go down to the political hell, and there you will find the worms of the natural Law, which you have broken, feed sweetly on your ghastly decomposition, and the penal fires, with exact science, prey inevitably on your vitalities. Law will be as beautifully exemplified in your disease, your decadence, and your decay as it might have been, had you let your Jesus take you to ride with Him in the high places of His political Heaven, where you may still find the same eternal Law ministering to your saving health. For the death of States, as of private souls, comes not of personal vengeance, which is but a word coined from the debasement of human despotism, but from the passionless necessity of the reign of Law. *Quem Deus vult perdere* only means in plain English, "If you are foolish, you must suffer for it."

So God be with you, good People, and give you wisdom, and peace always by all means.

SOUTH BERSTED VICARAGE, BOGNOR, SUSSEX.
December, 1885.

P.S.—If any one cares to remark on anything here said, or to have any answer to any objections, perhaps he will kindly send me what he may write. Otherwise I shall be none the wiser—and this I desire to be.

ENGLAND THAT IS TO BE,

OR

WHO IS TO BE NOT RECEIVED INTO THE HOUSE?

"Whosoever goeth onward, and abideth not in the teaching of Christ, hath not God: he that abideth in the teaching, the same hath both the Father and the Son. If any one cometh unto you, and bringeth not this teaching, receive him not into your House."—2 JOHN 9, 10.

THIS charge was addressed to those whom St. John calls "the elect lady and her children" —St. John, who knew more of the mind and heart of the Master than any one else then or since.

Some have regarded the elect lady and her children as the Church at large. Whether this were so or not, a piece of divine advice given to one family would hold good for the whole Christian family on earth, and for any national branch of that family. Therefore to England, if she could only be regarded as one happy family, the Apostolic advice would apply—"If a man rejects the Son, and therefore the Father, receive him not into your community, much less into your house— your House of Representatives."

This application of the text obviously, however, goes upon an ideal, on which, as things are now and as they are likely for a long time to be, it is utterly impossible to act. It is a sad thing to have to confess, that our beloved country cannot act upon the order of our beloved Master; but now, as a matter of fact, I repeat, she cannot. The Master Himself, by His Spirit working in His present and living Church, says: "No; ye cannot bear this now. Ye must receive such into your house; My laws cannot be now carried out into their fulness of detail." So, like the sap in winter, Christ's Ideal draws itself back into the root of State-life, and must lie hidden for awhile in "the law within the law." In the coming summer of humanity, when leprous sin shall melt from mortal mould, and shall have died down out of the spirits of men, then, and not till then, Law will "commeasure perfect freedom" in the full foliage of action. Then the day will come when those who do not acknowledge Christ, and therefore God—for these, in the nature of Personality, stand or fall, are honoured or are dishonoured, together—will be allowed no place in the government of the State, probably not even as electors, much less will they be received into "the House."

Yet do not for a moment suppose that Christianity is going to back-water in the river of freedom; for Christ says, "If the truth makes you free, ye shall be free indeed." All the true freedom which men now enjoy is in fact due to Christ; just as all those delicate shades of morality, about which men and women write such pretty books, are due to the working of the Spirit of the same Jesus Whom their authors and authoresses so jauntily deride. Truth will be found to work in this way:—mankind will grow free as they grow truthful—free from false ideas that confuse them, free from demagogues that mislead them, free from unfair class-interests that hamper them, free from selfishness that cramps them, free from that residuum of the old Adam type which lingers in their blood. Thus they will look into the perfect law of liberty; they will not be forgetful hearers of the Word, but doers of the work of God; they will shake off a thousand shackles of misconception; they will discover that Christ is their only intelligent

Counsellor; they will find, when they probe the matter in a businesslike way, that Christianity is, after all said and done, the only true political economy; for Christ's principles, as they will come to learn, can alone reach to the roots of moral disease, and save the ratepayers from the ruinous waste of poor-rates and gaols. And when men see that Christ is the cheapest as well as the best Guide, then they will not allow the right of citizenship to men of other principles, and will not receive stunted and defective natures into their House, any more than we now allow votes to those whom we already regard as imbeciles.

But I am anticipating. For reasons which would be too long to go through here, we cannot now as a matter of fact refuse to receive into our House of Parliament anybody whom this or that constituency may choose to send there. We cannot realise for a long time the ideal of the Christian State, the Church-State of the future. The Christ that *is* can only be potentially regarded as "The Christ that *is to be.*"

The Roman Catholic Church has all along been trying to realise this ideal—a grand but foolish endeavour; and this is why she clashes, and why, precluding herself from reconsidering her decisions and replanning her course, she always *will* clash, and will clash more and more, with the growing world. That Church has for ages been in confusion, and has thrown the world into confusion. Her imposing order covers organic disorder. More than half these national troubles and disasters are the result of that inveterate badness and congenital madness of Rome. She first made her House different in many main matters of construction from the House of Christ, framing it so that some of the best men must decline to cross her threshold; and then she arrogated to herself in the plenitude of her earthly grandeur, that she was forsooth the only possible form of the House of Christ; and thus she refused to go upon the principle of Open House, and she shut out from her portals the divinely-growing ideas of the human race. Therefore, however numerically strong—as Turks, Infidels, and Heretics of all sorts are at present strong—she has more and more isolated herself from the current of human progress, and the modern world goes on without her. We see how her Bishops, because they clash with the fair needs of the State, are dislodged from Germany; and how her Jesuits, because the enemies of ordinary and necessary freedom, are ousted from the best and freest France there ever was. If they find shelter here, it is only because Great Britain is free enough to let all extremes, from Northampton to the Propaganda, speak the thing they will. England seems to go upon the common proverb, and to think it well to give every principle, even the absence of principle, *sufficient rope*, under the calm conviction that, if that principle be a bad one, it must in the long run make away with itself. I do not say it is always wise to give this rope, but suffice it to observe that it is at present the character of our nation and the recognised mode of our progress to do so.

This is perhaps not the best place, nor certainly would you spare me the time, to attempt now so hard a task as to mete the limits of tolerance, or to discuss whether it ought to have *any* limits; but it is a fact to which we must bow, that even the intolerant, even the godless, must now be tolerated, nay, be received into our House if the constituencies send them.

The matter runs into such infinite ramifications, and so many things, most of them important, present themselves to say, that the difficulty is to choose what not to say, even more than to choose what to say.

I will say a few things which will naturally come uppermost in your own minds.

I would point your attention for instance to this:—that, lamentable as are the antecedents of the individual whose name has latterly been unhappily prominent, these are but accidental, and are not essential to the question at issue. To speak of this man in public is not trespassing on the reserves of private character, for he has "gone before to judgment." It is certainly the most offensive thing which could have happened, that this particular man, with the restless arrogance which marks the irreligious, should have been the man by whose demand this relaxation will necessarily be made for receiving anybody and everybody into our House. I have not seen it so taken, but I should indeed myself have thought that the unrepentant joint-author of a book condemned by the Judges as being of a criminal tendency and injurious to the State, might on this ground have been self-excluded from our House. For he has open to him now a career in which he may himself come to advise the appointment not only of Bishops of the Church, but of the very Judges of the land. The great talents which have enabled him to paralyse ministers, and probably to remodel the Constitution, may carry him or others like him to the highest place, so as even to be the first servant of the Queen, or of a Commune. The people of Northampton find very wide sympathy among kindred masses throughout this land. The franchise is soon to be extended so as to embrace vast constituencies of unfit folk. Since this man is succeeding in shutting out God as the acknowledged universal Power from the House, which must lower its conditions to receive him, and thus from the Public School of the *men* of the nation— so it will soon follow that it will be deemed an intolerable intolerance to name the Name of God in the public schools of the *children* of the nation. These children will be the voters, the masters and lords, of the proximate future. There is nothing to prevent, but much to induce them, as the awful years roll on, to send a majority of such persons to be received into our House, and some other Bradlaugh, if not this, may one day be the leader of such a terrible majority. The Church by that time will have *gone* as a sovereign element of the State, and probably the Sovereign also will have gone. There must however still be Judges, and we cannot suppose that Judges will be appointed who would differ from those who appoint them; and thus right and wrong in the land will have scant authority to distinguish them. The majority then will be at liberty not only to think and speak, but to write and publish and to teach in the schools what they will. This being logically the possible result of receiving men into our House on whose book the Judges have passed condemnation, I say that on this ground one might fairly have thought that there was at least some *primâ facie* reason for declining to discuss the reception of this particular man into the House.

It might seem at first a pity that the claim was not set up by, and the doors thrown open to, some quiet and so to speak inoffensive infidel, and not to one whose words and works make his reception so offensive. And yet perhaps this is only a piece of the irony of Providence; to show, I mean, by a patent example and in a strong blaze of shame, the condition to which that nation is reduced which begins in its House by the dishonouring of the Son. By so clear an example is it shown to History and to the world, that when a public body, the representatives of a nation, enacts that *Christ* need not be acknowledged, the Father and the Holy Spirit soon also say " Let us depart." Thus perhaps it is quite in keeping with propriety, if I may so say, that the man through whom this is done is one by whom our common sense of decency has been publicly outraged. The lesson would not have been so marked had a man like Mill, in some respects a fine specimen of the first Adam type, been the first in English History to refuse to say as well as to mean "So help me God": but, as it is, we can see better what we are being driven to. "It must needs be that offences come—." The rest of the sentence I leave to the Judge of all mankind.

Parliament is also punished, let me add, for having long ago ceased to be a distinctly Christian body, by its being thus called to suffer the loss of corporate honour. It used, till the other day, to be a Club that had an united sentiment, a feeling that could be outraged, an honour that could be trampled on, a dignity that could be offended, a majesty that could be hurt. That was a sentiment which this man is now blowing to the winds. No other assemblage of men in the world would think of admitting to their membership a man who had plucked off their sacred form and blown it in their faces, even supposing it *were* but a form. Henceforth, however, our House will, alas, have no public honour that can pretend to be hurt; for as soon as the Breath of God has ceased to inspire its organism, what does it become but a dangerous miscellany of individuals, representing isolated groups, and having no living Central Presence to overawe their vices and vagaries? Having been forced to swallow this affront, and having no longer any public recognised divinity to hedge it, there will be no deeper mire through which it may not henceforth be dragged. But when the Spirit of God is thus trampled upon, it is natural, and perhaps well, that together with *His* honour, the common honour that cometh of men should go along with it. So condign is our punishment for having once dropped the Christian ideal in our mode of national expansion. Such is the penalty that descends on a people who grow free, not *in* Christ, but *from* Him. God grant that our end be not that we perish for ever!

In Germany there are some sects whose deputies need not say "So help me, God!" But why? Because they regard the Great Name as too sacred to use. Even in Spain the deputies lay their hand on the open gospels, and the President solemnly says, "If you do your duty, may God reward you, if not, may He call you to account." Even in the United States, whose republican institutions are, we had thought, the model of what are called with grotesque arrogance "advanced politicians," every representative, even of communities where civilisation has been running to seed, still solemnly says, "So help me, God." While here in our own beloved and favoured England—the shelter of fugitive kings, the refuge of all distress, the most Christian nation upon earth (as far as inorganic Christianity goes), a man must now be received into our House who comes in with open blasphemy on his lips, and branded with immorality by the sentences of the Courts. He takes his unblest place, like one that says no grace before his meat, to stamp his vile principles with the name and authority of a legislator, and to strive to undo that Church, of which his Sovereign is still the earthly Head, and Christ always the Heavenly Master. Surely the nation itself may well say, "Help us, God!"

Except all indignation be henceforth counted intolerance, the man who has done this must expect such feeling as I have expressed from the ministers of Him against Whom he lifts himself; unless indeed we are to imitate that courtesy with which a man thanks his executioner. Yet let us not forget, when we pray, as we now more earnestly should do for this High Court of Parliament, that all its members come in for the benefit of our prayer.

The Parliament has been described as going through a series of convulsion fits. Well; we read that, when evil spirits were *cast out* by the power of Christ, the spirit tore the man so that he wallowed foaming before he came to his right mind. Perhaps it was to be expected that, in a great human institution, when the converse occurs and the evil spirit *enters in*, we should witness the like phenomenon. Those convulsion fits do not seem to me to have been other than natural.

There are many lessons which I could gather for you from these debates. Let me choose some. There have been expressions used by leading men to which as a minister of Christ I must take exception. One has described the infidel's state of mind as "unfortunate"; and another has expressed for him a maudlin pity, as though he were merely to be commiserated, and were in no way to be blamed for not having "the power of belief." Time does not permit that I go deeply into this matter: but I will only say that, if a man from childhood up refuses to pray, puts God from his knowledge, feeds on infidel food, does not open his soul to the inflow of Divine Grace, forgets his baptism, tramples on his privileges, lets himself be carried on by the set of the current of his fancies, calls the blood of the Covenant by which he was sanctified an unholy thing, and thus does constant despite to the Spirit of Grace—then surely God is not to be blamed by those who comment on his condition, and he has the wrong word applied to him when he is called "unfortunate."

This man says of himself that he could not choose his opinions, but that he grew into them. If, however, anyone eats bad food or none, his body suffers. If he chooses wrong mental food, or takes none, his mind suffers. So surely if a man ignores

*

his highest life, does not take food convenient for it, reads the Bible merely as a carping critic (if at all), cuts off the channel of Divine nutriment from his spirit—then also by the same rule his *spirit* is bound to starve, and his best faculties must run to waste and die. It is a man's own fault, generally speaking, in a Christian country, if he loses the faculty of faith ; and it strikes me, at least according to the ideal standard of things, as a marvellous and lamentable thing, that any man should be chosen to represent a constituency in a Christian country who is palpably defective in the characteristics of advanced manhood. But this men willingly are ignorant of, while they blind themselves to the Truth in this combat which is so rapidly deepening between God and His enemies.

But what a singular perversion of language it is to call the opinions of such men, and many others, "advanced"! There is a sad and curious prostitution of our mother-tongue in this word, which is now so commonly used of any unusual folly or any marked extravagance. If a man now-a-days goes beyond his fellows in any line of stupidity, if he apes the airs of any effete superstition to an extent which no sober-minded man would dare to do, he calls himself, and his dupes call him, "advanced" and "high"! And so in politics, when any mountebank leaps beyond all the bounds of decency, and transgresses all the received limits of moderation—if, like that tribe of Scythians, he shoots arrows at the thunderstorm, and lifts up his voice against the order of the commonwealth, and the reverence due to God and the Queen—he calls himself, and his clique call him, "advanced"! Instead of calling such men "unfortunate" and "advanced," let them be called by their right names. Let them be styled monstrous ; let them be regarded as retrograde ; let them be noted as self-degraded.

Let me however give you a few words of comfort

and of caution. I know not by what arts this man may have persuaded the men of Northampton to send him to be received into our House. I would fain hope that it is not *by reason* of his avowed Godlessness that they have sent him, but by reason mainly of his supposed advocacy of what is called political freedom. For let no one suppose that either all those who take up his cause in the nation, or who have voted that he should be received into our House, have done so from sympathy with his irreligion. For example, the labourers by the voice of their " Chronicle " have distinctly disclaimed this, and have openly based their advocacy of his cause on the constitutional ground that, having been chosen by the people, he must be allowed to sit in the people's Parliament, however lamentable they consider his avowed views to be. It seems to have been felt, and therein I suppose it is common-sense to agree with them, that—apart always from the question of his mode of treating Parliamentary forms, and apart from the *status* to which the judicial condemnation of his books has reduced him, either of which aspects might, as aforesaid, have excluded this particular man—it was not worth while, out of sympathy for the past, and from love of a standard which we had lost, to preserve any longer the sorry rag which was left to Parliament of the raiment of Godliness— that shred of profession which had been left by a sequence of concessions too late to recall. Still, it was to be expected, and in truth it is seemly, that our national avowal of God should not be let go without some such struggle to keep this Holy Name among us. As for the speeches and the votes, probably the right thing in this remarkable conjuncture was to say one thing and to vote for another!

At the same time, I do not envy the feelings of those men who, being themselves religious, have by their incessant clamours brought England to this pass of humiliation. Little did the pious member of the Society of Friends (as if, by the way, all Christendom did not purport to be such a Society!) or the reverential Roman Catholic, or the solemn Jew, or the religious Nonconformist think whereto this would grow. Perhaps had they foreseen this, they would have rather forced their good conscience a few years ago to bow themselves a little in what they regarded as " The House of Rimmon." But this is what they have brought us to, and it is they whom we have to thank for it. A still greater remorse however will await them, when they have cut out the spirit of the Church from the body of the State, and when they see the consequences of that vivisection. Their work will then be done. When they find the carcase of their Mother cast outside the House, they will then have nothing more that they can do. It will, however, be the State which will be left dead. We have truly in our political life set ourselves in no good way. We are tied and bound by the bands of our old sins. We are now reaping in the manhood of our nation the neglects of our youth. The fact that dissent—*religious* dissent—should have sprung up is now found to be the least of the evils sown in her field while the National Church was sleeping. In this effect there was indeed something inartistic, something which spoiled the beautiful picture of a nation in its highest acts at unity with itself. Yet, if thus alone the Church was to be roused, and if Christianity, in whatever form, was thus alone to be kept alive in England, Dissent, however devoid of culture, was surely to be counted a compensation and a blessing. While in so far forth as these religious anomalies are due to *political* revenges, there would seem to be a dramatic propriety in these losses and humiliations which are now suffered alike by the nation and by its Church.

But, however this may be, we have now to confront the larger calamities which have sprung from that faultful past. We have awoke indeed, but it is to gaze with dismay at worse tares than those sown by all other kinds of enemies while we slept. The Church finds the whole nation, as a national organism, slipped away from the control of the Spirit. How could it be otherwise ? Was it to be expected that bygone generations of uncared-for masses were so to generate the population which we see around us, as that they should be of a gentle temper, of a nature easy to be entreated, and ready to our hand for the uses of God and of the State ? Not only the mass, but the mind of the nation has been growing. Freedom has been marching with strides more rapid than religion. The Soul of the land has lagged sadly behind the Mind of the land. The lower nature has outgrown its higher. Yet the godless must be governed, as they must be buried. Nay they must, in this phase of free institutions, subject as yet to constitutional limits, govern *themselves*. As they insist on being buried in what place and way they like, and even, if so it please them, without any *post mortem* credit for faith, so they now insist on *living* without any public credentials of faith, and on governing themselves without any recognition of God. Well: England has bred them to be what they are, and she must take the consequences, be they what they may. She must make the best of her own failures, as parents have to do with their spoiled children. An imperfect nation cannot any longer have a perfect ideal forced upon it. Corruption has set in upon the national organism. The Church, as a test of fitness for legislation, was, by reason mainly of her own narrowness, given up first; then Christ Himself went; now God the Father is going; and it is obvious that a day may come when the Speaker will have to call to order any appeal to Conscience, which these " advanced " thinkers regard as an effete remnant of that natural religion which they consider also to have gone!

Already the leader of Nonconformist religion in the Lower House has stated that a conscience without God is as good as the conscience of a man who believes in God; and has stated that he makes no reference to God in his own affirmation. Now if this merely means that he makes no *express* reference to God, his argument is destroyed by his implying that he makes a tacit one. If he means, as he seems to do, that he makes no reference at all, then I say that this is the most astounding confession which was ever made by a religious public man. If a legislator admits that in entering upon his work as a maker of laws he, while believing in God, discards God from his legislative conscience and discharges the sense of the presence of the Source of Law from all the law-making which he is elected to do for his country, this is certainly a novel conception of the uses of religion, and one from which the whole sense of Christendom must recoil. It is the main comfort of our common faith that in Him we live and move—which, I presume, includes the moving of resolutions. The Quaker was by common understanding admitted to "affirm" solely because of some verbal difficulty as to taking the name of God, and because an eccentric but quiet community opined that it was as wrong to take the Holy name in verity as to take it in vain. The House thinking more of the Quaker than of the Quaker's God, and little thinking that this door, thus set ajar, would let in the flagrant Atheist, took it for granted that "the Friend" was at least so far the friend of a legislative God that his affirmation included a *tacit* acknowledgment of that God for the uses of the State. But now it turns out that his affirmation has no inward reference to God at all, and that the remission of the sacred form, made in the case of the Society of Friends, is claimed by the modern spokesman of that Society as affording a cover for the admission of the openly and avowedly Godless! Whatever private functions he may leave for his God, surely that member of the Society of Friends who makes no reference to the source of Truth and Light and right judgment as a member of his country's Parliament, is a questionable friend of Society. This public avowal shows, I may add, what is to be looked for by the Kingdom of God and the Church of Christ from that Nonconformist faith which at such a hinge of affairs has thus already stood apart from God in the English House of Representatives. It is strange —and, to those who look to find a perfect nation come out from the old lines of European and British ecclesiastical history it might seem hopeless —to find that Christianity, in this its favoured home, has been brought to a national level far, far below that which was attained in States by the first Adamic species under mere primal religion.

To pass by the wisdom of Egyptians — from whom Moses learned, "I am that I am"—look for a moment at the simple beauty of the religion which Virgil makes Æneas to have found at the Court of King Latinus—a court the more interesting from its locality being that of the future Empire, and the future Church, of Rome. If the story was bodied forth without perhaps much substance of fact by the imagination of the poet, it shows us at any rate what a pre-Christian genius and the guide of Dante felt to lie in the sweet ideals of that early past. He draws a picture of a heathen State, a State without even the benefit of such revelation as was vouchsafed to that Semitic race, in the line of whose stem Humanity was to flower in the Son of God. I am tempted to give you the whole story, but you will find it in the seventh book of the Æenead. The coming of the Trojan strangers, you will some of you remember, surprised the youth

of the Latin nation as they were engaged in martial
exercise. One of these youths, as became him,
rode at full speed to tell their prophet, their priest,
and their king. Latinus, in no alarm but in full
reliance on the guidance of Heaven, summoned to
his presence the heroic estrays of the fallen Troy,
and sat to receive them on the throne of his
ancestors. The palace in which he welcomed
them was a vast and august Mansion, standing on
a rising ground, supported by a hundred columns,
hardly less grand, it would seem, than our House
at Westminster by the precincts of its Abbey. The
sanctity of the place was enhanced, it was said, by
the mysterious gloom of the mighty woods which
encompassed it, and by the associations of an
ancestry reaching back, as they believed, into
sources which were divine. Their Temple was the
scene of their feasts, for their very feasts were
sacred. Whatsoever they did, whether they ate or
drank—not at particular times, but always—they
did it all to the glory of God. Church and State
were naturally one, and their refreshment—if I may
carry back these words to those times—their very
conviviality, was sacramental. *Hae sacris sedes
epulis.* The Houses of Lords and Commons in
one, the gathered company of their old men, were
wont to feast there off the flesh of sacred rams at a
long Board, and round them, carved in cedar,
were the effigies of their departed kings. They
appear to have had no " religious difficulty," nor
any question of " local option," for in the entrance-
hall stood the images of the first planter of the vine
with a symbolic sickle in his hand, and of the
Father of the gods. Also the War-god was there
with two faces, looking one for the deeds of war
and the other for the works of peace. To show
that this established State, with its established
Church, had reached its tranquil era through no
untroubled history, there were also many statues of

old kings who had bled and died for their country. On the door-posts and from the holy pillars there hung battered armour and disused weapons of the past, shields, spears, horse-hair crests of old-fashioned helmets, chariots taken in land fights, the beaks of vessels captured in sea-fights, and mighty bolts wrenched off the gates of cities which they had stormed. Such was the Palace-hall and such the Cathedral in which old Latinus sat, sceptre in hand, when he summoned those strangers, the waifs and strays of Troy, the early colonists and fathers of the Roman Empire, into his august presence. When they had been ushered in by the youths aforesaid, whose martial games had been checked by the portent of their arrival, he addressed them with the calm dignity which became so mighty and firmly-seated a monarch. "Sons of Troy," he said, "—for think not that your city and your story is unknown to us,—say what is it that you seek? What reason has brought you through so many waves to our shore? Have ye lost your way, and are ye driven hither by the storms? For men that fare on the sea have many such chances to run. Ye have come up our river, and, it seems, are settling in our haven. No uncouth people are we, to dislike you because ye are strangers. Let me tell you at once that ye need not fear us. We are the Latins, and we are God's people, and we are just, and fair, and walk in the ways of righteousness. Not under constraint of any laws, but of our own free will and natural desire we follow the guidance of Heaven."

Well, such is the picture which I said I would draw for you from history as handed down through the great poet Virgil of the old ideal of a pre-Christian State under natural religion. Now, I would ask you, is not that a state of things before which the Parliament and people of England, who have professed to be guided by the Son of God for above a thousand years, may well feel abashed?—a people whose Parliament, in this present year of grace, in virtue of their very growth in freedom, are on the eve of banishing the last token of the presence of God from the form with which they receive members into their House. How would a Bradlaugh have stood before the State and Council of Latinus? Had such a man, without any god at all, ventured to ask leave to take part in the deliberations of that venerable people, had he said, as he has said to England, "I cannot choose, and have not chosen, my opinions; I have grown into them"—Latinus, who was, as it appears, his own Prime Minister, would have said: "Man, I understand not what thou sayest. Surely thou art no Latin; nor do I think that thou art a full-grown man. Thou hast a terrible organic defect in thy nature, which must exclude thee for ever from our council-table and from our State;" and he would straightway have bidden the young men who brought him thither to convey him thence, that the winds which bore him to the shore of Latium might blow him back to that strange and defective race in which it was possible for a man to have grown down into an ignorance of God.

Look once more at that other great people, the Greeks, also a pre-Christian and non-Jewish nation; to whom the race of Man owes so much of its culture, for that was the part of the stem along which in them the human plant long up-ran, just as to the Latins we mainly owe the knotty joints of human law.

Herein let me choose for you one sublime Chorus, or holy song, from the Antigone of Sophocles—one, so to speak, of their canonical prophets. This song, as far as the idea goes, might have been conceived by any observant child first opening the eyes of his soul upon the world in which he found himself; while the language could only be the outpouring of a poetic spirit, rare and practised, and using all the weapons of words and, without knowing it, all the secrets of Art. The name of Antigone leads the Chorus at once to the thought of her father Œdipus, and to that riddle, the great riddle of Man, by solving which he had saved his country, and lost himself. It was a riddle to which the Theban king had only added a fresh and terrible entanglement—one which our Christ alone, the God-man, was destined rightly to unravel. Man, who by the original game-license of Eden inherits dominion over the beasts of the field, the birds of the air, and the fish of the sea, over disease itself, and over all things but death, finds himself the victim of forces which he cannot control; and mere ignorance makes the best of men the sport, so runs the old song, of this worst disaster. Having pondered man in his early gregarious and uncultured state, the Teacher comes to think of him as a sower, a plougher, and then as a citizen. A possessor of thought and voice, he begins to mould society into manners. But, adds the poet with a truth which is not Greek alone but is eternal, man foregoes his high name of citizen when that which is evil is present with him. Then only can he rightly be named a high-souled citizen, when he binds together the laws of his native land by righteousness, when he brings God into his form of words, and when he owns *the validity of an oath*. If an ancient Greek could regard his word as good as his oath, it would only be because his word like his oath *had God in it*. So that, as we see, under " natural religion " the great and cultured mind of Greece, like that of Rome and of course of the higher type of the Hebrews, held the taking of the name of God into his solemn duties as a citizen, to be a sign and token of Truth bound up with the deepest consciousness of his position as a man.

Alas, my brethren and fellow-countrymen, what

a sad contrast to these pure aspirations of "natural religion" both in Rome and Greece, is now set forth in our House of Representatives, which is the very cream of our English citizenship, by what I must call its un-natural irreligion! Here in civilised England, at the close of the Nineteenth Century of Grace, that which has been regarded in pre-Christian Empires, as well as all Christian States, as the deepest and most inviolable bond of all the sacred Past, the Name of God, is being rudely and violently undone. The highest legal authority in our popular Chamber derides the very conception of an Oath! Sad indeed is the immediate prospect of the truth among us, seeing that by a majority it has been pronounced to be thus separable from the God of Truth. And the matter is not mended when we feel, as we must, that, upon the line of license to which our national constitution has long committed itself, this separation was necessary. The steeds are racing down-hill, and the reins are being thrown upon their necks. May we not well exclaim with the Prophet, though with a converse significance, "The chariot of England and the horsemen thereof!" We have handed ourselves over to forces which can thus already for a time destroy legislative Godliness, and which must end in the ruin, I do not say of National Christianity, but of our national and natural Religion. I say *for a time*—for let no man suppose that this is to be the *denouement* and final catastrophe of English Christianity. The course which lies before our country will be *this:* let me advertise to you in a few words what must come to pass. I have already glanced at it by anticipation.

Our beloved State must run—she is *bound*, I say, to run upon the line of country which she has marked out for herself; and to run, I fear, till she drops. There is no present discharge from that obligation, except indeed men wake up and shake off before it is too late, by some gigantic and premature effort, that illusive trifling by which we see them at present to be mastered. This will not be done by any exclusion of Godless and Christless men from our House. It is, as I have said, too late now for that. I take it that we shall first be called upon to learn by bitter experience the ruin consequent upon Godless Government. The principle of toleration which excludes God from the House, which is the Public School of men, must soon exclude Him, as I have said, from the Public Schools of children. These, trained out of the knowledge of God, will soon, very soon become, I repeat, the voters, and thus the masters and governors of England. It were long and sad to trace—but easy, alas, to foresee—what a change this must soon make in the details of our national life. The principles of Christ are those which alone lie at the root of conduct and contentment. These principles will be *gone*, for it is ridiculous to suppose that the random efforts of sects (of which the Church will only be one) to teach Truth in an hour and a-half of the Day of Rest (if that Day of Rest will then be left) will suffice to keep national conduct wholesome and right. Sunday Schools, to which there is no compulsion, will draw but few of those children, who all the week have been forcibly taught aversion from their God under the high authority of the State and Queen. Into all these questions of "conscience," as it is grotesquely called, how can those poor lambs be supposed to enter? The masters of England will grow up, or rather grow down, *without God in their world*. The code of morals contained in the duty to God and our Neighbour will be forgotten; or if in some form the latter will be taught, it will be based on an authority which must fail to fill the place of religious instinct in the national soul—which soul, from want of energizing its faculties in social life, will speedily die out. The region in which resides national conscience and individual principle will, I say, be *gone*. Earthly codes, the only codes left, will not touch the anti-family vices. There will be nothing left to control common impulse, and the population will sink towards the level of the swine of Gadara. It will not be long before the whole herd will show signs of rushing violently down the steep places of Sin, to perish in the revolutionary abyss.

This being our prospect at no great distance of time, how, you will ask, is the Kingdom of God eventually to come?

On this wise. Men will before very long begin to cast about for a remedy. It will be seen by the very masses, who are after all " English natures, freemen, souls," that the heart and kernel of conservation remains with those of their fellow-citizens who are *Christians*. Those, in their unpublic way, will be seen to have made marked advance—the more so because they will have retired into the splendour of contrast. Their isolated polity set on its hill cannot be hid. The best of the Christian sects, notably the ancient Church (though the name of England will, if that ever be possible, have been taken from her) will let it be seen that in the teaching of Christ they alone possess the secret of the only true political economy and of national salvation. It will then, in the search for a remedy for national evil, come to be demanded (and the energy of surviving Christianity will all along make effectual, fervent efforts to this end) how the principles of the higher Type can be brought to bear upon the conduct of the country. Then some day, when the hour is ripe, either a Royal, or Presidential, or it may be even a Communistic Commission will, with nervous anxiety and hot haste, be issued to ask what there was which may yet be useful and generally necessary to National Life in the old teachings of the half-forgotten Christ. The sooner, let me say, some such course is taken by ourselves in our own historic juncture, the better chance we shall have of providing a substantial Christianity, and the better shall we be able to meet impending perils. The result, however, whenever this is done, will be that some rough code of public Christian morals, better than none, will be arrived at, and acted upon. This will be made imperative in all the elementary schools of the day, gentle and simple. Then at last will begin again to grow up a nation with a bright, lively, and steady hope. For as that half-heathen people will come to know, with something of the charm of novelty, the solid comfort of the indwelling Spirit of Jesus, the more they will yearn to know. The meagre divinity granted at first by trembling and incredulous statesmen will put the people of successive generations upon the track of further quest. To that end they will fall into the gospel-nets of the thousand sects into which religion will be split, and those sects will prosper most which most commend themselves to be in keeping with whatever of sound truth the schools shall have taught. Then it will be our own beloved Church (if one of her humblest ministers may venture the vaticination) that will re-gather, with paramount success, the souls that she had lost, and will come, with splendid triumph, to the rescue of our country. Thus, by due degrees, the Truth in the Scriptures, the Truth as it is in Jesus, will be again believed and loved. The people, with fresh delight, will begin to recognise their Saviour, and smile on their Mother Church who has kept Him for them. They will perceive that Dissent was not the true mother of the Christ-child, for she was willing that He should be given to neither, but should be slain in the quarrel. England will then erelong grow up into Christ in all things, and—oh! blessed resolve—

will finally and once for all say, "Lord, to Whom shall we go? Thou only hast the words of eternal life and saving health. We will never leave Thee again."

But the time of figs is not yet. And—oh, dreadful possibility!—the fig-tree of England, cumbering the ground, *may* be cut down before that time shall arrive. For, between this present and that future which I have so roughly sketched, who can say what may not happen? The nation that forsakes its Ideal will only find it again through much tribulation. Yet pray God that the many righteous men and women found in our land may arrest the natural penalty of destruction!

Meanwhile, dear brethren, let us, for our own single parts, take infinite care, first of all to receive the Spirit of Jesus into the house of our hearts. And, next, let us take earnest heed to send men of the right sort into our National Assembly—men whom no member can charge with disregard of the Presence of God and the *validity of an oath*. For remember that, as things now are, whatever members any constituencies, however reckless or evil, may choose to send up to represent them, will henceforth be received into the House.

Wertheimer, Lea & Co., Printers, Circus Place, London Wall.

THE TIMES OF ENGLAND IN THE HANDS OF GOD.

By the Rev. W. B. PHILPOT, M.A., Vicar of South Bersted, Bognor.

"My times are in Thy hand."—Psalm xxxi. 17.

IF the voice of a man may say this, much more may the voice of a nation. Except we can say to God "My times are in Thy hand," there is no comfort for us as private persons. So neither is there any comfort for us in our civic capacity or in our patriotic moods, unless we can feel the same with regard to our country. If we be not convinced that they are in the hands of God, we may well be filled with fear when we contemplate the times of England.

I think I hear some one say, "Let us have no politics in the pulpit." Suffer me at once, my brethren, to forestall any such remonstrance in the minds of my hearers. Far be it from me to desecrate these few solemn moments at my disposal by subserving the ends of any party in the State; but at a time when great changes, affecting all of us, are working in the Constitution of our country, you will most of you expect that the ministers of our national Christianity will have something to say, at least as to the principles by which our political course should be guided.

If there is any valid reason at all why the ministers of the Church of England go unrepresented as a class in the Parliament of England, it is not because the priesthood is a separate interest, too spiritual to involve itself in earthly struggles—an idea come down from times even more dark than these; but rather it is that we are called to reserve ourselves for the duty of preaching peace and right to all parties, involving ourselves in the selfishness of none. If parties should ever cease—a supposition not untenable—a consummation to which clear thought leads — and to which the shades of party names, till the present struggle came on, had seemed already to be fading —then the ministers of Christianity will find a political Public House in which, without soiling their Master's honour, they can mingle their counsels. Meanwhile it is our duty in this place and hour, of which authority and custom still give us possession, to say that which we believe our Master would have us say, and that which we have the more right to speak because none of our body are in the House of the People's Representatives. And what our conscience puts into our mouths, whether it favour one side or the other, that must we speak.

And first—on the very threshold of all social and political considerations—what is the teaching of Christ? Why, the teaching of Christ is clean against adherence to any party at all. "Call no man master upon earth: for one is your Master, even Christ, and all ye are brethren." Useful and necessary as it may be that those who in the main think together and feel together should also act together—useful chiefly because of the banded union of factions which would persecute opinion, and force their selfish projects; yet, the moment your united action becomes inconsistent with your individual conviction, the moment that a man votes about any matter more important than party ties in a way in which he thinks it wrong to vote, the man who so acts with his party calls that party master and breaks the law of Christ. A limit must therefore be reached in the region of casuistry at which a good man is bound to say "Party or no party, I can go no farther." Nor is it the least wholesome and hopeful feature of our struggles that so many, from a sense we will presume of duty, break off ties which in less crucial affairs conveniently bind them. Where this is honest, it of course reads the very lesson, and illustrates the principle to which I am adverting. In some cases it undoubtedly is so; in others, God in the conscience and in the world is still the Judge.

In fact the only sanity in party government rests on the readiness with which the claims of party yield to those of reason; and he is the only safe leader of a party who seeks to strengthen his hands not so much by encouraging any dogged opinion of staunchness, as by commending his measures to the common-sense and high principles of the nation. Perhaps, however, to bring party politics to any test of reason were out of place. They tell you that necessity knows no law, and that to strain after ideals is to wind ourselves too high for mortal politics beneath the sky. Well: there is a measure in all things, and idealists, like the rest of us, must set an example of self-restraint. Yet a nation that strikes root downward must and will strike shoot, and bear fruit, upward. This is why it seems to me to be well to allude now and then to things as they ought to be, except we are to disregard the Voice which says, "Be ye also perfect, as your Father which is in heaven is perfect."

And it is closely connected with this aspect of political duty to say here that it is hard to see how a reasonable and honest man can help being coloured with every light and shade of politics. Of all the questions which come before the councils of the State some will seem to his conscience,—which may be more enlightened, or less,—to demand for an answer the maintenance of certain institutions to the last breath of his sympathy. With regard to those he will necessarily be *Conservative*. Other questions will seem to be capable of a temporary or of a two-sided solution. With regard to these he will be guided by some nicer distinction, dependent on the circumstances of the case before him. With regard to these he will be " Liberal-Conservative" or " Conservative-Liberal," as the case may be. Other questions will seem to demand for an answer, as rigidly as the first, the destruction and extinction of some practice or some institution which he regards as wholly mischievous. In that aspect of his politics the Christian must be utterly and entirely *Radical*. While in all things, if the word has any meaning at all, he must be liberal, if he is a Christian. The fact is that these names throughout confuse and harass society; and make as though the difference between right and wrong depended upon how we looked at them, and not on what they are. It is the same in what are called Church-matters—as if, let me say in passing, *all* matters were not Church-matters, or at least Christian matters, where they involve conduct. In Church-matters, I say, this man is called *high*, as if the heights of Christianity were not reached by lowly hearts that lean on the love of Christ—aye, though they never may have worshipped save in the precincts of some mountain Bethel, where their " Church " has never been able to follow them. Another man is called *low*; as if anything were lower than to hold matter, manner, and ritual—which slew the Lord, Stephen, and Ridley—dearer than Spirit and Truth and Right. Another man will be called *broad*, in positive contempt; as if it were a virtue for the soul and mind to be narrower than God meant them to be. The term, used in obloquy, springs of a priestcraft that would keep the key of knowledge and hide it away, even from themselves. What ignorant presumption it shows, but what a tale it tells, that this word *broad*, as applied to opinion, should ever in any circles have come to be used as a reproach !

And so it is in all things, in politics and in religion—for in common parlance the two are unhappily thus divorced. The enemies of all order thus confuse the nature of things by forging and foisting upon us false names and pitiable watchwords. Well saith our Peer-Poet—

> Nor deal in watchwords over much.

But having thus cleared the ground, and come, I hope, to a spirit in which to regard these changes and struggles aright, let us see what matter for thought, for comfort, for indignation, what matter of prayerful contemplation for all parties, is afforded by this crisis—a crisis in which great changes *in* the Constitution may lead to great changes *from* it. What is there to hope? What to fear? What to denounce?

1. What is there to *denounce?* To begin with, we denounce that man, whoever he may be, who thinks there is no class in society whose interests are to be consulted except his own. We denounce that "working man"—(a misnomer again, and a most incomplete term—as if those Princes, Peers, magistrates, and the rest, who do their duty in that state of life to which God has called them, were not working men as much as he who labours at trowel or loom)—we denounce, I mean, disclaim, that selfish "working man," who —not content with the enviable blessing and the high pleasure of truly and fairly getting his own living, and his family's living, by the sweat of his brow—wishes to make laws which shall cancel the Commandments of God as reissued by Christ; and would fain grasp at the living of him to whom the Disposer of humanity has given the liberty of working in his own scope and doing, within due limits, what he will with his own. That man, I say, we disclaim.

Again, no less, but the more (for he should know

better), do we disclaim that idler into whose mouth fortune drops, and who thinks there are no claims but his own; who wishes his own class to be the sole arbiter of hard-wrung gains, of whose creation and disposal he for his part cannot be supposed any degree feelingly to know the nature. That man also we set aside. I make these remarks, I again beg you to remember, not politically, but morally. If they cannot help being political, it is because morality is necessarily social, and because Politics involve the working of the inner life.

2. Now what is there to *fear?* As there is something we see to be condemned on both sides, so is there something to be feared from both. It may perhaps be feared on the one hand, that classes never before entrusted with the reins of government cannot at first be trusted to govern the reins; that, changing all that is to be changed in the parallel, those scenes of disorder which we find in races newly emancipated may be enacted in England herself. It may be feared that the taste for making new laws may with some be coloured by the habit of breaking old ones. It may be feared that the delightful sense of the possession of the power of dividing property may lead to its division with a view, it would be said, to benefit the rich and idle, by giving them some practical knowledge of the pleasures of work. This result might have its advantages;—only take heed that the measures of attaining it be just. Not that I profess here to say anything whatever as to what the Nation may ultimately arrange touching limits and modes of property. The whole question of "mine and thine" will one day find a solution which, let us hope, will be fair. What if it should be found, in the far future, that St. Paul's apparent paradox "having nothing, and yet possessing all things" was a description of the status of a citizen in a perfect polity?

It may also be feared, as the Church has not till lately done much for the masses, lest the masses when in power may not do much for the Church—except rase her beautiful temples to the ground, with all her material and spiritual designs, leave the Nation without a National Church, defile the sacred precincts of our fathers by the abnegation of worship, and vivisect the spirit from the body politic. It may be feared that, as the masses have not been religiously educated by us, they may revenge our neglect by a reign of terror, and that so freedom *in* religion may become freedom *from* it. Ghastly phantoms, which God avert!

It may, however, on the other hand—to be fair all round, as in duty bound—be feared lest, in dread of these calamitous issues, the classes at present dominant should have the folly to feel it their duty, by a too prolonged resistance to the laws of national and rational growth, to provoke this awful, mysterious monster, which is imagined to lurk in the masses, into some such violent revolution as that at which I have glanced. It may be feared that our failures in legislation for the poor and the criminal population may be perpetuated till the homeless and voiceless people are beyond the control of Statecraft, and no longer open to any invitation to providence and thrift. It may be feared that a kindred policy to that which in some way has alienated and driven into the arms of the Italian Priest the natives of our Sister Island, with what results we too plainly see, may alienate, not only from the Church but from the Throne, the dense, strong, and stubborn population of our own. It has been well shown in a story lately written of the times of Charles the First, how the evil influence of the Papacy helped in the overthrow of the English Throne—not from any sense of the demands of freedom, but because Rome could so best compass the overthrow of the English Church. It may be feared that our reverence for and attachment to old privileges may be over-strong and over-long for wisdom. Thus, our ancient institutions may fall from their own weight, and the garment become too old for piecing. It may be feared that the Oak of Old England, rotten at the root, and over-flourishing at the top, may come to the ground. So that you see, my beloved brethren, to put the matter candidly, there are fears which arise from all quarters of the State.

3. Now, lastly, is there nothing to hope for? Alas! how little time is left us to dwell on an aspect so delightful. As in life itself, so in these reviews of it, and these advices on it, much of that breath must, it seems, be spent on thoughts of fear and denunciation, which we would fain spend in the pleasure of hope. Is there nothing, I say, in our country's future left us to hope for? Much, thank God, every way. What does our text say? Our times are in the hands of God. We live in the midst of probabilities. We believe in Salvation itself because its truth is more probable than anything else. The upshot of Faith itself is the hopeful leaning to the probable. The whole of our life is in matter which allows many ways of making up. It is the part of men, and women, and above all of Christians, thankfully grasping at the best probabilities, with a buoyant remembrance that our times are in the hands of God, to go fearlessly forward. We may rest well assured that our Race—if only the conditions of our planet so long suffer its survival—nor need we abandon the hope that our Nation—will reach the highest state possible to Man. All power on earth as well as in heaven is given to our Master—and in Him, to *us*. He has shown us the Way. He has given us the lead. If we follow it—come His Kingdom must.

For are there not many gleams of hope breaking from every side? Take a survey of the classes, brief and summary as it must be. Look how society is at present composed. You may indeed gaze in the dust till you find your eyes filled with it; you may contemplate with blurred vision the vices of your country till you become horrified at the extent of power largely held now by a class as notable in common estimate for luxury, dissipation, arrogance, and folly, as the opposite class, who are likely to hold it, may be for brutality, drunkenness, and venality. But to take either the froth, the scum, or the dregs of England and regard them as if they fully and fairly represented the classes in which they are unhappily found, is not only uncomfortable, but it is unnecessary, unwise, and unsafe. For look frankly and manfully at the elements of which society is made up. Examine the classes generally supposed to be antagonistic. Take specimens of both, numbers of whom must have come within your own knowledge and your own love. You must certainly know — we all do — numbers of men, of "the old school", of ancient integrity, unbroken faith, high honour, and uncompromising courage; men whose nature is as noble as their name, and their character firm as their everlasting hills; whose virtues, like their oaks, abide from generation to generation. They may be fewer in number—though that I doubt—than those vain, ungenial men of their class who from congenital imbecility, from youthful excesses, from their education not having been rightly inspected, or from ignorance of the laws of wealth and its responsibilities, misuse the gifts of God. But even though men of a certain passing influence among their classes, these are not the men likely to carry their way; these must be swamped, I believe verily, by the magnificent phalanx of those in our dominant ranks who work, and feel, and think, and who no doubt would suffer to the death rather than forget that they are English Christians. You know also, I am sure—I for my part am happy to say that during all my life, in all times and all places, I have known and regarded with esteem and affection—large bodies of working men, in the more limited sense of the word, in whose hands, conjointly with the sound elements of that other class of which I have spoken, anyone would feel that the destinies of their country would be fairly safe. As for ancestry, these men also, as may be seen in the registers of their parish churches, come of families who, labouring on the land, have held, longer perhaps than some of its lords, a patent of hereditary nobility of toil and a steady self-supporting integrity of industry, though helped by no supplementary blessings of fortune. And if you were to examine the general run of the great factories and the best managed regions of mineral production, you would find a grand staple of hardy, noble-minded men who from generation to generation have been clinging to the same places in an incessant course of honourable work —men who, if any, may be fairly trusted not to bring ruin on the country which their laborious self-sacrifice, and their splendid but perilous struggle to live, has helped to provide with its material comforts and to raise to its pitch of greatness. There is doubtless a vast array of the opposite character in the ranks of these as of those. The vexed, and vexing question before the legislature and its leaders is—when, and how far, power can be entrusted to the whole community. If on the one hand there is danger lest it be delayed too long, there is still more if it be granted too soon. Once granted, it can never be recalled. Clear knowledge should precede the boon or the bane.

But one thing is clear, that you *must* give the whole population a voice gradually louder on the questions affecting their own life :—*gradually*, I say, for there is the rub. I, for my part, should be sorry to think that it was allowed to be the perquisite of any one party in the State truly to honour, and wisely to trust a people, which, though hitherto neglected to the verge of danger, are after all born Englishmen, born freemen, and constituted with the high faculties of human souls.

Let us, however, thankfully acknowledge it to be a hopeful sign, that, where the popular element has already prevailed, it has worked mainly for conservation. I think we need not fear for Christianity, however its present form may shift, even if that should come into the hands of the people. The common folk, now as heretofore, hear Jesus gladly: nay, it is the people who always save religion. As for the form of it, that is too large and interesting a question on which here to dwell.

I cannot, for lack of time, say all that could be said, and much that ought to be said, on this head of hope. But I think I have said enough to suggest to the fearful some grounds of good cheer. Come changes must. It seems to me wise, though we fear them, always to make, not the worst, but the best of them. Yes, my beloved brethren, our " times " are in the hand of God, and He will take care that the basis of the soul of England shall not decay. All we want, if our desires are honest, is that justice, and truth prevail; and of that, so we do our part unselfishly, Heaven will take care. We must trust God fully in our public as well as our private lives. He in whom the race has come to be what it is will take care of it in all stages of its growth. None can say to what, in the course of ages, God will bring England : no more than any can say to what He can bring our private souls—if we allow Him. But we must be careful not to hinder Him. That man, that nation, must prosper most which hampers least the highest working of Him in whom we live and move and are. Never are there times when our prayer for Parliament has more meaning than in times of constitutional change. Oh, may "all things be so ordered and settled upon the best and surest foundation, that peace and happiness, truth and justice, religion and piety, may be established among us to all generations." Whether societies have, in any but a fantastic sense, a future life, or a life at all,' is known only to Him in whose lap are all life's forms and all its ideals. In mysteries like these lie half the pleasures of existence and all the interest of reverential speculation. May God help us in this country to do for our Nation what we can, and to help her to the utmost of our power to gather her children together under the wing of Christ; and then, having served our country fearlessly according to the will of God, may we ourselves fall on sleep, and wake prepared to enter on that perfect state which we believe that Christ has gone before to prepare for us.

Wertheimer, Lea & Co., Printers, Circus Place, London Wall.

LAW THE FORERUNNER OF THE GOSPEL.

BY THE REV. WILLIAM B. PHILPOT, M.A., VICAR OF SOUTH BERSTED, BOGNOR.

SERMON PREACHED (THE FIRST AND LAST PARTS) IN WESTMINSTER ABBEY, ON DEC. 4TH, 1882, BEING THE DAY OF THE DEPARTURE OF LAW FROM THE COURTS OF WESTMINSTER HALL.

"He must increase, but I must decrease."—JOHN iii. 30.

JOHN THE BAPTIST said this of Jesus; and as humanity grows this is happily the language which all law can use of Gospel—nay, *must* use; for most thoughtful persons will take note that the coming of Christ's kingdom, while a promise of Divine revelation, is no less a prophecy of spiritual science. To grow up into Christ in all things, till men and nations arrive at "the Christ that is to be," is not only that which was prayed for by Him whom we know that "the Father heareth always," but, even looking from below at the course of events, it is the direction in which mankind is bound to commove.

No mistake could show a greater mental or moral twist, than to fancy that between Law and Gospel there can be any the faintest contrariety. It holds in morals as in facts, that no one truth can contradict any other. A higher truth may displace and supersede a lower, but that is only "by law and process of great nature," and in the growth of the soul and of the race. Between the Spirit of Jesus and the spirit of John how could there be anything of rivalry? "I have need to be baptised of Thee," said John, "and comest Thou to me?" "Suffer it now," said Jesus, "for thus it becometh us to fulfil all righteousness." Then he suffereth Him, though it is likely enough that in his vague wonder he failed to catch the full sweetness and far-reaching import of the reason. The Moses met the Jesus, but it was on a Mount of Transfiguration. So the seed falls into the ground and dies; but the bud sets, and the bloom opens. If Law's *decrease* was in a sense Law's *decease*, this meant only its apotheosis and immortality. Mortality was but swallowed up of Life.

Let us ask how our moral and spiritual natures stand to Law. What *is* Law? Law is indeed a wide term. As Love is of God, so Law is of God. As God is Love, so God is Law. Our Father who is in Heaven is not only Personal Love but " Personal Order." (This expression is so just that I must not put it forth as my own. It was a remark made to me twenty-five years ago by no less a voice than our Laureate Poet, with whose Christian teaching you are, or ought to be familiar.) The idea of Order would seem, however, to *come before* the idea of Love, not only in the lower working of the Universe, but in human society. It is by Law we live, all round. The Deity is not *all* a distant Mystery. Even before the fulness of His Godhead (so far as a phenomenal man could ever set Him forth) stepped with His highest Truth and His vocal Love bodily upon the planet, *some* of God men still might know; and this is indeed part of one of the arguments of St. Paul.

Indeed, what movement is there of our life, or of any life—nay, what phase of slumbrous vitality in the mere coherence of things—which is not based on Law? In us and about us Law reigns. The offspring of Personal Law, as well as of Personal Love, in Law we live, and move, and have our being. We know something—and under the wide wings of that Truth which alone can make thinkers truly free, we are ever coming to know more—of the laws we live by. We make this advance by gazing up at the far things and peering down into the little things. Yet all these things, great and small, went on, and infinitely more of such things are now going on, undreamed of by the wisest of the sons of men. Nay, their times and their seasons were not even known to the Son, for so He Himself said, but only to the Father.

And just as the whirling star above the optic glass, and the wheeling rotifer beneath it, reveals itself more and more clearly as we fix its focus, so Law is sure to be found in its hiding-places, whithersoever you may be shrewd enough to catch its clue and bring it within your disc. Nor is the Law that works in Matter dead. How could that which works be dead? What else is it but a variation of the operation of life. The fact that the most fairy-like wheel goes round shows that the great Power is telling upon it. Nor can even matter itself ever be dead, for in it Law works. If matter ever seems dead, it is only that as yet it sleepeth. All nature has life in itself, that is, in the Power by which it is. Christ, indeed, said (though the special work of Him that sent Him was that of a master of the science of the *Spirit*), "The earth bringeth forth fruit of itself": but He knew, none better, that this earth and all the earths that have been, are, and will be—have had, and have, their being and their hope of being, in the living God, by Whose real presence in Nature, without any superstition at all, all things cohere.

The material Universe, in a word, is, as it were, the body of God: a truth which of itself also makes all food-matter—which to man is the most important part of matter—in the Christian's eyes sacramental, even before any outspoken and representative blessing on our priestly part. Did not Christ show us this when in that masterstroke, comprehending all life and duty, He said of food "This is my body." I and the Father are one; I set forth His moral fulness in bodily shape of a man; this food causes my body in subservience to my spirit to be: do this, that is, *eat*—always take food—in remembrance of me, bethinking you how I used this bread-fed body to work the will of God. And the Christian Church, in its blessed Sacrament of the Lord's Supper, recalls this sometimes in a special manner—why? It is to set forth the fact that Christians eat in this spirit always. In fact all matter stands to the indwelling, immanent, vivifying Spirit of God as the body of a man, yea, as the body of the man Christ Jesus, stands to the spirit of the man. This, in fact, is the first meaning of our being made "in God's image." And it is this likeness—and nothing lower—which concerns us here and now. We leave the lower types of being, and all the laws by which, as we have seen, God guided and guides them, to their devout students, for such we love best to handle subjects which are nowhere and nothing, or at best have but little interest for men, except they form part of religion. We have lightly touched on those things to day, because it seemed necessary to trace Law throughout.

But the Plant of Being shot up a fresh joint when its stalk reached to Man. It then entered, though it only *entered*, the region and kingdom of Spirit. Here is the more proper study of mankind. Then in the year of the Lord—*annus mirabilis*, if ever any other year was wonderful—this topmost joint of the Stalk of Being broke into Flower, into the last Phenomenon of life, into the Standard and Model of conscious existence and spiritual excellence, into the God-Man, CHRIST JESUS. Thus there have been two species of Man, the Old and the New, the First and the Second. And if the proper study of mankind is man, his highest study is the highest man, and God as in Him set forth.

Now when we come to the study of the first kind of man in our enquiry as to the scope of Law, we find that here also Law works. How should it be otherwise? That which held through unconscious and all other animate being, naturally holds when we come to the first Adam. It does not, indeed, hold so pleasantly or so evidently in a type which without Christ was not finished "The stars are kept from wrong, and the most ancient heavens are fresh and strong" because they follow a law which no indwelling will of their own could break. And when in the ripeness of growth a type of Being arises Who says, and by His law of Self-sacrifice induces the rest of the world to say, "Lo I come to do Thy will, O God: I am content to do it; yea, Thy Law is written in my heart," then it is that Law comes forth from behind the clouds, clad in a new form, exceeding fair. Her whole aspect is transfigured into what, with the best reason, we call Gospel.

Meanwhile the race of men is living before the *social fulness* of this time is come, and I have glanced at Jesus by anticipation. I have spoken of Him merely as a Fact, so to speak, in the course of natural history and the last human Phenomenon in the growth of Being—a fact pregnant with promises of which as yet but a small part have worked their fulfilment. In studying how Law works in humanity we must go back and confine ourselves for the moment to the imperfect race.

Take men at their earliest, and do we not note Law? No community, however small, can hold together where every one is allowed to do what is right in his own eyes. Every one who lives with other people must more or less sacrifice himself.

He that saveth his life—that is, indulges himself at the cost of others—shall lose it. He that loseth his life—that is, goes on the principle of give as well as take—saves it. This law of Christ, which is, in fact, "live and let live"—which means "if you do not let others live and enjoy, you will have no outer guarantee, nor inner capacity, for your own' life and enjoyment"—this early form of self-sacrifice was thus necessarily the seed or germ of that splendid form of it which came afterwards, and which now promises to save the world. Such oneness is there in Man, in virtue of the Oneness which is in God. So clearly is the Law of the Gospel to be traced in the very earliest rudiments of the gospel of the Law. When society is in its infancy, or rough boyhood, Law is like also to be rude and rough, but still there it is, and, involving self-abnegation, it is divine. It is set over against desire. It is the voice of God, through the voice of the man or men whom that community agrees so to constitute, and who are therefore ordained by God as His ministers for the good of that society, great or small: it is the voice of God saying to all irregular impulse, "Thou shalt not." "Thou shalt love thy neighbour as thyself." Wherever there is the seed of men, there doubtless Love also, in some rough sort, lives; at first perhaps in some low forms of mutual regard, and bound up with selfish considerations. But, with this saving clause, it may be laid down that in every imperfect society Love is preceded by Law. And this must be the sterner, the more imperfect the society. Were there not stern law at first, how could any society grow to its gentle and neighbourly atmosphere at the last? This power has double action. Those who will not live by law must die by it. The roots of this great tree strike down as deep as the sprays of it play out on high. *Quantum in cœlum tantum in Tartara.*

If I go up to heaven Thou art there; if I go down into hell thou art there also.

And if in an Empire which has grown into general freedom there are regions which have refused to outgrow the rude state, then that Empire must, in regard of them, return to its early and summary modes. The calamities which should befall men of "lawless and uncertain thought" and act, but which sometimes, alas! only fall to their duty-doing victims—the penalty and fine, the shades of the prison-house, all the groans of duly exacted suffering or justly demanded death—what are these but signs of an imperfect state, the rolling of the terrible wheels of the sublime chariot of Law till she can come upon better roads.

If at any periods again

> In the corrupted currents of this world
> Offence's gilded hand has shoved by Justice,
> And if 'tis seen the wicked prize itself
> Buys out the law—

or if faction gathers such head that it trips the course of Law, and the innocent suffer whilst the guilty go unscathed; wherever such cases in this mixed state of things may have marked the miscarriage of Justice below—and looking back over so many centuries we cannot but think very humbly over the great array of such :—however it has been below, it is not so above :—

> There is no shuffling, there the action lies
> In its true nature.

And in some way in that eternal world, where we are brought face to face with heaven, those who have suffered wrongfully will be found, let us thankfully remember, to have rested their souls safe on the bosom of God. And for those who have passed unjust sentence, or, having wrought ill to their neighbour, have escaped the penalty, what shall we say of *them?* They also are carried by the Great Apparitor to that Supreme Court of Appeal in relation to which all the highest Courts of earth are, after all, but Courts of First Instance.

But the best hope of what Law will be, out of what it is, lies in this :—that it is what it is out of what it has been, yea, that it is what it is out of what it was when Justice first held her Balances and her Sword in these precincts which she is leaving to-day. If there is much to depress, there is more to encourage human hopes.

How encouraging it is, on the one hand, for Humanity to stand by and see at any time in its annals young communities, in their struggles to vindicate the divinity of their origin, mastering like an infant Hercules the ingrained remnants of ancestral ferocities. Thus it was in the State of Rome, to whom the Courts of the civilised world owe their best Law to this day. How pitiful, on the other hand, to behold an adult Empire so bound by the bands of old sins that, with laws too fine for rough and half-forgotten work, it fails by its most patient counsels to curb the madness of a portion of its people, and even to save its own Ministers of Justice from being the unavenged victims of a list of lawless resolutes sharked up by the selfish hands of a policy of sentiment.

But, except where a society is in a state of decay, which no society can be in which the Christian leaven is given fair scope to work, the life of Law, by the law of its life, sooner or later recovers itself, and upon the whole moves on triumphantly. It becomes more and more one with the Voice of the Supreme Lawgiver, and then happy are the people that are in such a case. If the Jews were happy when their God was their King, much more blest will that nation be, where, in still fuller reality as well as in name, Kings reign and Judges decree justice by Him to whom in these last and better days all judgment has by that Father been committed.

For the path of Justice, like the path of the just, in a nation as in a man who follows his best light, shines ever more and more to the perfect day.

It is obvious that in all Law which takes a lower range than that of Christ, there is a most dangerous, but yet a necessary, shortcoming. How much there is of moral disease and of wrong action which demands to be dealt with and to be cast beyond the threshold of society, if we would attain, as a nation made up of families and households, to anything like security and serenity! That very freedom of the subject—with which, beyond certain limits, no laws in any country, much less in ours, no laws however well devised, could ever dare to meddle—must, it is obvious, involve much general freedom to be foolish and even to be criminal. For instance, to Christ's gracious words, "Where two or three are gathered together, there am I in the midst of them," there is a dreadful counterpart—for any two may agree on earth and have in the midst of them only the Enemy. Nay, it is possible, as far as law can go, for all the individuals of a nation, so long as they keep themselves close, to feed without fear on half the pleasures of sin. With this, though it sap the soundness of the State, no law which man can make is of avail, I say, to grapple. Therefore is it not plain to the meanest capacity that society must be conscious of a most dangerous blank, and must from the depth of its heart raise a pitiful cry for the play of another law —a law within the law, and behind the law? And what other law, I ask, can come to its aid, but our Gospel, the Law of the Spirit of Life in Christ Jesus, to deliver a nation from that law which, as we see, works in its members, the Law of Sin and Death? How manifestly, if a nation would grow to its best estate, must it recognise that New Commandment which writes across the wall of heaven not only "Thou shalt not," not only "Thou God seest me," but "THOU GOD LOVEST ME." What else but this can touch the core of Imperial decay?

This then is the New Commandment under which the old ones have been leading us up to live. It has been issued by Jesus, and by Jesus alone. Our "sweet Master" speaks with an authority which all the world, as its perceptions become exercised and its traditions freed from superstition, must eventually recognise.

If before Christ, or since Christ, this fine and delicate spirit has been anywhere abroad, it has been for Christ that the world was waiting to develop those premonitory whispers into an authoritative Voice. He spake as never man spake. All the voices, through all time and in divers portions of the planet, which have been good and true, reissue now from Jesus as their natural, while supernatural, Well-head. He who said "No jot or tittle of the Law"—of the heart of the old eternal Law, written or unwritten—should "pass, but all be fulfilled", covered all the needs of men by this brief and new commandment "Love one another." Christ would not have said it was new, if it had not been so. The Jews were the first of the nations, but He found they had it not. Every other enactment which is honest and useful, plays under the range of this. And when everything which is of a passing nature has purged itself away, like the leaves and skins and refuse which float to the scum, or sink to the dregs of the winefat, this Law of Jesus will sweeten all the body of social compact. And God endorses it, saying, "This is My beloved Son; hear Him." To the fearful this may sound as the voice of thunder, but to genuine human souls, to honest and good hearts, it will always be the voice of Him who is still more our Saviour than our Judge. If you would know that there is a Law far above and beyond any usage possible to human tribunals, here is a reminder. In one breath, in our *Te Deum*, we say "We believe that Thou shalt come to be our Judge;" in the next we say, "We therefore pray Thee—*therefore* pray Thee—help Thy servants, whom Thou hast redeemed with Thy precious blood"! Could ever Law be more magnified than in such a glorious paradox as this? "Just, and yet the Justifier." "Charity itself fulfils the Law." What a safe position, brethren, is that of the believer! The Law of the Spirit of Life in Christ Jesus has made him once and for ever absolutely free from the Law of sin and death, and he acts the Law he lives by without fear.

I have said, The path of Justice in a society of men is like the path of the just.

Watch then, I pray you, with me the advance of righteousness in the case of one man. And, since it clearly would not serve my present purpose to instance one who, having learnt the Law of Love at his mother's knees, has all along grown up into Christ in all things, a case even already happily becoming less and less uncommon — take, by way of illustrating the working and growth of Law in an imperfect state, the case of a person who, coming to years of discretion, finds, to his alarm, that he is far from being discreet, and that he has a very mixed nature wherewith to go through his life. He finds himself full of vague longings, and is apt to be the prey of a variety of dangerous desires, springing, some from the cesspools of sloth, others in the fever of false activities. For many of these he cannot, perhaps, be held accountable. But he is naturally honest, just, and good, and, by the hypothesis, sane. Now what course does he at once adopt? This is what he does. He brings to bear upon these elements of inner disorder, *Law*—the inner Law of which he is conscious, the law of his mind and common sense, upon which the debased law of his passions is making such impetuous havoc. He may be aided, indeed, by some fear of the statute-book; but to dwell on this would also of course mar my illustration. Well: he resists the devil, and that Enemy flees from him; for this also goes by a law. Desire after desire, possibly after hard struggle—which may be in part dependent on constitution and circumstances, though, perhaps, in greater part upon antecedents for which he is responsible—impulse after impulse goes under, and he soon has the comfort of finding these wild and wandering tendencies subside, and give place to the calmness of order.

Now this, take note, can, as we see every day, be done—I do not say without the good spirit of His God—for every good working of Law must come from that living Source of Law Who has been called Personal Order; but it can be done, as I pray you to observe, without admitting that highest light of Him who in these last days proceeds to us also *from the Son*. The man has been turned indeed to God and His Law, but not yet to that fulness of God which is manifested only in the face of Christ and His Gospel.

But we are speaking of one, who, having a sound conscience and a sane mind, is ever on the look out for light. Doing the truth, to this Light he now comes. For every man who is constitutionally complete has in him, more or less in activity, a natural craving for his best religion, which in England we still nationally hold to be Christ's. One of the seeds of that ripened and risen Flower of Being, one of the spores of the atmosphere of this new life, whether by a text, or a friend's word —or sometimes, haply, God grant it! even by a sermon—falls into his old nature. He is thus *converted*, he is born again: old things pass away, behold all things become new. He changes his mind, which any man may do about anything, high or low, perhaps in an instant. He starts up a new creature in Christ Jesus. New desires now spring up in his new nature. He soon finds ample cause to be thankful that he could not rest or be content with any finality short of his Redeemer. Out of that calmness which now rules in his life—which calmness was his reward for not having been a "child of disobedience"—a still higher reward now comes. *Christ* has come to him, and His reward is with Him. Our friend has been obedient hitherto to lower law; and now that which is best and strongest in him asserts itself. The Spirit, pleading with his spirit, urges a claim for that something which is more touching, more constraining, more penetrating, more elevating—in a word, more human and humane even than Law. Law was only his kindly pedagogue, but that old family servant has led him to the School of Jesus.

As Equity is not better than Justice, but is a better justice, so the law of the Spirit of Life in Christ Jesus is not better than the Moral Law, unwritten or written, but is a better Moral Law.

The man's old conception of Law, good and useful as it was so far as it went, had yet about it something driving, something hard, something ungenerous, yea, even mean, in comparison with this glory that excelleth. But all *that* is now taken up, absorbed, refined, and has passed through every phase of change which can bring it to its essential perfection. No jot or tittle of the teaching of that old pedagogue, which did such good service in mastering bad desire, has passed away. Rather it has ascended into this new spirit which now comes over him, shedding an indescribable lustre over his life. Law was to him but the grey half-light before this bright and balmy effulgence of his Morn. Now out of his newborn soul spring up, as aforesaid, a thousand new desires. These are of a better class. The old ones demanded—I do not say extinction, in so far as they were human, but they called for much repression. Being inherited from a long line of low-type ancestry, for *them* obviously repression was the rule. But for these new impulses, these supernal forth-reachings, which now are astir in him, repression would rather be the rare exception—I say rare, for repression may here also be sometimes needful. Do we not see plainly that there is such a state, not only in persons, but in the best movements of the masses—a spiritual ecstasy which may turn to be as much the worst of all states, as that of which it is the corruption is the best? The same Voice which cast out the devils from the Magdalene, refrained that changed and sweetened maid, when she would fain have flown to Him dazed with the delight of seeing Him in the flesh once more, and calmed her again to order. But generally these desires which have now sprung up in the nature that we are dwelling on, are such as require to be co-ordered and indulged rather than to be checked. The law of his life, which has set him free from the law of sin and death, is not now so much "Thou shalt not," as "Thou shalt." "Do to others as you would they should do to you," which is clearly but a beggarly element in morals, is now transfigured into all the splendour of that bloom of self-sacrifice, of which we saw that he had nurtured the germ when he was but battling with his baser besetments. The chord of self has passed out of sight in the harmony of the hymn which rises now from this new arrangement of his being.

So it is I say with the individual man who, having followed Law, becomes at last a new creature in Christ Jesus.

Now, as surely as a man is part of a nation, it is clear that some corresponding change, some movement of the like nature, must come about in the life of the Nation—of that Nation which is following on to know the Lord. This change will not be to-day, nor will it be to-morrow, though signs of its approach are not wanting throughout the land; but it will be in some day hereafter. Law well observed and well administered in a nation, as in a person—except from other causes that nation shall decay before the Gospel comes, or except it put out its desire of light—Law is bound to be the Forerunner of the Gospel. This were a consummation how devoutly to be wished, and, as it seems to me, to be aimed at beyond all things by Statesmen. How can any genuine statesman stand unconcerned in the presence of such an element as Christianity among the citizens? And what a glorious theme for any preacher to launch into! Would that in lieu of twenty minutes I hae twenty hours with you, for I guarantee that thd beauty of the idea, despite its handling, would enchain you to listen.

When Law has thoroughly done its magnificent and beneficent work—when, like a hawk, brooding over the coveys of crime, the certainty of swift penalty has repressed all irregular impulse in the population—when that sunshine of the popular breast, the sense of fair play all round, which does so much to brighten the utilities of each, has taken the cloud of discontent from the brow of all, thus not only repressing their bad impulses but replacing them with good ones—when the free overflow of the reservoirs of the charitable and rich shall have descended, far more than now, and poured itself with all wisdom into the empty cisterns of distress—when thus under the kindly action of the Law of Jesus, there has arisen a communion of saints which shall forestall the communism of sinners, and a certain understood participation of blessings shall have taken all the wind out of the sails of Revolution—when better-considered poor-laws shall have helped to make temperate a people leagued to be provident—when Christian culture in all schools shall have rendered the masses fit to be masters—(*Christian* culture, I say, for what would happen in the land if those masters of the future shall have learned nothing of the Spirit I speak of?—aye, what, indeed, would happen? But I will spare ill-omened words to-day)—when superstition, standing even now where it ought not, has been ousted not only from the State but from the Church—when, in a word the nation shall say as one man, " Lo, I come to do Thy will, O God, yea, I am content to do it, Thy Law is within my heart "—why *then*, I say, Law may take a long breath and stand aside for the advent of LOVE.

You will look for a few words from any one who stands here to-day upon the great occasion of the hour. They shall for every reason be but few. How can this be nothing to you, oh ye that pass by? Would that there were in this Temple at this time not only the sleeping dust, but the vocal spirit of another: of him, I mean, who loved above all things to light up for us, as each went by, the eventful changes of our history. For methinks that sweet and powerful soul would have said this evening something wise, something solemn, something affectionate—in a key which who now can touch?—to express the emotion with which the people at large, and you, brethren, in particular, must regard this exodus of Justice from these precincts of yours, which for at least eight centuries have been her home. By your journals, which now so largely supersede the voices of your preachers, the event is duly chronicled, and by them every association, which memory and their imagination could summon, has been so brought together, that the mind of the nation cannot but note what a change it is.

What then is left for a preacher to say? This—which, after all, is the best that anyone could say. It is left for him, whoever may chance to stand here, at this hour when Justice is gathering up her robes and saying, "Let us depart," humbly, and so far as he may, to breathe for her, as she passes to her more splendid palace, but to a less historic home, the blessing of her country's Church—the blessing of Him who was heralded as the Lawgiver to be raised up from His brethren for the guidance of the world—the blessing of Him whose way Justice is making ready.

Ah me! but is not that blessing yet warm from the lips, and signed in the last writing, of him whose it was to convey it?—breathed, in dying loyalty, but undying affection, to the earthly Head of this State and this Church—to Her, to whom therefore it was above all things most rightful that Her Primate should send the blessing of Her Church, in sending his own last farewell. That wreath of royal cut flowers, sent to please his last eyes, serves, alas, but to deck his bier. A supreme grace, done, as it might be, for his burial. For know ye—too well ye know—that our Master was taken from our head but yesterday. "My father, my father, the chariot of England and the horsemen thereof!"

Thus do our great souls pass, and our great

institutions arise and abandon, as now too narrow, their primæval homes.

But whatever, and wherever, may be the future of British Justice, and however commodious may be her newly-chosen apartments beside the public thoroughfare, it never will be forgotten that here it was, under the holy shade of your venerable towers, she grew to be what she is—that here it was that she passed through all her early ordeals—here it was that she "broadened down from precedent to precedent," weaned herself from her old superstitions and her rude mistakes, and so foreran that Just One in the best teaching *she* could give of that righteousness which has already exalted her native land.

Time may have broken and crumbled her marble seat; ruin and fire may have blotted out well nigh all her ancient landmarks; all things which can fade or be shaken may have been shaken to the ground and faded into the crypts of the Past—nay, it may not be without some sighing on your part, and perhaps some natural tears on his, that "the parting genius" was sent from this place this morning.—Though as for any fears on your part for loss of dignity, you will bear in mind, that, if Judgment has left your Hall, "a greater than Solomon is here," in your Abbey.—However all this may be, Justice is not a thing of place. The Judge of all mankind abides always, and the Queen, by whom, under God, her Judges decree Justice, wherever they fix their tribunals, abides over them still. So may the path of British Justice ever grow brighter and brighter to the perfect day. If she is doomed to decrease, may it only be because Christ increases. Go whither she may, God and the Queen go with her.

Then, when the full Christ shall have come—

"the Christ that is to be"—come, "His fan in His hand, His reward with Him, and His work before Him"—come not only as we know Him now, by His words and in His standard excellence, but come in His social realisation, then at least, if not before, He will be treated by all men with the fairness which He has died to win for all, but which He Himself beyond all has found hitherto denied to Him. Men look, nor vainly, for the Justice of which Jesus is above all the Advocate and "the Counsellor." How right then it were that all men should learn to render, in that consummation which we have foreshadowed, not only to the Queen and our fellow-subjects, but to God and His Christ, that which is their due.

Wertheimer, Lea, & Co., Printers, Circus Place, London Wall.

THE WITNESS OF JOHN.

By the Rev. WILLIAM B. PHILPOT, Vicar of South Bersted, Bognor, Sussex.

Sermon Preached at South Bersted.

"And this is the witness of John, when the Jews sent unto him from Jerusalem priests and Levites to ask him, Who art thou?"—John i. 19.

IT would be a flat and trifling truism to say that John the Baptist was a remarkable man. His place in history is more distinctly marked than that of any one except of the New Man Himself. He who "knew what was in man," and therefore what was in John, points him out as the greatest up to that time born of woman. When I speak of historical greatness, I mean a far higher range of historical greatness than that of your Alexanders, Tamerlanes, Cæsars, Napoleons, or even of Bacon and Shakespeare. Of these, the men first named disarranged, upset, or rearranged divers nations, with confused noise and garments rolled in blood; but they simply made a seething in the existing elements of the world: and the last two, though living in newer times and more or less professed servants of Jesus, lifted mainly the platform of Mind. But John, take note, played his part in the highest regions and ranges of humanity, moving and working on the upward line, breasting the steep and straight path of *spiritual* advance. He was not one of those common great ones who battle and strive and whose voice in the struggle for pre-eminence is heard amidst the dragging of captives and the parading of trophies through the shouting streets of triumphant capitals. John was "a voice" indeed, but a voice in the wilderness. If his place was wisely chosen at the fords of the Jordan, and if he sought to gain the soldiers and civilians who passed to and fro thereby, his aim was to win, not their swords nor their suffrages, but their souls, to the Kingdom that was coming. Great he was, but he was great in the sense in which Christ said His servants aimed to be great—in ministering to the advantage, not of themselves but of mankind. In this sense Jesus, the Man-God, the God-Man, the First and the Last of the New Race, and the representative not only of Man but of God, pronounced John to be the most remarkable instance of the former Man and of the now fading type of Being. He was, as Jesus said, "the lamp that burneth and shineth," who bore witness to the truth by preparing His way before Him. John, as he himself avowed, was not filled with the Christ-Spirit. He was to decrease, while Christ was to increase. As the saurian, the mastodon, and the beasts of the caves had faded before Adam, so the old man was now to fade before the New. John came in point of time before One who, in point of type, character, and position in humanity was altogether on a higher, nay, on the highest possible platform of visible Being; and John's greatness lay in the fact that he was the first to recognise that other as the Coming Man, and to tell the world that it was so. He stood by, feeling unworthy to stoop down and unloose the latchet of Christ's shoes; and as the New Man, the Divine Master approached, he pointed Him out in the following beautiful and striking language:—"Behold the Lamb of God, which taketh away the sin of the world." How simple and magnificent was this record that He bare of our Master! Speaking after mere earthly modes, John was indeed His cousin; but, bent on his own prophetical mission, he had not seen his playmate since the time when, as Raphael loved to imagine of the Holy Family, the twain had blended their infant lispings round the knees of Mary. When Jesus came among the crowds to stand in the shallow waters and bend to the dipping in that symbolic stream, John did not know Him even by sight. But he knew Him by a sign. His heart, a prophet to his heart, forewarned him that the sacred form on whom the pure emblem hovered and alit was there and then receiving in fulness the inflow of the Divinity, and that He it was whose way he was destined to prepare.

You cannot understand Christ's words that "the least in the Kingdom of Heaven was greater than John" to mean anything else than this:— that, great as John was in comparison with the pre-Christian man, yet he who in any degree should afterwards receive into his old nature the seed of the new nature, and the leaven of the Spirit of Christ, was thereby turned into a higher kind of being than even the highest and greatest of the old. So great and so essential a thing is it, my brethren, to be converted, to be made new creatures in Christ Jesus and to be renewed in the spirit of your mind. If you receive the temper of Jesus, if you are changed into Christ's likeness, if you let the Spirit of the New Man bring you to what is called "the new birth," you have then a patent of nobility compared with which all the honours of earth are like dust in the balance. I fancy some of you think that what we so often say about the need of this change is in the air, and will not bear examining. I only have to say that it is a fact which is based upon the most patent facts of all natural history. We are borne out by the laws of growth and development in a sense which no truly scientific man can dispute, when we say that, if you do not rise into the Christian man, you continue to be a lower kind of man, or sink even to be lower than man.

Now let us look closely, while briefly, into this witness of John, for his ministry is part, though the elementary part, of *our* ministry.

Our Gospels for the last two Sundays in Advent are drawn from John's record, and one collect prays thus: "Oh Lord Jesus Christ, who at Thy first coming didst send Thy messenger to prepare Thy way before Thee, grant that the ministers and stewards of Thy mysteries may likewise so prepare and make ready Thy way by turning the hearts of the disobedient to the wisdom of the just, that at Thy second coming to judge the world we may be found an acceptable people in Thy sight, who livest and reignest with the Father and the Holy Spirit, ever one God, world without end." I say John's ministry is only *in part* ours, for if we had nothing else to say beyond what *he* said, we should not be Christ's ministers, but John's. Our ministry, to you who are rejoicing already *in* the light of Christ, is obviously not to bring you *to* that light, but by His Spirit to help to show you, if so we may, ever more and more the glory of these bright revelations. But to those of you who have not yet tasted (of course I do not mean merely baptismally and formally, but inwardly and spiritually) of the good gift, and have not yet experienced the powers of that higher life which Christ has for you, to such of you our message and John's is one. And that message is "Behold the Lamb of God which takes away your sin."

Now, let us note the main drift of the teaching and preaching of that herald of grace.

The people of the Jews were struck by John's coming. Here was a wonderful prophet. Those who had visited the fords at Bethabara told of the strange being, in garb like their prophets of old, recalling the voices of the holier past, and of the best teaching of their country's history; and this was not an apparition to which they durst be insensate. So they sent a chosen deputation for the express purpose of ascertaining what voice it was. The Jews, I need not tell you, were *all* a remarkable people. They dwelt alone. It were beside my immediate purpose to remind you here of the thousand traits by which this Semitic type proved that theirs was the stem out of which the flower of humanity was in its time to break. Christ could not have been an Egyptian, could not have been a Greek, could not have been a Roman; nor could he have been an Indian, nor an Englishman, nor in a word anyone but a Jew. All those other races had indeed their longings, their inspirations and their aspirations, and had their great men round whom as their best they naturally gathered, notably their Confutze, Zoroaster, Buddha, Plato, Aristotle, and the rest. But CHRIST, the newest and last Type of Man, was the desire of them all; and all other nations can now be lifted up by receiving the seed of this Spirit of Christ—a consummation how devoutly to be wished! But historically and by the lately lit upon laws of what is called Ethnology, or the science of the grouping of humanity, our Christ could only, I repeat, have been a Jew. As it was from among the mammals, that is, creatures that nourish their young from the breast, that the living soul and conscience of the First Adam was to spring, to be evolved, or rolled forth, to be developed or *dis-covered*, in greater or smaller instalments, coming from below or from above upon those former natures out of the Life-fountain of the invisible Father, so it was out of the special Hebrew branch of man—for life here also grew by subdivision, humanity in its groups as in its individuals breaking into variations—it was out of the Hebrew branch, I say, that in His own divine order, by spiritual generation, there was to spring this quickening Spirit of the New Man. Hence was it that the Jews were never to be reckoned among the common nations of the earth, any more than it would have been reasonable to reckon the mammals among the lizards. This was why the lips of Balaam, though his eyes lusted after the gold of the princes of Balak, were spellbound into blessings which no power of his could reverse; and, sorely against his will, he bore witness and said: "The Lord his God is with him and the shout of a king is among them. Surely there is no enchantment against Jacob: neither is there any divination against Israel." It was, in short, of no earthly use to resist the growth of humanity. And the Jews could not but know this. Though, by reason of the strong admixture among them of the more debased types of being, a thousand times they had rebelled against Him who nourished and brought them up—though they were a seed of evil-doers, and laden with iniquity, yet the voices of their better men, from time to time vibrating among them with an instinctive pertinacity, which can be laid to nothing but that good Providence which was longing to reconcile and skilled to bless them e'en against their will—the Jews clung to the record of these voices as if they were indeed the rule of their lives; and they kept their Psalms and Prophets till Christ came, and read them and fed upon them, and uplifted them, and found Himself in them. Thus it came to pass that they were ever on the out-look for that coming Man whom those prophets had taught them to expect. And so now, when they found this most wonderful person, John the Baptist, speaking strange sayings—but sayings strangely in keeping with the voices which were read every Sabbath day in their ears—it was no wonder that they sent this deputation of their most learned Priests and most zealous Levites to find out whether at last this were really the Christ who was for to come. John indeed—whether it was that, faint and broken down by the misery of his prison, he had lost the memory of the sunshine and the dove, and had gone back from that full assurance which had possessed him before, when he pointed with triumphant exclamation to the Lamb of God—whether or not this was so, I know not; but John himself sent afterwards to ask Jesus if indeed it were He that should come, or whether they were to look for another. In like manner, though with a far different spirit and with minds not only unprepared for but set against the truth, the Jews sent their cleverest Pharisees to ask John if he were the Messiah for whom all men were waiting.

Now what did John say? He said "I am not the Christ: I am the voice of one crying in the wilderness." And what does he say that he cried? It was this: "Make straight the way of the Lord, as said Isaiah the prophet." It is possible indeed that he did not know that he was the Elias which was for to come, for great men in their natural simplicity are mostly greater than they know. And when they questioned his acts as not suited to any except to the One whom they looked for, he turned their minds from all symbolic and outward observance, and said, "I baptize you with water: in the midst of you standeth One whom ye know not, even He that cometh after me; the same is He which baptizeth with the Holy Ghost and with fire"—those inner fires of renewing grace and quickening and purifying love which we, dear brethren, by this time should know so well. Such was John's answer. The deputation went back; and in less than three short but momentous years they for their part definitely refused to receive the Christ, though He was their own, though He was a Jew and sprung of the same human stem, and though His voice was only the higher key of the old voices of their own prophets. They said, "We will not have this man to reign over us." They interpreted their prophets according to their own carnal mind; they killed the spirit in the letter; they closed their eyes to the light;

they stopped their ears, and with one accord rushed upon Him, cast Him out of the city, and nailed Him as a slave upon the Cross, thus killing the body which was the Temple of the Spirit of Christ.

Now, ye men of Upper Bognor and inhabitants of Bersted, this is virtually what you do, if you refuse to prepare in your souls the way for Jesus, and to make straight the paths of the Lord. You will not find Jesus down any crooked path. The soul of man is filled with base and low desires, some of one sort and some of another. If you wish to rise to the highest humanity, to vindicate your due position in the race, to sit with Christ in His heavenly places, ye must make straight paths for your feet. Ye ask and receive not, because, like those Pharisees, ye ask amiss. I am here addressing those who have not found, and do not care to look for the Lamb of God. Submit yourselves, I pray you, to God. Instead of saying to your *desire*, "Thy will be done," say to *GOD*, "*Thy* will be done." "Resist the devil, and he will flee from you." "Ye cannot serve two masters." "Choose which you will serve." If you have reason to believe that God's enemy will prove himself *your* friend, follow *him*; but if He who loves you so as to send His beloved Son to save you—if He be God, *since* He is God, then follow *Him*. "Draw nigh to God, and He will draw nigh to you." "Cleanse your hands, ye sinners" in whatever respect your conscience tells you that you need cleansing; in whatever matter ye know that your heart needs purifying, purify your hearts, ye double-minded. "To him that knoweth to do good and doeth it not, to him it is sin." To go on against your conscience, this, be well assured, is not preparing the way for the Lord; this is not making His paths straight. How can that sweet Spirit of Jesus enter your soul in any muddy by-path of pleasure?

If your paths are leading down to the grave, those are no paths up which your Christ can come. It is from above, along the straight path of a good conscience, that Christ comes bearing for you the gift of His salvation. To have a genuine desire to be right, rather than to enjoy any wrong pleasure, this is to make a straight path for the Saviour. If you do not really desire to go straight, you cannot hope to be saved. So long as you or I are presumptuous and self-willed, bent on wrong pleasures, reckless of the welfare, the feelings, the salvation of others, if only we ourselves be gratified, then I do not scruple to say that we have in us—how have we not?—something of the nature of the *criminal*. Nobody here would perhaps mean crime with set purpose; but show me, if you can, any essential difference, any difference in kind, for I do not say in degree—but show me, if you can, any difference in kind between the character of the criminal and the character of the man who by any selfish act plants in the nature and conscience of another some sin which draws that other from the way of life or keeps that other in the paths of death. Of how sore a punishment, think you, is not he worthy, who, to do some sweet pleasure to his own vile body, damns precious souls for whom Christ gave *His* pure body to those bitter pains of death? In fact if any of us allow in ourselves any wrong desire whatever, if we let any sinful wish gather head, we are full of danger to others and to ourselves. So let every one of us take heed to ourselves. If we are not making straight our ways and preparing for the coming of our Saviour's grace into us, we are preparing the way for the devil, and preparing our own way *to* the devil. If our souls are not well banked up with good breakwaters, there will come on some terrible night a tide which will carry us away roof and basement to perdition. The strong influences of temptation and the high winds of some violent occasion are sure in some hour to unite and prevail, and sweep away those who have not built themselves firmly on this rock of Christ. When the different classes of persons crossing the Jordan-ford came to the Baptist and asked "What shall we do?" you note how directly he drove at their special besetments, and warned them each and all to battle with and overcome those. Observe how ethically correct John was. Look how the matter stands. A besetting sin pervades and fills the soul. An allowed desire and an obstinate self-will, be it of what kind it may, leaves the soul absolutely unprepared to admit the sweet and safe Spirit of Him who comes to give peace on earth, good pleasure among men — peace among men in whom He is well pleased. The Spirit of Jesus will not take for His Temple a house with the dry-rot. No man would build himself a house without making a way to get to it. When the colonists build a town, the first thing they do is to make a road or a railway to it. This is the only course of prudence and of common sense. So I will leave with you and myself this sacred and solemn record of John, "Prepare the way of the Lord, and make His paths straight." Now may the Spirit of Jesus bless this witness and these words to all our souls, and may that gracious redeeming Spirit come along the straight path we make for Him. May He enter in and dwell here in our hearts, so that our last state may not be worse, but infinitely better than our first. This may God in His mercy grant for Jesus Christ's sake, His Son, our Lord. Amen.

THE NAME WHICH IS ABOVE EVERY NAME.

By the Rev. WILLIAM B. PHILPOT, M.A.,
Vicar of South Bersted, Bognor, Sussex.

Sermon Preached at Stratford-on-Avon in April, 1882, on the Occasion of the Shakespeare Commemoration.

"A Name which is above every name."—Phil., ii. 9.

YOUR Vicar has warned me that whoever speaks here on one of these Sundays must give to what he has to say the colour of the occasion. It is *indeed* an occasion of great and natural interest to you who have had thrust upon you the honour of being born in this town, which gave birth to the most famous poet, as we like to think, of all the Planet; to you who have come to pass your days here; and to you who may perhaps have made a pilgrimage from the Transatlantic England to pay honour to the genius of the place. You will take any teaching we can offer you the more kindly when it comes stamped with the reverential sympathy of your Bard, for I shall call to-day on the spirit of Shakespeare to help me to bring you to Jesus. This is also a Saint's day. Our Church does not allow us indeed to invoke him as our Patron Saint, but we have an omen of fair courage from the day of St. George, and hope that the Spirit of God will help us with him* to "swinge the dragon" who is the enemy of our Master's Name.

It is the name of "God over all blessed for ever" that we come hither to praise; and the name of His Son Jesus, which is above every earthly name. Nothing, I am well convinced, would be more abhorrent to the sweet and graceful soul of the poet than to see any one rise up in one of these churches of Christ, especially in his native place,

---

* ἀντιπάλῳ δυσχείρωμα δράκοντι. Soph. Ant.

and begin to trouble his rest with praises, without remembering from Whom all those powers flowed into him, and to Whom alone all praise is due. If we were now to see those stones move, and that pale ghost of the Bard burst his cerements and revisit these glimpses of the sun, he would, methinks, stretch forth his hand—canonized, if ever any was, by the consent of mankind—and he would say, with an air of hurt majesty—" Behold the Lamb of God, who has taken away my sins and yours; what mean ye to break my heart with your glorifications? A greater than Shakespeare is here. Bow down, oh people of my birthplace, before the name that is above every name.".

And yet what a piece of work was your poet! How noble in reason—how infinite in faculty—in apprehension how like a god—the beauty and glory of the common world. Did not Christ remind His own people from whom and to whom first He came—" I have said ye are gods and all of you are children of the Most High"? Even the only-begotten Jesus said, " Father glorify Thy Son, that Thy Son also may glorify Thee "; and thus if we glorify this Stratford child of God to-day, it is only that we may the better see how in him God was glorified. Let us note what place this mighty Mind occupies in the progress of Being.

There is a good deal said now about Evolution, the exponent of which beautiful idea was on Wednesday last hearsed in death and laid, as befitted him, in our National Mausoleum of departed worth. Darwin may have made mistakes, and Quatrefages has shown clearly to my mind that species can only spring from species, from something newly given by the Life-Source out of the Unseen into what before was seen; that man in fact could only be " a son of Adam, which was the Son of God." Darwin has also left unsaid much which he did not make it his province to say, though at the close of his interesting and elaborate books he mostly pointed out that further truths might be evolved from his doctrine. And surely it is the province of every man in all such thoughts of his heart to make for the knowledge of his Cause. I for my part should have thought that science, whose function it is to search for the causes of Being, only did its fair part when it distinctly confessed, as Christian men of science do, and as Faraday always did, firstly that there is a Personal First Cause; and secondly, when it candidly acknowledged that this Throne can only be filled by God as shewn to us by Jesus. But it has long seemed to me that some such idea as Evolution, in a wider sense than perhaps even Darwin dreamed of, was wanting to explain to those who had leisure to look for an explanation, and mental range to take it in, *the great fact of Christ Himself*. While the fulness of the Godhead morally is also God in phenomenon, He no less, but infinitely more, than any other divine phenomenon, physical or Personal, invites and demands enquiry. He who said "What think you of Christ?" "Whose Son is He?" "Handle Me and see," not only frees from the charge of irreverence, but welcomes with the frankest and most friendly challenge those who are fain to put the reality and the real place of His Being to the test.

For look how the matter stands. You must indeed take for granted—everybody must—the ground existence of a Fountain of Universal Life. For if not, you break that canon of the Master of them that know (as Dante calls Aristotle) in which that great mental authority lays it down that everything has some scope, and that design pervades nature; and thus you make this vast and delicate universe one monstrous and aimless puzzle. Every effect, and therefore the earliest stirrings of life, must have a cause. It were surely bad science, and but a clownish philosophy, as Socrates calls it, for a man, with such limited senses and frail faculties for the apprehending of vasty ideas, to have found all along, ever on and up, cause after cause, after a uniform and consecutive purport, and then, at a particular point in his analysis, namely, when he comes to the necessary end of it, to stand off and say there is no further cause—why? merely because he cannot find one, and cannot here see, with his microscopic eye, what the cause is which till then he has owned that in every thing there must be! By what law of thought, I ask, does a man follow a series of links which mark design — if design has any meaning at all for us—and then peak like John a dreams and say nothing—nay more, say there *is* nothing and No One, when the clue of his chain of causation has led him to the curtained Tent of the very Designer Himself? Is not this the very moment when Science and Truth should meet together, Knowledge and Faith kiss each other, and with united voice, standing on the edge of the gulf impassable to sense, proclaim the great Original, and joy together as with the joy of harvest in the presence of the found and trusted Father? It is the worst and most mischievous form of dogmatism, this dogmatism of negation. What has happened, I repeat, in the universal law of causation, that the universe itself should have no "*causa causans*"? Nothing—except indeed that a blindness of heart, as well as of eye, has fallen upon that faithless enquirer. Blindness moral and intellectual is the cause of Atheism. Let any one else say what he likes: I for my part say this.

I have shown you that you must take for granted that one Source of life. But as the highest life, of all that from our own experience and our own consciousness we know, is *Personal* Life, therefore the source of that and of all life must obviously be a Person. How could any of our personality spring wholly from a mere vegetable or animal cause? Such a source would be ludicrously inadequate. Personality may indeed, in some sense, spring out of these as a lily from a pot of loam, but nobody could be such a fool as to fancy that the loam accounted for the lily, except the person who would say—which certainly Darwin did not say—that the dirt, or the ape, the monad, or the monkey, sufficiently accounted for Man. The Father of Man—of a being who has been shown to have in his microcosmical composition the nature both of plant and animal in subordination to his personal nature—that Father, however far in His own nature he may be beyond the reaches of our souls, must, I say, for the production and nurture of man's personal life, be not only of a nature to supply all those lower ranges of life which adorn the planet and subserve the uses of man, but must also Himself be, as His best known creature is—a Person. If it be admitted that there is a First Cause, which I have shown you that you must take for granted,—for such a hypothesis, however inexplicably mysterious, is, as we have seen, demanded by Science itself—and which when thus taken for granted explains all that otherwise would be a conundrum, idle, unmeaning, and without an answer,—seeing that there must be such a Cause, that Cause, that Life-Source must in fine have infinite Personality. We cannot conceive, nor need we look for, any higher entity. Into what ranges and changes of Being this may reach —who can expect to know? But, be that how it may, the Most High must be some mode of Personality.

Behold we show you a mystery. The fact, brethren, is, God the Father is *immanent*—that is, He is abiding in nature and in man. And He must have been conscious from the beginning, for otherwise that which was obviously designed could obviously have had no designer. Things were designed with equal clearness in all their ranges *before* man stepped out of the Unseen. If, as the sweet-souled Emerson is represented to have said, (though probably he, like most great men, is likely to be mistaken and misrepresented)—Emerson, whom also we mourn to-day—if God only and first became conscious in man, then, you see, all that order of nature which led up to man must have designed *itself!* Such a creed is only to assert the confused and confounding dogma that there is no other God than man. The fact however is, that God is dwelling in the universe and the universe in Him. In Him we, universe and all, live and move and have our being—we in Him and He in us, that we may all be made perfect in One. *The material universe is,* so to speak, *the body of God.* As the spirit of a man inhabits, and lives in, and uses the body of the man, so the Spirit of God lives, and works, and is, in all the matter of the universe; and this is the main meaning of man being made " in the image of God."

Well now, if you have followed what I have tried to make clear, you will see how, in the way of evolution, God has fulfilled, or, if you like, finally evolved Himself in Being. In Him the universe has lived, lives, and will for ever live, and in all its rising grades and phases it has and will have its Being. First there was the formless void—a chaos, still to be seen by the miners and those who drive the tunnels through the hills; not organised at all, but only *eatenus quatenus* living in God by force of the fact that His Spirit with all His potentialities of future phenomena was moving over, and in, and under the face of its mysterious deep; growing ever into those novel forms of beauty and vigour which He was risingly showing. Every atom and molecule in this sense has God in it bodily—God and power of life in atomic phase; capable under certain legalised conditions of moving towards its fellow-atom for communion and for germinating cells of organism; atoms which one day would in due course enter into the matter and composition of higher beings; clay which could rise and turn hereafter into an "Imperial Cæsar," yea, and a greater than Cæsar. For then there came for our planet, with which alone we have now to do, those rising changes described by the poet of the Creation. As the last book of our Canonical Scriptures is the Apocalypse of the Future, so the first book of Moses, called Genesis, not less dark amidst its brightness, is the gathering together of all the traditions and intuitive aphorisms of the earliest intelligence, and thus forms the Apocalypse of the Past.

But does the account of things there given affect to be scientific? It is as far above science as intuition is above argumentation. Science is quite a later, the latest, if not the last, evolution of mere mind. Science, in its common acceptation, is a kind of material revelation given through mental processes to thinkers and seekers after God, whom Christ's truth has, so far as men will let them, made freer than before. Science is a mode, newly found and growingly ingenious, of acquiring a kind of knowledge which is not necessary by any means to salvation, but which still may be very interesting to us saved folk, upon whom the ends of the world have come; to those of us at least who have taste, capacity, and time for enjoying its study or mastering its results. For my own part, though that is neither here nor there, I grant I have hardly time even to note the bare conclusions of material scientists, curious and pleasant though they be, being professionally and by predilection absorbed in the study of that science of the soul which may teach me better how to bring your souls and my own to that spiritual Type which is the ideal. You cannot expect me, for instance,—you cannot expect the Christian minister, I mean,—to go into very great raptures over anything which even the greatest naturalist has discovered in the habits of a worm, when I have open to my enquiry a region of fathomless mystery and of infinite sweetness in noting and reflecting on the image of God found in His people, and in watching the genial impact of divine Charity on the dormant molecules of my human soul, and humbly and prayerfully reflecting upon all this for my own personal growth in the knowledge and love of my God. Yet mistake me not. As long as that lower science knows her place and bides in it, we pay her the most amused and respectful regard. And science, as I was going on to say, finds the germs of its own being in those brilliant touches of the aphoristic poetry of the early Scriptures, in which we can see, glancing from earth to heaven and from heaven to earth, the very same kind of courageous intuition and magnificent imagination, which, in the interests of humanity, the Source of all knowledge imparted to our Shakespeare.

Well, this account in Genesis, borne out in its main and grand features by the lagging and late-coming discoveries of modern days, tells us that out of the mud and clay of things there arose plant, fish, bird, four-footed, and then two-footed creatures, not *self*-evolved—except it be in the sense in which Christ Himself says, " The earth bringeth forth fruit of itself "—but rolled forth one after the other ever into higher and higher and more and more delicate organisms, filling the beautiful earth with forms of diversified life. Then, and not till then, God said—for those great poets of the past personified God's monitions and acts into voices and words—God said, " Let us make man after our own image in our likeness." Then He gave forth a new. species. He caused to spring forth out of His invisible reservoir of varied and potential vitality a being with dominion in the head and breast, not only with consciousness, which doubtless the former type in some sort had and have—not only the power of affection, which the creatures had who must have been Adam-the-First's immediate precursors and *entourage*—not only with ingenuity and mental acumen, such as the beavers and bees had and have—but with conscience, with reflection, with the power of looking up, with the faculty of faith—which is man's requisite and constitutional instinct—with the power of prayer, and of talking in open vision with the face of God; a being of large discourse, looking before and after with that godlike faculty of reason, which was an advance upon the former merely animal instinct, and of a certain intuitive appreciation and apprehension of all of God that was perceptible by the grade and type of his being.

This was the first Adam. You will take note how Being in its evolution, all according to God's design of fulfilling Himself, thus entered for the first time, but only *entered*, upon the kingdom of *spirit*.

Nor does it matter to me, as a Christian minister, by what theory of development these grades of rising life at any period of the history of Being may, either now or by any more enlightened researches, be ascertained to have been generated; whether by minuter instalments called "variations," or by larger down-givings and by that more marked mode called "species." For all changes and additions, small as well as great, admittedly and incontestably come new and fresh out of the Unseen. Mental science can say no less than this. The spiritual science of the Christian faith says more; for in that Unseen we recognise by Revelation, through our developed intuition, the Personal and immanent Source of all that lives. This is GOD, and Him Christ teaches us to call in the fullest sense "our Father." And this down-giving of traits successively new from the unseen into the seen, we call *Creation*. It explains but in no way mars this conception of the work of God, to find that this creation goes by His law of development. This rather enhances our sense of its unity, its order, and its beauty.

In the form of that creature whom we call man, Being, you see, advancing beyond the mere plant and the mere animal, crossed the frontier, sallied beyond the boundary-line of sense and instinct, and, carrying these along with it in expanded and elevated forms, became partaker of more of the Divine nature than any kind of being before him. But as yet this Man knew nothing, save and except by way of forth-reaching anticipation, of that farther and last range which was to come after him—"the desire of all nations"—and in some sort by the uniform law of growth to be evolved out of him. This first Man fell, superior as he was.

Now be careful how you understand "the Fall of Man." Those former types being complete in their own kingdoms and rounded off into their several functions without the element of Will to disturb the internal economy of constitutions born to the necessity of obedience—those other types of beings, you observe, could not fall. Why? Because they could not sin, nor go in any other way than God had made them to go. Adam and his species after him fell because they willingly and of choice refused to keep up and to rise. Having a will placed in the midst of desires, that type of being to which, before we became new creatures in Christ Jesus, we all belong, chose—which by constitution and make they were at liberty to do—not to abide by God's will and not to reach forward to some nobler perfection. Thus it was that the first Adam could fall, and thus it was he fell. And are we, I beg to know, in the position to quarrel with the Potter for having chosen to inspire His clay with the power of Choice and the characteristic of a Will? For it is to this that the whole question comes. Adam came forth from the Life-source perfect in his type; of *a* perfect type, but not of *the* perfect type, being a type of but penultimate perfection. Or else, as you must see, he would in fact have been at once the Christ. Down into that spiritual kingdom, on which the nature of being had, as we have seen, only entered, something more, a new Nature, was bound to flow, before God could fulfil Himself in setting forth the last Phenomenal Type of Being.

Nor was it to be expected that the design of God should leap from the Ape to the Emmanuel without the intervening grades of the first Adamity. And even if it shall be shown that the previous grades of Being *had* advanced by slight variations— always more or less marked, as the circumstances of their generation were more or less propitious—still it was to be expected that this new and last variation of Man, the fulness of the invisible Life-Giver in human form, would be more marked than any before Him. Nor would it be sane to limit growth in this region of Spirit by any law which we may have noted in the region of the dust.

The species that fell, fell because without further inflow upon his nature he was not and could not without Christ be made perfect. The common but fallacious view of the Fall, which regards Adam the First as being, not only the best kind of being that could then and at that stage come forth from God, but as the best kind of being which could ever and was ever to come from God, wrecks itself and displays its fallacy in this: that we should thus be brought to dishonour God's last manifestation of Himself as being only Adam-the-First over again; and as though God had no further manifestation of Himself to show, but, in sending His only begotten Son, was only correcting some old mistake; a view which carries its own contradiction on the face of it.

Indeed, now that Christ has given us Light, how plainly do we see that the best specimens of the old Adam were far, very far, from being the best and most commanding type that the Author of Being had to show; but that He had yet a Name in which to utter Himself which was above every name, at which every knee should bow (for how could every knee bow to the apple-loving disobedient Adam-the-First or to any of his frail posterity?), One to whom no knee has bowed with more marked and affectionate reverence than the knee which now rests out-stretched beneath the stone in that chancel.

When we speak of the mind and the morality of the old Adam—the pre-Christian man—and when we dwell with sorrow and humiliation on the fact that even from his own ideal he fell—fell because, as I have shown, he had not the Christian ideal of the New Man to lift him and draw him up—it is yet well, if only as an interesting study in Natural History, and indeed part of the "proper study of mankind"—to look into his nature, and to give him credit, or rather to give glory to God, for the grandeur of those powers and the loftiness of that *morale*.

We can only, or at least mainly, judge of the faculties of our pre-Christian Fathers by what written or remembered notices, thoughts, and ideas they have been able to leave on record. Men of action left their records in their deeds, and these have been mainly written in laws and in blood. But to-day we naturally turn more to men of letters, men whose remains are handed down in literature. And herein it is only fair to remember that it is most likely that through all time the greatest thinkers and keenest observers have never written, set down, or perhaps even revealed their thoughts and ideas at all. It is probable that, as with the Apostles, and even with Jesus Himself, the recorded utterances of the best and greatest men of our race are but brief and imperfect signs of their real nature, and that many of their best conceptions are wholly lost to us. Even if they communicated them, they would rarely find disciples or hearers capable of recording them; and therefore we can never, I say, really know how great of soul, how wide of thought, and how large of imagination the old Adam and his type have been. Think how much richer literature would have been had the special correspondent and the daily telegram come earlier into play!

Poetry was a very early vehicle of emotion. Lamech had slain some rash, hot-headed youth in self-defence; and the first piece of rhyme handed down in the annals of the race is, as far as I know, the dirge which he made on that sad occasion for the benefit of his family circle and the vindication of his memory. The early Ægyptians were the depositaries of that early wisdom which Moses took his singular opportunities of mastering in order to keep up among mankind the knowledge of the true God, whose man he is especially called. Abraham was "the friend of God;" but, though he probably guarded in his deep Oriental memory holy traditions, which also Moses used afterwards, he is not remembered as an author of books. His was, however, that straight, up-running Semitic stem on which the New man was bound in the fulness of time to come to flower and to seed.

Looking now to the side-shoots and variations in the human species, the Greeks produced, as you know, their Homer, their Solon, their Socrates, their Plato, at least three great tragedians, Aristotle, and many powerful orators and sweet singers of the splendid music of their tongue. But there was no Christ in Greece; and so their empire found nothing in all those mighty minds, nothing in their best morality, to keep from decay the whole fabric of their dominion. Rome conquered them, and was conquered by their literature and their art; and thus the Greek mind gave to Rome, and they and Rome to Europe, the elements of culture indeed, but not of self-preservation. This first law of nature in its true sense was being kept as the secret to be told us thereafter by the Master of Grace. Hence it was that from Rome arose men like Vergil and Horace, the Cæsars, Livy and Tacitus, Juvenal and Marcus Aurelius, whose aphorisms are not far from the kingdom of God—the wisest of all Christless philosophers. In all the above—and time would fail me if I were to tell of more—we find wide mental range, firm and loving grasp of such truths as they could reach, deep and sweet emotion, divine power of righteous indignation, and a sad but valid sense that the soul was immortal. Great however as the minds of Rome were, and splendid as were some of her moralists, without Christ neither could they, as we have seen, be made perfect. So the Empire of Rome, like the State of Greece, declined and decayed:

and their literature and absorbed culture, and above all their masterly law, fell back, like those of Greece, to swell this our last magnificent wave of human advance, and to enrich the inheritance of Him who was to be Heir of all the ages—the Name that was to be above every name. Few except those Greek tragedians wrote dramas. The Romans were for the most part but imitators and adapters in this. The man who makes dramas has the advantage of his fellows. By art and imitative action—in which men will always take a singular delight—he sets forth, if he be fortunate enough to find those who can so far forget themselves as rightly to render him, the working of all the ground-emotions of that ongoing humanity, which, in its basis, is one and the same through all its changes, for worse or for better, from first to last. Thus the dramatist, according to his ability, is more likely than any other kind of writer to speak to us by his spirit after his body is "encloased" in the tomb. The mantle of the Greek drama was to be taken up in later and in Christian times.

Those whom we have spoken of were, as I said, among the side-shoots of the great plant of humanity. The main stem of the human race, ethnologically speaking, was coming down, remember, in the Hebrew line; which accounts for the super-eminent traits still shown in most ranges of mental power by men who are of Jewish stock. The Jewish prophets, as can be told by any noscent taster of the wine of thought, and any discriminating critic of the vintage of feeling, have a finer smack about them altogether; and as any ear can tell that is master of the music of language, has altogether a purer ring. Of all the First-Adam thinkers, feelers, and writers, the literary men of that Jewish branch alone indicated that, however the Greek and Roman were in their own line darkly feeling after something better, it was they alone who were on the line of bringing to flower the New Man, the Omega, the Crown of Being, the end and consummation of this design of God. Æschylus and Sophocles never could have uttered the same kind of high spiritual truth which came from David and Isaiah; and the higher the truths, the lordlier was the march of the music that alone could match it and convey it. Christ could not have been a Roman or a Greek, speaking merely from an ethnological point of view. Christ came to His own, and out of His own. God evolved Him, so to speak, out of that special stem and shoot, and was thus, as we have seen, leading up to Him. You might as well look to find a pyramid in Attica, or a Parthenon at Coomassie, as to find the Christ anywhere but as the Lion of the Tribe of Judah. Thus He naturally fed and grew on the highest literature of His preceding type and His special stem of it, fulfilled the law and the prophets, imbued Himself with the hymns of His sweet ancestral Psalmist, recognised His place in His Father's all-embracing economy, felt He was the one and last New Man and that He and His Father were one; took on Himself consciously and deliberately His mission and position in accordance with His internal Revelation; rejected the dominance of mere mind, and withstood the great temptation of being the King of Men in that outward sense to which the Enemy tried to lure Him. How easily could the people and the soldiers who came to the fords of Jordan, by an arrangement with His Forerunner, have carried Him on, with His miraculous adjuncts of power and by the sway of His Mastermind, to the overthrowing and superseding of that enfeebled Empire of Rome. How possible it would have been for Him to salve over the world's wounds and lay to the soul of society the flattering unction of a more pacific rule, mastering all opposition by the spell of His transcendent genius and the wand of His consummate wisdom. But no; His kingdom was not of this world, and He knew it. The ulcer of sin was not to be skinned and filmed over thus. So he gave forth His own living and eternal panacea to witnesses chosen before, and thus delivered to mankind the new secret of *Salvation* by the healing power of *self-sacrifice*, first His own and then ours. Or how easily He might have retired to His loved Galilæan hills, left the thankless race, Jew and Roman, with all coming generations, to perish if they pleased in their selfish aims. Who of *us* could have blamed Him, had He gone back to the lake and the mountain, and passed away in a good old age, reclining in serene converse with God beside the nectar of His divine contemplations, careless of mankind? How easily—but for the voice of duty and His sense of His crucial post in this planet. This was a conception which no one formed or could have formed before Christ, and which since Christ's day has become wholly unnecessary, even if it were possible for anyone else to conceive it—a conception not open to a Socrates and a dull anachronism for a Comte. So with set face and high composure He said to His Father, "Not My will but Thine be done," and, knowing fully the consequences, said His great say and died that great death which was to become, and is becoming, the life of the world, and of all individual hearts who accept this mode of His atonement and reconcilement with God—all who let Christ save them by making that living principle of resignation and self-sacrifice their own. Thus He established His church. Hence, brethren, sprang this splendid structure of Christendom—a temple still only in course of building, though its ground-plan is before us.

Well, it was into such a state of things—for to this I have all along, as you will perceive, been leading your minds—that your Shakespeare was born into the world and in this place.

As for your poet's mere mind and imagination, you note that, while he was more strong on the wing, and while he had a wider and older and therefore richer world to deal with, yet these are essentially of much the same make and mould with those of the poets and dramatists of old; being but a gorgeous variation of the old Adam type. Though beyond any of them he was specially grand and beautiful—head and shoulders, as mankind agrees, above them all—still, like each and all of them, he was but a special and individual instance of the old humanity.

But now I pray you·to mark this: that had we found even our Shakespeare unaffected by the surrounding atmosphere of Christendom, not baptised, or entirely forgetful of his baptism (probably in that very font which you guard there in your vestry), elated by his mental endowments into that light-minded and shocking irreverence which, alas, some leading thinkers and writers of to-day consider to be compatible with their highest ideas of humanity—had Shakespeare been a positivist, a humanitarian, an unbeliever, or a teacher of any form of contempt for God—had he sought to put himself and his humanity, rare as it was, in God's place—had he trampled on, or not realised, that self-sacrifice of Jesus—why then, much as we should still have admired his First-Adam class of mind, his range of imagination, his knowledge of mankind, his power to raise our emotions or interest us by his acted stories and his high tone of moral nature, then, O men of Stratford, you would not have had this same poet of yours to be so proud of and to be so thankful for. You might indeed have raised him a memorial theatre, but the mention of him could have had no claim in this sacred place to-day; and the world could not have looked to you, as it does, to further the restoration for a memorial church of this building which is the shrine of his dust. You would not be called upon, as now you are, to save his bones from the desecration of lying among the unsightly remains of a fabric no longer in keeping with the age. May God speed you and your minister in paying this honour to God and to His poet in the name of Him who is above every name, and to whom every wisest knee gladly and thankfully bows.

Many other things you might well expect me to say, had I not drawn largely on your time already, but there are a few more for saying which I crave your further indulgence.

There are some things doubtless in his dramas which scandalise those who love Christ even more than Shakespeare. But, I would beg you to remember, for it is only fair, that since Shakespeare's days the leaven of our Master's Kingdom, the principles of Jesus, are doing their work in the world. As within the borders of some civilised empire or well governed colony, there is seen to reign industry and order, justice and serenity, while beyond the lines of its frontiers there is no less markedly the wildness and confusion of barbarism, lust, rapine, and the anarchy of brute-force; so outside the pale of Christ's righteous, peaceful, and joyous Kingdom—and that even in a nation which is in name Christian, but which is yet only growing to be Christian in reality—there is always raging in common life the turbulence of human passions. And just as in the former case which I have pictured, tribe after tribe begins from outside to recognise the neighbouring blessing of good government and the security of goods and life in that civilised colony—which is in fact not only an illustration but an instance of what I mean—so also, in this nation of nominally Christian England, family after family keeps coming in under the sweet range of Christ's real control. Public opinion becomes modified to a higher and more Christian tone, and what is low and godless is left to remote places, or to the streets and lanes of the cities—places like Northampton, in which the beautiful feet of the servants of the King have not yet, it would seem, gone forth. When they do, I doubt not that those good cobblers will make their best shoes for them, and return only Christian members to the House of Commons!

And can we not see already how this blessed change is working in the interests of the drama itself? Our poet lived in days when humanity was bursting forth, as it were, in every direction, and he was its spokesman—the spokesman of its beauty and its tenderness, its grandeur and its aspirations—but also of its wild exuberance, and I may add, of its swinish propensities in all their reckless humour. It is hard, I grant, to conceive the same mind and heart which set forth with genial delight the sweetness of a Cordelia, the purity of a Juliet, the devotion of a Romeo, the philosophy of a Hamlet, and the reverential religion of Christian kings—giving vent to the coarseness of a Falstaff, the license of his clowns, the vivid animality of some of his minor poems, and the general looseness of the low pleasantry of his day. But the fact was that, rightly or wrongly, he took men and women as he found them, good, bad, and indifferent. He did not aim to be a teacher except, so to speak, incidentally. What he did was to "hold the mirror up to nature." He left it mainly for the New Man, his Master, to hold the mirror up to "Grace." And Shakespeare, it would appear, was, like most of us, only partially renewed in the spirit of his mind, and therefore only partially subserved in his art His Master's ideal. Yet very distinctly did he set forth also the traits of the highest life. In some of his plays, as in the Twelfth Night, which has been so well put upon the stage and acted here, he raises your ridicule at the disgraceful antics of the drunken—which I grant is wrong, for we should never laugh at so dreadful a thing as sin; yet it may well be said in his defence that in so doing he gives the stronger effect to such sentiments as that which he puts into the mouth of Hamlet,—"To my mind, Though I am native here, and to the manner born, It is a custom more honoured in the breach Than the observance. This heavy-headed revel, east and west, Makes us traduced and taxed of other nations : They clepe us drunkards, and with swinish phrase, Soil our addition," which means in plain English—they call us hogs. In this he spoke forth the words of truth and soberness. And none would have rejoiced more than our poet, could he have looked forward 300 years and pictured even the stage of to-day. It would certainly have given him much natural pleasure to think that his countrymen would put his dramas upon the boards with such beautiful adjuncts, such consummate effects, and such sympathetic rendering, as he might, were he among us, witness in his native town in this week. But we may safely say that it would have given him a thrill of far more exquisite satisfaction, could he have known that in after days not only would the manager be able to draw houses *without* the low libertinism with which he found it necessary to tickle the palates of the vulgar—but to know that the improved taste and more refined manner of the coming ages would demand the entire omission of many things which ought never to have been said even before the audiences of his day— no, nor even in the Christless time of an Aristophanes.

Moreover, we cannot but note, in our endeavour to reconcile with so sweet and pure a nature that which is now and then so much opposed thereto, this also :—that, just as he uses comedy to heighten tragedy, so his art told him that perhaps he could in no way show forth virtue more forcibly than by relieving it against the blackness of vice. For example, we could not appreciate the sweetness of Desdemona so truly had it not been for the villainies of his Iago—and so in like manner he exalts purity by setting it, however questionably, against its opposite.

It is obvious, however, let me say, that a time must come when the whole tone of drama must be changed. Oh what a drama will be that of the wholly New Man! What houses will be drawn when Christ has His proper place in the world of the stage, and on that stage which is all the world. For neither should this region of the Drama any more than others—nay, it should, by reason of its unfailing attractiveness, less than any other—be exempted from the range of that influence which is the best. There is something grotesque and alien to that Christian life into which our nation is happily and surely rising, in the fancy that audiences in this century cannot be interested and amused without all these murders and adulteries; or by teaching that there is anything grand in making, as the ancient dramatists did, suicide the main escape from the difficulties of life, or the despairs of love. Is there not, I ask, something horribly out of place in dramatists, nay, even in the great and new musical composers of the Christian era, going back for topic to those ghastly stories of the heathen and pagan stage? For in fact it *is* the heathen stage, in the dramas of Greece and the terrible trilogies of the Christless past, which has given on these matters the lead to the most readable and hearable of existing plays, and has channelled out the course in which all drama has been running. Just as most French Comedy—from whose piquant incidents so much of our home supplies have, the more's the pity, been more or less skilfully adapted—depends upon holding up to ridicule the purity of domestic life, and showing how the sweetness and kindliness of homes may be invaded by the trickeries and lecheries of the foul fiend of libertinism; so it would seem as if dramatists thought that tears could only be wrung from human eyes by reducing some tempestuous hero or some distracted heroine to some suicidal entanglement. Thus the invention of poets, and even of the New Opera, racks itself to devise, and to rake mediæval antiquity for, horrible conjunctures from which, in the poverty of genius, none but bloody solutions

can be imagined. Whatever fine passages there
may be put into the mouth of dialogue, purple
patches among the rags of nonsense, the drama
never can furnish such teaching as may consort
with the demands of a Christian age, till all this is
clean swept away, and higher issues be found
out of the disastrous complications of a tale. Oh!
reform it altogether. I may instance the direction
of what I mean by referring you to that notable
and splendid passage in our poet's Hamlet. The
idea of suicide was suggested to him by the Enemy.
He stands with his bared sword in his hand, but
he makes pause, contemplates the folly of his act,
and sheathes it again when he thinks of the mystery
of immortality, and the "something after death."
Is not that a passage which moves the audience
more than almost any other? Why? Because they
feel that he is right. Look again at the King on
his knees in the same drama. Does not this give
a teaching such as what preacher could ever hope to
rival in setting forth the true nature of repentance?
And yet the audience holds its breath more than
elsewhere to watch the awful interest of that struggle.
Much as I could wish it, my time does not now
permit me to do more than glance at such passages by way of showing you that the drama
need not depend for its interest on breaking upon
the stage those laws which are the bonds of society.
Suffice it to say that the highest glory of Shakespeare—as you may see even by his little birth-
day book, and the book which parallels his sentiments with the Bible—rests on this:—that his
dramas are alive with the noblest Christian sentiments, such as no dramas of the future will either
rival or discard.

And now look lastly, from even a dramatic point
of view, at what God the Father has done in
giving us His only-begotten Son—"the Name which
is above every name." We highly praise that
author who can first conjure up for us the most
painful and apparently insurmountable array of

circumstances, and who then in a manner which we could not have surmised, with supreme delicacy and with the honour of hero and heroine unsullied and intact, brings all out into smooth water and sunshine. We are at first held with awe and wonder, and are next filled with rapt interest and breathless expectation as we watch the unfolding of such a masterly plot. Well, with what feelings then are we to regard the work of the Author of Authors in the management of this Tragedy of the World and the remedies for its disasters? Here we have the treatment of the greatest of all subjects—not in a fiction, or a dream of passion, but on the largest scale of actual misery and in the most painful and entangled of all possible conjunctures—even that of humanity itself —humanity ready to perish. Nor has the Author of this drama, as of those, with cold and calculating skill Himself first tied the knot which He was to unravel, and imagined the complications which He was to solve. But His work is that of the sublime Lover of mankind, who finds before Him for solution a plot thickened by the perversity of His creature whom He has made—made not to be evil, but made with the noblest power of choosing the evil and refusing the good; and Who has to deal with an entanglement of death and disaster foisted upon His beloved race by some Enemy to us inscrutable. He notes in the growth of this field of Being deadly possibilities of mischief, and in surveying it He says "An Enemy hath done this."

It is out of such an imbroglio of misery that the great Dramatist of Humanity has to rescue mankind, with His truth unimpeached and His divine honour untainted by a breath of failure. Do we not, surveying this—not at this moment as those who are personally involved in the issue and *denouement* of the drama—but regarding it simply as the work of the Author of Being—do we not, I say, stand by with adoring marvel and watch with breathless interest and unspeakable admiration the consummate skill, the infinite knowledge, the unimagined tenderness of that power of Love with which our own Almighty Author out of all things evil is bringing round all things good? What are our feelings when we observe how in the mere following out of the unity of His plot in His great Law of the Growth of Being, He has let His all-seeing eye glance from earth to Heaven, and from Heaven to earth; and as His divine Imagination bodied forth the form of One before unseen, has let His merciful Hand turn to shape the New Man, the Person of Jesus, and given to this Flower of Being, a Name which is above every name and a local habitation among the sons of men? So splendid a Drama, I say, speaking merely as a critic, if one for an instant may dare to do so, has the Poet of the Universe made for us here, with Paradise Lost and Regained for His subject, Satan for the Enemy, and Christ for His Hero.

But let us, dear brethren in this Redemption, come off from the standpoint of admiring critics; and let us remember that we are ourselves the very persons concerned in this great Personal Drama—all the world a stage, and all we men and women actors and sufferers in its successive scenes; and let us glorify the great Author of this Drama of our being by bowing, as our human poet did, before the Name which is above every name—the Name of "our dear Redeemer."

Wertheimer, Lea, & Co., Printers, Circus Place, London Wall.

THE GREAT AUTHORITY.

" He taught them as one having authority."—MATT. vii. 29.

THERE resides in what is called an "authority" a power which we shall do well to contemplate. When I speak of an "authority" I mean that position as an adviser which is gained mainly by diligent study, and habitual, practical research; or else by the inherent endowment, always a valuable if not an essential adjunct, of special gifts or of a superior nature ; or, in fine, as in the unique case of our sweet Master—the First of all that know—by the full possession of that Nature which is Supreme.

Take the Medicine-Man. He has studied the laws of health, and he has watched and learned how best he may master the workings of disease. He knows the conditions of life, and he can tell you, as none others can, the causes of death. You or I, with our mere common sense (if we are so fortunate and exceptional as to possess even that in any high degree), untrained and uncultivated as as we are in those regions of observation, live we know not how, and fall ill and die, we mostly know not why. And if in any intricate or unusual case we hazard a conjecture, it is such as to cause a melancholy smile to play round the lips of the men who know. The *medical* man is the only person whom we can regard as entitled in medical matters to speak to us with authority.

Take again the *legal* man. From his youth up he has been versed in the study of that—shall I call it science, or system?—which treats of the regulation of the agreements and differences (so far as they can be distinguished, for these mostly spring from those) between man and man, and about the adjustment of rights. It is idle for you and me to pronounce upon how a knotty, much less how a clear case is likely to be settled. But your legal authority can pierce by a kind of magic through the hazes and pretexts, the falsehoods and subterfuges of litigants, discern by intuitive decision the merits of the case which you bring before him, and specify to you the vantage-ground possessed by the man who may be in the wrong. It may seem to us indeed, in our rough estimate, that the thing is as plain as the day-light; but the masterly acquaintance of our legal man with the precedents and technicalities of Courts will give us in a few words advice which may save our ignorant innocence from plunging into certain disaster; so as to make us rather "bear the ills we have, than fly to others which we know not of." Thus you see in *legal matters* the only person entitled to speak with authority is your *legal man*.

And so in philology, and indeed in all specialties—providing always that one-eyed men in their several realms of study be not permitted, to their neighbours' detriment, to reign wholly unquestioned!

I will not, for obvious reasons, take that profession of "the divine," to which I have the high honour to belong; but the honest man of puzzled conscience *should*, here and there, find some of us an authority on matters which perplex him; and indeed this brings me to eternal topics, and therefore touches closely on what I have now to say.

For let us leave the contemplation of professional examples, and go into the region of the highest life. There are those, we know, who lead such a life. We have among us, happily, and have had from the beginning, men who are genuine students of the law of the Spirit of life in Christ Jesus. All the day long, all the long day of their life, is their study in it. They are not like those fish that come only now and then to the surface to breathe that upper air; but in these supernal regions of contemplative insight they wing their way as in their native element.

There are, and always have been, vain persons—notably pseudo-scientific men—who, living mainly among laboratories and dissecting-tables and the ephemeral natures, parade their one-sidedness and boast of their blindness by even venturing to cast discredit and ridicule on the very existence of a God of Whom they know nothing, nor care to know :—and that, although they see around them the most high-minded and trustworthy of their fellow-citizens living, and moving, and delighting to have their being, in that very God whom *they* deride. Standing on their lower level, with which they assume to be contented (though this nervous anxiety to displace God from the faith of others does not, methinks, indicate any very serene satisfaction in having displaced Him from their own!), they mock at the invitation of Him who says, "Friend, come up higher," and set down as the victims of self-deception those who accept the welcome of Heaven. But take note, I pray you, what a small-minded thing this is, and what a cramped imagination it betrays in these men—to do what they dare not do, and would not dream of doing, in medicine, in law, or in any other line of profession, and to reject the authority of students in matters which they themselves have never seriously studied. For merely to study *objections* to a region of thought in which they do not live, and to which they do not practically devote themselves, or even use themselves at all, is not a study in that sense of the word which invests men with *authority* How could it be so?

Who would regard as an authority upon law the writer who bent his main endeavour to show that law was futile? Would you go for a cure to that empiric who had spent his life in proclaiming that physicians were unable to battle with disease?—Or take, if you will, the every-day instance of the man of business. I was talking the other day with a bank-manager, of large and long experience. Without going into other people's affairs (which neither would I have done, nor he allowed!), that gentleman made it in a short time very manifest to me, that his was a post demanding such special knowledge, such practised acumen, observation at once so wide and so minute, such insight into the subtle turns and delicate twists of social requirement, that I went away convinced more firmly than ever that none but a bank-manager could manage a bank. I saw something of what it means to be an *authority*.—In fact, who but a station-master can manage a station? Who but a signal-man in his signal-box, or the man who instructed him, is an adept and an authority upon the signals?—Nor should we, in fine, ask " What must I do to be saved?" of anyone who took no delight in, and made no study of the way of salvation?

No: it is proverbially hard for any one to prove even a bare unopposed negative. But when a positive and rational affirmative is opposed to it, then naturally the negation, by the weight of its own folly, falls heavily to the ground. For the sustained intuitions, the deliberate convictions of time-long successions of the sane—intuitions and convictions which in those who entertain them grow with the growth of the best civilisation—these, I say, have in themselves the force of positive affirmation, and would stand on their own base—being in fact the form taken by Revelation—even if they had no traditional Revelation to stand upon. This is the unreasoned Reason of Faith. You may set it down as certain, that all the negations made by the specially ignorant must fail to weigh down one intuitive perception, one clear assertion of the man, who from habitual converse with God is specially conversant with his subject, and who tells us that he knows his Father. You might as well tell Livingstone there is no Africa, or dispute with Stanley, the traveller, the fact of a Livingstone. If ten thousand people tell me they do not believe that the Queen exists, because they have not seen her, how can that invalidate my single statement that, having seen her most religious and gracious Majesty, I know that she exists? The thing is preposterous, and such negations set against such affirmations, so far from being "humanitarian" and "positive," are in fact positively inhuman, and absolutely null.

Of course all this stands to reason, and may seem too obvious to dwell upon. But why, I ask, is it to be different in Religion? How plain it is, that in spiritual matters the student of spiritual truth is the only trustworthy authority. The carnal mind knoweth not the things of the Spirit of God; they are foolishness unto him, because they are spiritually discerned.

A clown goes into a lecture-hall, and hears the lecturer discoursing on Hydrostatics, on the Theory of the undulation of Light, or on any other mathematical or scientific topic, be it abstruse or be it simple: and he cannot for the life of him persuade himself that the man in cap and gown is not a born fool. He stands at the door with his mouth wide open, and a grimace of incredible incredulity and comic contempt marks every feature of the face of that honest rustic. He could tell the Professor many things about the sheep and the pigs, but for the matter in hand his ignorance is patent, simply because his faculty is latent. And this is none other but the very attitude in which the infidel or blasphemer stands, however much he may know about protoplasm and other animal matter, when he hears the high-souled student of the Holy Book, or any genuine believer, expatiating with divine fervour on the things of the Spirit of God, taking the things of Christ, and with constraining power labouring in vain to show them to his unwoke capacity.

Alas! I for my poor part know but little compared with all which I know that by this time I *should* know, of these blessed topics I tell of; but I *do* know thus much, and thus much I tell you; yes, tell you professionally if you will :—I know that when I read the words of Jesus and His Apostles, I find in them that subtle spirit of knowledge, that intimate acquaintance with the relations of God to man, that refined aroma of experience upon the instinctive Science of human life—upon that Science of sciences which indeed concerns us all, but in which only its practical students can claim any weight—which forces me thankfully to declare that *they* know what they are speaking about and what they testify. These, above all others, nay these alone, let me inform you, or remind you, *speak with authority*, and with that authority which none by any other study can attain to; with that very authority which our inmost needs demand, and to which it were best for you and me with our inmost souls in all humility to bow.

It does not argue wisdom to desire over-much to know more than it has pleased our Father in this stage of our existence to tell us. Admitting all legitimate range of human enquiry, and applauding as highly natural the thirst for all that men may hope fairly and usefully to know—yet, to be for ever perplexing ourselves in the endeavour to re-adjust the Universe—desirous, if we could, even to re-issue its conditions, and contract to make it work on simpler principles and easier terms—this is not a sign of a sound mind; nay, it is rather the mark of a mind which is radically unsound; for this way lies the worst form of madness.

For is this not so? Look with me for a moment how madness works. A mind may run off the rails of reason either in the way of delusion, fatuity, incoherence, or passion—which while it lasts is a brief madness, and, if it be habitual, is habitual madness.

That is to say, a poor spoiled brain may make a man think that to be which is not, or that not to be which is—seeing or fancying that he sees "more devils than vast hell can hold." That is delusion.

Or again, he may sit with leaden eye that loves the ground, drivelling and making moes, and muttering sounds which are unmeaning. That is fatuity.

Or again, he may ramble on in his mother-tongue, like a babe that strums on some goodly instrument, with ideas that follow each other in no sort of order —either mildly inconsecutive, or aimlessly ferocious. That is incoherency.

Or else, in fine, he may be seen and heard by his paralysed and useless friends, indulging in angry extravagance, and inveighing with absurd perturbation and misplaced or excessive indignation, against things which cannot be helped. That is the very ecstasy of passion.

All these are but the common forms of insanity, and are profoundly to be pitied, and carefully to be guarded against by all in their earliest indications. But, mark me, no way lies more direct into mental dissolution and the decay of intelligent perception, than that which can simultaneously lead a man, as we see, into the passion, the incoherency, the fatuity, and the delusion, of first denying his God, and then fighting angrily against the God whom he denies!

Look what takes place in the moral nature of such an one. Instead of allowing his godlike faculty of faith, which is only reason in its highest form of self-affirmation, to grow up sweetly towards Heaven, he cuts it summarily down, and keeps no longer any spiritual leafage through which to nourish his best nature with congenial air. All of that has withered. He bends himself back on his own poor, finite, and now truncated self. Having transplanted himself from beside the rivers of wholesome water where his God had planted him, he isolates himself into a little earthen pot—a little potter's vessel soon to be broken in pieces—where the roots of his nature become cramped and matted, and at last putrefy, while his blossom goes up in dust. He brings forth none of that best fruit which to the straight-growing, upward-shooting soul is seen to come in its season; or, to change the image and use the words of David—"he is like chaff which the wind driveth away."

With those quiet and interesting questions, those sweet and holy mysteries, which are so highly fascinating and so wholesomely delightful to every genial and thoughtful soul, he deals in a temper the very last which should be brought to them, and in a mood the most fatal of all to the sanity, as well as to the success, of the thinker. The man of sane and holy meditation hopes to know, by following on to know, the Lord. This is to him the harvest of the quiet eye. Upon *him* new lights keep ever breaking at every turn of the road along which his Father leads him. Instead of hating a happy light from which he falls, he loves the happy light to which he rises; and when he comes to an acknowledged difficulty, to the bottom of a sack, to a point at which it is obviously impossible for any one, or at least for him, to advance, he humbly bethinks him who he is, and what he is. He remembers the infinity of his subject-matter, and the years of the right hand of the Most High, from Whom both he and all proceed. Thus before such a problem he reposes as a wise man should, and quiets himself with the common-sense reflection that, in the presence of a manifest impossibility of advance, the mind may rest as calmly as before an ascertained and acknowledged truth.

But far otherwise is it with the man who puts God out of his knowledge. He cuts himself off, as we have seen, from the fountain of living waters. He fights and beats his weak wings against the bars of the cage that he makes for himself, and in which, like that cruel Cardinal of the Eleventh Louis, he is doomed to durance vile; or, like an ill-broke, runaway colt, he dashes himself against all the impassable walls which impede his wild career. He lifts his head on high, and snorting in terrible blasphemy, he lets his tongue run dangerously loose among the simple and ignorant folk that throng the thoroughfares of society. Turning the freedom of the Press, granted him by his country and his time, into unwarrantable license, of which he is sometimes sternly reminded by the Courts, he leaves nothing unsaid. Availing himself of that questionable liberty, which has let him fling up his heels unhaltered in the commonwealth, he flies at high and hallowed institutions, and, by sheer force of arrogance, plunges through them as if they were sheets of a newspaper. Have we not lately seen such an one paralysing the very Legislature, and saying of the Deity, as Cromwell said of the Mace, "Take away this bauble"? And at such a bidding we may be in fact constrained, and that by the very stress of our constitutional precedents, to put God Himself out of the recognition of our Parliament, so that, alas for England, no man who goes thither to make our laws can any longer be called upon to seek from the Source of Law the wit and the wisdom to make them! *Tantum irreligio potuit suadere malorum.* Into such a dark labyrinth of sin is that nation led, which forsakes its ideal, and expands into freedom *from* Christ, instead of freedom *in* Him. But I only mention this class of man in speaking of the various forms of madness, by way of showing that, of all those forms, spiritual madness, notably when flinging about fire among the masses, is the most dangerous and the worst.

Let us go on to consider, in such lights as may come to us, the importance of finding in Jesus the one Authority in the affairs of the soul, and also of the mind, when brought up against eternal questions.

There is a class of mind, or rather say, a habit of mind common to all classes, which seems to delight in nothing so much as to fathom the unfathomable. Such are those at whom I have already glanced. There is no irreligious gluttony more vulgar, and in vogue with men of a certain stamp of intellect (and that, I need hardly say, by no means a high one), than to keep grabbing at that tree of knowledge of good and evil, which still brings forth its Dead-sea apples in the midst of the garden of thought, and in the most open walks of enquiry. It demands no great subtilty of wit, no vast reach of imagination, to be puzzled, for instance, by the sufferings of the just. Any fool at the first blush of the matter is led to fancy that here is some injustice. In fact a distinct act of piety, a piece of express resignation, and the remembrance of "Thy Will be done" is requisite to contemplate this common example of apparent wrong, and yet to make inwardly no graceless rejoinder. It is only the soul who believes in God, that, in presence of such a fact (to take the most crucial of all) as the sacrifice of the meek and lowly Jesus, can say with His Master "Thy Will be done", and can then expect the issue in repose. Yet, if He, the Christ, felt and said this about His own case, we may surely use the same language about ourselves, and about all the minor instances of unmerited calamity, which in this journey of life come under our ken. In this thing, above all, we had surely best look to *CHRIST as the great Authority.*

No fool's paradise is so anti-human as that of the individual who has unmanned himself of his faculty of Faith—unable any longer to recognise, that in this self-mutilation he stands outlawed of the Universe and wrong towards the whole range of being. What a spectacle he makes of himself to all the Intelligencies ! The more, if—in place of humbling himself with bitter repentance, and tearful, strenuous endeavour to regain his lost inheritance, so that the thought of his heart may be forgiven him—he holds his head on high, and leads uncultured folk to imagine that in his stagnant abnegations he enjoys any equivalent to " the peace of God." His serenity, if he has any, is but that of the lull of the tempest and of the heart of the Malström.

The fact is, that of our imperfect conditions Faith happily forms an integral part, even more than our ignorance does. Are not these set over against one another for our great and endless comfort? We cannot in some things help being ignorant, but we should avoid being fools. We are to blame if we strap our best eyes with fresh bandages, instead of stripping off those which bind them already. The man who does not keep in exercise the divine faculty of Faith, which Spiritual Science shows to be the highest faculty we have, is pulled up by his human ignorance at every turn, and must always be in conflict with Providence—or with whatever Power his vain imagination, conscious of dependence, must set up in His place. The very purpose and use of Faith is to turn ignorance into bliss, and to give us tranquillity in the practical perplexities of life, with respect to most of which it were sheer folly to seek to be " wise above that which is written " both in Scripture and in the experience of life.

What a calamity it would be for us, if in this half-fledged condition we knew all about ourselves, and all that God is doing for us! In the mere striving after this too wonderful knowledge, how horridly do we shake our dispositions with thoughts beyond the reaches of our souls. We all know what a nuisance in society we consider an over-forward and too inquisitive child—a child that is always teasing its elders and betters with questions beyond its years, and philosophising about matters which, if not in themselves unknowable, it imports that children at least should not know, and about which all wise and well-behaved children of modest mind soon come to see that they must cease to make enquiry. But the last absurdity was reached by that child who said to its father "Why mayn't I say 'Why?'" And yet the father of that child was a man who made a point of satisfying every seemly and well-proportioned enquiry.

And does not the whole human race, including those persons with the kind of mad-intelligence I have spoken of, stand as a child towards Him Whom we are privileged to call our Father and our GOD? Why, even in the most common, familiar, and vulgar matters, we acknowledge the advantage of unconsciousness, and count ourselves fortunate not to know what we are doing, and whither we are going, content to be guided by Heaven. You are sitting, say, in a railway-carriage that is at rest. Others in motion are passing by your side. You seem to move, when you know you are at rest, and the others seem to be at rest when you know that they are in motion. Nothing will persuade a child that it is not so, nor a man, till he brings his late learning to correct the sportiveness of sense. Again, sitting in your garden, you know that you are in motion, while you have every apparent reason to believe you are at rest. Did I say in motion? Why, you are being whirled along by a complicity, possibly, by an infinity of motions! You are a traveller on the grandest scale. You are journeying round your earth's axis. You are whirling round yonder sun with a speed not only unconceived but inconceivable. Yonder sun of ours is whirling again round some other sun—perhaps, as some have said, under the sweet influence of that little twinkling Alcyone who sits in the choir with her six sisters in Heaven; while she again, and we with her, may be wheeling with frightful velocity, suns and all, round or towards some other far-off star, whose rays have never yet reached our planet with all its far-glasses and helps to vision! In God we not only live but move, but all the Universe in all its ranges of actual and potential life is high-busy, and we with it, bent on the beautiful work of flying upon the bidding of our Father. To a large extent the Will of God we *must* do, and must abide—whether we have faith in God, or whether we, who are the first of His earthly creatures, choose to murmur and sulk, and let our best faculties slink behind in this glorious and universal rivalry of implicit and unquestioning obedience.

But only imagine what a ghastly thing it would be, if we were so constituted as to be conscious and sensibly aware of all these motions at once—of which nevertheless, willy-nilly, we are, as we have seen, the blest but passive subjects! What brain could stand a tithe of such knowledge? Would not the lightning flash of such a revelation, the moment it fell on our perception, blind the line of our gaze, and scorch up the mental retina of the wisest among men? Well did the sweet King-Poet of Israel say: "Such knowledge is too wonderful and excellent for me; it is high, I cannot attain unto it." Would it not, I say, drive us clean out of the few poor senses that we have, even to feel, more than we do, all the movements we have? We should never know whether we were standing on our heels or on our head. You would, indeed, in such a physical case as I have instanced, be irritated, confounded, and distracted.

But yet, believe me, even if you *could*, as for the sake of our argument we have somewhat freely imagined—even if you could have your frail senses aware at once of all that complicity of motion—your brain would not reel with so dire a dizziness, nor would you be dazed and astonied with amazement so sore, as that which would come over you in this other case :—if, I mean, you could become, in your present state and in your terrestrial framework, vividly conscious of half the problems of life and mind, of good and ill (if there *be* such a thing as ill), of which nevertheless—nay all the more—in helpless but natural unconsciousness you are enjoying the combined and harmonious action. It has been well observed by one of the greatest orators and philosophers of Rome, in his Tusculan disputations, "Non valet tantum animus ut se ipsum videat." ("The mind has not so much power as to be able to see itself.") "At animus, ut oculus, se non videns alia cernit." ("But the mind, like the eye, discerns things outside itself, though itself it does not see.") Just as a person who is well is not conscious without a direct effort of will—which can even produce local pain—of any particular one of his vital organs, or of the fine network of his nerves; so the mind, when sane, will not be unduly directed to any of the intricacies of its own machinery. I say *unduly*, for God has given us, within certain limits, the power and the pleasure of reflection.

Now, why have I gone through all this? Perhaps only my more studious hearers—to whom also we are called to preach—may have felt able to follow me throughout; but my drift, I am sure, must be clear to all. You, at any rate, who are the advanced scholars of this school, are not unaccustomed to these lines of thought, and you do well to go forearmed into the larger arena of the great University, where you often do yourselves and your master such high honour—you at least can follow me. Why?—except to say with the more reason—that which the most rustic intelligence can understand, and understand perhaps better than some who occupy the place of the learned—namely this: that it is obviously best, in all the difficulties of life and its conduct, to look humbly and thankfully to our Father, Who will bring all right in the long run for His children; and, in a word, to turn to the Rock from which our spirits are hewn, and the hole of the pit whence our bodily clay is digged. And with that view, I urge you to listen betimes to Him Whose voice is certainly from Heaven, for it could not have been from earth—to Him Who said to the wonder-stricken disciples from the bright cloud that overshadowed them, "This is my beloved Son; hear Him." "Truly," as the centurion said under His Cross, echoing that voice from Heaven, "Truly this is the Son of God." *He knows.* Never man spake like this GOD-MAN. Christ alone speaks "*with authority.*"

We have lately learned among the laws of solar light which have been revealed to us—for science also has its late and lagging revelations—the astonishing fact, that beyond the atmosphere of our world, as of all others—even till the eye again reaches the airy envelopes of sister worlds, and catches the bright particular stars which are the sources, direct or mediate, of the rays that play upon its tiny pupil—all is blackness of darkness. And so we find it to be round all the circle of science. Round every world of knowedge there is also a shade which no knowledge of ours can penetrate. We live and move and have our being upon the edge of a ring of precipitous and abysmal darkness. But, as we have seen to be the case in the fiery citadels of Heaven, so we Christians believe it to be in the moral world; that, dark as its surroundings are in respect of the origin and workings of evil, and of all the problems that hang about this enquiry, there abides above and beyond all a Paternal pavilion of Light. God is a central and Personal Sun, Who gives light to all, and borrows none from any; and in Him, as Jesus shows Him forth to us, " is no darkness at all." In that Light Jesus dwells, "having no part dark"; and from that Light He speaks to us, and teaches *with an authority which is unique.* Well, to whom else shall we go? *Christ, our Saviour*, O dearly beloved brethren in Christ, *must, in all matters of the soul, be our great Authority.*

THE STILLER OF TEMPESTS.

"Even the wind and the sea obey Him."—St. Mark iv. 41.

WHEN we are in the act of considering any one of the parables or miracles of our Lord, or indeed any of the facts of His life, it often seems to us at the time (at least so it is with me), that no other can surpass that particular one in aptness, in richness, and beauty. And so it is with each in succession as we throw ourselves into the prayerful contemplation of it. There are hardly any, if any, other sayings or narrations in the study of which we feel the same emotion; for there is usually in common writings so much to offend the moral or the mental sense, that, when we look into them closely, we seldom draw near to a perfect satisfaction. We may at times be conscious of a kindred feeling before some great works of art; and perhaps in a still higher degree in the presence of some remarkable landscapes, where we see in clearer form the works of God; but that which I have observed seems to hold good in a peculiar manner with the sayings and doings of the Master. It is an unintended homage which we pay to the infinite beauty of all, that we thus find ourselves rendering in succession unsurpassed admiration to the excellency of each.

Let us, by the help of the Spirit of God, Who has caused all these things to be written for our learning, ponder this morning the given details of this miracle of the stilling of the tempest; and let us dwell upon some few of the many good things which the Spirit here means to take and to show unto us.

Our Divine Saviour teaches us sometimes by deeds, sometimes by words, sometimes by silence. His silence speaks more than the words of mere men; His words do more than all men's deeds together; while his deeds themselves possess moreover an infinite eloquence. We have in this miracle, as we shall see in the sequel, all these modes of teaching combined.

It was evening,—an evening that followed, as usual, a well filled day of work. He had been preaching among the villages of Israel, for therefore, said He, was He sent.

It would seem, as far as we can gather, that on that particular day He had been sending out many words which once from His Divine Lips were never to pass away. It is probable that He had been giving forth that constellation of parables which are recorded in the 13th chapter of St. Matthew. In these, under a variety of aspects, He had fore-imaged the changes and growth of His kingdom in the heart of the world, and in the world of the heart. He had then unfolded them to His disciples, so far as it concerned them to know, and so far as they were able to bear their disclosure. It was a work of the Spirit to bring all these things to their remembrance, and to ours, in the after days, so as to meet the needs of each occasion and of each soul.

He had been showing them how "the Prince of the power of the air," by his Harpy messengers of mischief, would pick up and carry off the good seed which *they* were to sow along the hard thoroughfares of the nations. He had foreshadowed the withering effect on shallow souls of the fiery trials that were to try them. He had been foretelling of the evil spirits which were ever to be at work—in times, for example, like these in which we are living; of that gnawing care for worldly advantage, and that deceitfulness of commercial prosperity which were to choke the seeds of Christianity scattered broadcast among these half-civilized peoples, both of the East and of the West. He bequeathed no fixed and no necessary scheme under which His kingdom was to be spread, nor had He promised success or foreboded failure to any which should be devised by His successors: "Go ye into all the world, and preach the Gospel to the whole creation" was His broad but explicit mandate. His only promise was to those who should believe and be baptised. Those only who should disbelieve were to be condemned. Yet He had held out the gracious hope that missionary labours would not be in vain. He had given His Apostles comfort in the forecast, that there would be places in the world where in honest and good hearts their good and honest seed should be manifold in its fruit.

He had also been showing them under what conditions it should grow; what tares of evil would be sedulously intermingled by "an enemy" among the fairest and most cultured fields—not however to be prematurely uprooted by man's headlong fancy, but to be left for the ministers of mercy and of wrath to gather off duly at the last.

In spite of all this, He had said, changing the image, that the little company which was springing from His side was to become the greatest of all trees, under whose boughs the farthest nations of world should flock for shelter.

Yet, He had added, ever ready with a fresh and homely similitude, His kingdom was not to come in a manner which men should always be able to trace and to mark. The influence of the Spirit in His words was to work like hidden yeast, till the entire bread of society should at last be made wholesome; that, whether a nation or a soul should find out His truth by heavenly chance or by diligent search, it would prove, to all who should light upon it and keep it, a blessing of worth untold; that, though evil should remain in His Church and His people till the net should be drawn ashore, yet a day would come when the bad should be cast away :—parables, let me say, in all of which the Master taught, that in this highest range of being, as well as in all the lower, God's great law would have its way, and that the full bloom of the Plant of Humanity was only to achieve itself through those slow grades, which Science, though in some minds with a godless meaning, has now beautifully termed "evolution."

Thus it was that, like His own good householder, Jesus had been busy all day long, bringing forth every form and phase of truth which might comfort and forewarn His Household. And having so done, He winds up His day by that act of marked significance which is now before us. Does He not in this parabolic miracle show to those who were the nucleus and kernel of His Kingdom, to those valiant souls who were with Him in His labours and were to be with Him in His approaching trials, that, let come what storm there might upon the Church and on the soul, He was with them still, and would be with them even to the end? He might seem unconscious of their danger and even appear to have forgotten them; yet they were to have faith in God, for that out of their worst calamities He would bring them to peace. On the one hand great would be the storms by which His Ark would be assailed, but that, on the other, He could, and He would, guide her course, and great should be her calm at the last.

He was weary in spirit with the work of the day which now was drawing to a close; and of that weariness a large part no doubt arose from the knowledge how little His words were understood, and how little even those which were understood would be acted upon. According to his wont He sought to be alone with His Father; and for that end, as on the evening when He heard of the murder of His cousin and Forerunner, He besought His disciples to go across to the other side, where the mountains abounded in lonely spots well suited for undisturbed communion with God. And so without any preparation, even as He was, they took Him aboard; and then made sail across the lake, accompanied by some other little ships, in which some of the more zealous of the multitude still kept to His side. Anyone who knows a mountainous country will readily understand what now took place. Down one of those ravines, which traversed the solitary regions in which He was to spend the night in prayer, there swept one of those dangerous, fitful, and often fatal storms, which,—as, alas, on our lost Eurydice—come suddenly on the mariner and find him powerless to meet them.

It was doubtless one of the manifold devices by which, as we shall presently see, that prince of the power of the air, that enemy and tempter of Christ and man, that author of all confusion in the world and in the soul, endeavoured—oh, vain and foolish attempt—to sink the hopes of the Church in the very outset, and before the course of Redemption should be finished. But here, as in all like cases, these permitted trials of Satan had a Providence that held them in check. How proudly and how savagely in that plague of the sky did the Devil come howling down on them as if there were no arbiter of Gennesaret to lift or to lay its waters at His will. Yet what were his fiercest sallies in effect but harmless play about the sleeping form of the Lord of the Lake? At the same time the water kept beating in faster than they could bale it out, and, as you can well imagine, the fishermen found themselves in a very sorry plight. Their boat was now sinking, as Matthew and Luke relate, and perhaps was actually swamped, as St. Mark relates, and was only kept afloat by the Power to whom in their terror they betake themselves. They would perhaps not have been allowed to reach that extremity, had they called at first on

Him on Whom thus they call at last. These faithless disciples, as Peter on another occasion, were allowed to begin to sink, in order to teach them, and to teach us, how vain are our own efforts except blest and inspirited by our God. Jesus was sleeping through the storm, with His head laid on a cushion or on the taffrail; slumbering, while all the rest in their terror were struggling with the elements—like Jonah, save that, while to *his* ship's company Jonah was the cause of their danger, Jesus was to His their only hope of safety. One was fleeing from the presence of his God, the other was that very Presence from whom none can flee. To Him at the last moment they fly—"Master, Master, we perish:"—much in the same way, though not so piously, it would seem, as the shipmaster of Joppa—"What meanest thou, O sleeper? Arise, call upon thy God, if so be that God will think upon us, that we perish not." And here was the Son of God Himself ready to prove His power and His love now that His hour for doing so was come.

How striking, how beautiful, how simple—in a word, how like Christ and the Gospel account of Him is this whole narrative. How unlike the common wonders of mere men. No parade, no endeavour by any mysterious form of words to make Himself an idol of dread. No straining attempt made by the recorders of His wonders to gain for Him, as there would have been had there been any lies in the matter, any useless applause. The fact itself was not to be surpassed in its pure and kindly beauty. To garnish it would have been but to tarnish it. Standing up in the stern of the boat, he rebuked the wind; or rather (as He would hardly have enacted the cold, unmeaning form of addressing a mere effect—a theatrical mode which would have been wholly unlike Christ) He rebuked the Enemy which was at work in the wind to trouble His people, just as He rebuked the power which had laid low the mother of Peter's wife. He in fact rebuked the same power through whom sin and sickness and all real evil has come into the world. He rebuked the wind, and said unto the sea—or rather, as I say, to the malicious Fiend, through whose allowed but restrained agency it wrought and was so tempestuous — " Peace, be still." And the wind ceased, and there was a dead calm. " Hitherto shalt thou come, and no farther; here shall thy proud waves be stayed." The waves of the sea were mighty and raged horribly, but He that dwelleth on high proved Himself mightier. To mark the miracle, the calm was great. There was not, as is usual after a tempest, that heavy swell, that dying down of its violence through many and long heavings and tossings, as of a steed that chafes and plunges in the course of its being mastered. He spoke to the wind—it ceased. He spoke to the sea—and, not obeying the common law by which it rocks itself to sleep, after the wind that woke it has passed, but acknowledging the higher law that overruled its wonted manners, it fell into dead calm on the instant.

Then it was, and not till then, that He turned His face away from the demons of the angry tempest, and spoke with a gentler voice to His people ; a voice in which, if there was something of reproof, yet that very reproof was love.

Now comes the lesson which all along it had been Christ's divine purpose to convey, not only to those who heard it then, but to everyone throughout the whole world who has read it since—yes, to you who hear it to-day. " How is it ye have no faith ?" or, as St. Matthew puts it, " O ye of little faith ; "—or, as Luke again has it, reconciling both, " Where is your Faith ? "—a slight discrepancy, which shows by the way, among many other like examples, that the inspiration of Scripture is far deeper than a verbal one. He saw perhaps that they had *some* faith, but grieved that there and then it was not to be found. How important it is, my beloved brethren, that in all the storms of life—nay in all the moments of a life in which, at any moment, storms may sweep down on us—we " have faith in God," full faith in Him who rules all storms; and that we not only have faith, but have it ready at the shortest notice for our use. Let us not be like that captain of whom we lately heard, who, having a true and correct chart in his cabin, failed to consult it while the weather was calm, but went below to look into it only when the wind and tide had drifted his barque upon the bar; and so, with his eyes upon the course he should have steered, felt the shock which in a few moments sent them all headlong into the abyss. Our souls are like a ship upon the deep; and as we sail over the waves of life, we must, like wary mariners, take the hints given us in our nature. If we see on the horizon a cloud of some possible temptation no bigger than a man's hand, though all else be bright and clear—if we hear but the first blast of some probable sin hurtling in the farthest caverns of our life—let us beware; for in that speck, in that remote murmur may couch a tempest ready to spring up and leap down upon our souls. Above all we should always have Christ aboard with us; we should have Him formed within us as our hope of glory; under His ensign and by the guidance of His voice we should all sail, as our only hope of reaching that Haven for which we are making.

Once these same disciples were in their boat on the same lake; a storm again came down upon them; Christ was not near them, as they thought, and they were sore afraid. But when the storm was at its height, they saw that familiar and beloved Form approaching; and, though frightened—frightened, poor ignorant souls, at their best Friend!—they received Him on board: and what was the consequence? Immediately they were at the land for which they were making. The fact is, when the Spirit of Jesus is with us we are in Haven. Is it not, indeed, to be in Haven—yea, to be in Heaven—if we are where the Son of Man is?

Too many Christians—nay almost all of us at too many times, though we *have* Christ with us, do not profit by His presence nor enjoy Him as we ought. We should not only have Christ, but, having Him, ah why have we not that faith, that assurance of faith, that full assurance of faith which can realize and utilize His presence? Are we living
> As beings breathing thoughtful breath
> As travellers between life and death?

Ask yourselves, my brethen, can the life you lead confront itself with that Power of Whom I speak, and to Whom in truth our life is at all times naked and laid open? Here is an immortal soul, a parish full of immortal souls, sent into this lower world freighted with eternal destinies; a God to honour, a Saviour to serve, a Holy Spirit to commune and advise with, a blessed and undivided Trinity to acknowledge and to enjoy; mankind to regard as brethren, the poor to think for, the wretched to commiserate, the ragged to clothe, the afflicted to console, and all men to love. We talk of living innocently and harmlessly! Is it innocent, I ask, is it harmless, to pass a life, given us for ends so high and so sweet as these, in honouring yourself, in serving yourself, in clothing yourself, in feeding yourself, in cultivating yourself, while your neighbour, while the Holy Spirit, your Saviour, and your God, if not consciously despised, are passed over and forgotten?

Did God send you into this world to live the life which we see so many leading around us? To scrape together a few hundred, or a few thousand pounds, which you will be said to have "died worth"—at a moment when your poverty will be the most utter and abject that the human mind can imagine? To devote body, mind and soul to the turning over of arable loam? To spend your time and devote your spirits to nothing else whatsoever beyond the common avocations of your daily life? Is there indeed *nothing* of marketable value besides wheat, and stock, and swine, and barn-door fowl? Are these, I ask, worthy to be the *sole* objects of the industry, the intelligence, the feelings, the principles of a class of men such as those to whom God has entrusted the agriculture and commerce of England? Important as it may be, interesting as it may be, highly desirable as it most assuredly is, to give to such works all the industry and all the intelligence they demand—let me remind you, that you have a higher work, a nobler calling, a more remunerative field of labour; and yet one of which the scope is to be found among those very works of which I have been speaking with apparent slight. Just as the pastures of Bethlehem were common pastures, and yet the Heavenly Host held their Session above them; just as the mountains of Galilee were common mountains, and the waters of the lake common waters, and yet they were trodden and crossed by the feet and the boat of the Son of God; just as Calvary itself, in short, was no more than a common hill outside a capital city, and now not even to be clearly discerned, and yet it was on that hill, in those selfsame streets, that the Son of the Highest did His greatest deeds and gave His life for us all—even so it is in our common work, in our ordinary employment, in our worldly calling, that there lies, so to speak, the raw material of our blessedness, yea, of our eternal life. Do not all these works bring you into direct contact with your fellow-men? Love them then, and act towards them as brothers. Does not every hour of our earthly life, common though it seem, hold us in direct and immediate dependence upon our Father and our God? In Him do we not all live and move and have our being? Bear this then in mind; and bear in mind Him who has brought us nigh by the blood of His Cross, and through Whom that God is no more a fire to consume us, but a Father whose Face shines on our reconciled souls in everlasting loving-kindness. Open your sails hour by hour to the secret impulses and the gentle monitions of that Spirit of Grace Who proceeds from the Father and the Son; and so these common earthly works, instead of being animal drudgery, or mere instinctive trifling, will be moved by the very breath of God. And whenever God calls you from them, and bids you leave behind whatever His Providence may have lent you, you will not grieve to lose them, and pine to stay with them, and murmur to quit them; but, committing your soul to your Faithful Creator, you will feel that the summons of death only means "Friend, come up higher."

We have, as I have said, a stormy world to go through; a world whose storms are aggravated by the wickedness and ill judgment of those who, more or less, allow the Enemy to use them for his tools. But we, both the Church at large and the several members thereof, like the boat in the miracle, have Him with us whom even the winds and the seas obey. Though He may seem to be careless of us, it is not the fact; it is we who are forgetful of *Him.* Though He sleeps, so to speak — though He may seem to our faithless hearts to hide Himself and forget us for the moment—His heart waketh, and a single cry to Him will let us know to our peace and joy that He is there. A blessed thing it is to enjoy, even sometimes—and is it not mostly by our own fault (though perhaps it may often be a trial for our good) that we do not enjoy at all times—that great calm which always surrounds

Him, however horrible may seem to be the raging of the waters of the world; a calm which He is always ready to make for *us*. Oh blessed fragments of that great and endless, yet unwearying calm which will prevail when we reach the happy harbour-mouth of heaven!

Before we part, let me give expression to what I am well assured all of us must be feeling about the terrible thing which in the past week has shocked the world. There are, you hear, winds and seas raging also in the minds of men—winds of revolution, and social seas that ever and anon rise as if they would sweep down all the barriers of Order. The noise of these waves and the madness of these evil spirits that have got loose among the Russian people—and peoples nearer home—will obey the Master when His hour has come; but meanwhile how disastrous they are even in their failures, and how alarming in the bare fact that they are possible!

Brethren, of late years, in England as well as elsewhere, we have been, and still are, earnestly (and not, as it seems to me, unreasonably) on our guard against the outward movements of that Empire. We of course think it hard and sad, that, in order to keep alive barbarous traditions of conquest, this overtopping flood of the Sclavonic race should keep all their neighbours in wakeful alarm, lest at any time they should come down, as they have lately done, in a deluge of war. Civilisation is tired of being turned into a camp.

Do we praise Russia in this? We praise her not. But, when we turn from the contemplation of this attitude which she assumes towards her neighbours, and behold her internal state, we stand aghast—how can it be otherwise?—with sorrow and compassion. For it would almost seem as if the penalities of ancestral slavery, long in arrears, were now being paid down by the very man who is most ready to impart to her all he can of the blessings of freedom. Nay, it would seem that his very efforts to educate and emancipate his people are recoiling on the head of this Emperor, who has done more than any before him to uplift the level of their nationality. That land is obviously possessed by such a legion of devils, that he who kept them in fetters and chains from breaking forth before into these sallies of madness, would seem in his generation to have been the wiser in his rule. Oh what a demon is man, whether solitary or in packs, when the culture of the head outruns the culture of the heart! How well have you done, both in your voluntary and your compulsory schools, to see that your children shall gain from us such pure Church-teaching as we *can* give them, and such residuum of it as we *may*.

But Russia, alas, seems to have been so unready for that freedom which long-taught truth alone can safely bring, that even the modicum which has been imparted to her population proves to be greater than she can bear. So far is she from being fit for more, that she is showing that she already has more than she is fit for. She is able to endure neither her evils nor their remedies. For what else are we to say, when we find, through her length and breadth, lurking hardly masked in the vitals of her twin Capitals and lodged in the very home of her Sovereign, this multitudinous demon of wholesale murder, which no law can reach, no scrutiny can track, no severity quell?—a movement which takes so little account of the conditions of history and of the Divine order of national growth, that sweeping away past and present at one fell swoop, it erects Destruction into a Creed! For it takes its desperate stand on the mad doctrine, that before all things it is necessary to hold a Catholic faith in "*nothing*"; making it the one religious principle of humanity by means the most inhuman to bring to nothing everything that mankind has ever held to be valuable and inviolable!

What compassion must this distracted nation claim from *us* within our quiet island home—from us, to whom the Saviour has given a land of settled government; where faction is less and less likely to gather head, and where "diffusive thought hath time and space to work and spread." For with *us* the industrious masses of our patient people are mainly wont by a kind of instinct (which, let the world say what it may, has been taught us by our National Christianity) to acquiesce in the slow gradation of national growth as the law which even Supreme Providence conditions Himself rarely to break—never before His hour. Thus we know how to bear what ills we have, using all earnest but quiet means to cure them; nor ever, here in England at least, in our worst and wildest phases of discontent, do we dream, by committing national suicide, to fly to ills that we know not of. What a deep blessing, I say, it is, that our very people are by nature *conservative*—I mean, are of a nature to keep our nation together. The main body of Englishmen are content to leave it to theorists (some of whom they may feel to be wise, while most of them they know to be foolish) to speak and write the things they will; to make what mark they can, and to lend what aid they may in our solemn growth towards our great ideals; but meanwhile upon the whole we move unitedly on, maintaining, through all the trials of life and all the changes of time, a sane love for our native land, and an increasing affection for our most religious and gracious Queen.

For this reason it is that from no nation more deeply than from ours will rise to-day hearty thanks to Almighty God that He has frustrated yet again the knavish tricks of these infernal regicides. And the more so, because that indiscriminate havoc of superfluous death—that "Gunpowder Plot"—recklessly meant to make a victim, among others, of the young wife of our Sailor Prince. This little congregation of ours is indeed thankful that Heaven has spared our Royal Family and our Queen, and therein ourselves, a pang which would have been so bitter.

If, as Christ teaches us, not a sparrow falls to the ground without our Father, much more is He like to take care of the innocent family of an Imperial dynasty. Nay, this repeated preservation from these repeated onslaughts—not only in Russia, but in Germany, France, Spain, Italy, and almost wherever men have the questionable fortune of being born to be Sovereigns—this marked recurrence of escape might, one would think, even teach these political murderers that, in the words of our English poet,

" There's such Divinity doth hedge a king,
That Treason can but peep to what it would ;
Acts little of its will."

At least, it may well be part of the serene faith of all Christian rulers, that the same Providence which exalts them into special danger will cover them with special safeguard.

Now, may God save our own gracious Queen: and not only Herself, but all Her Royal Family, whom He has made Princes and Princesses in so many lands less safe and happy than our own.

February, 1880.

Wertheimer, Lea, & Co., Printers, Circus Place, London Wall.

"NO PART DARK."

By the Rev. W. B. PHILPOT, M.A., Vicar of South Bersted, Bognor.

Sermon Preached at South Bersted on Sunday, January 22nd, 1882.

"Having no part dark."—St. Luke xi. 36.

I CANNOT do better than read to you the whole of this passage—at least that part of it in which a new thought wells up in the mind of the Divine Speaker. I shall give it to you from the Revised Version, which, whatever exception may rightly or wrongly be taken to it, is of course the best which is now open to those of us who are not professed and self-sufficing linguists. "No man when he hath lighted a lamp putteth it in a cellar, neither under the bushel, but on the stand, that they which enter in may see the light. The lamp of thy body is thine eye: when thine eye is single, thy whole body also is full of light; but when it is evil, thy body also is full of darkness. Look therefore whether the light that is in thee be not darkness. If therefore thy whole body be full of light, *having no part dark*, it shall be wholly full of light as when the lamp with its bright shining doth give thee light."

Here you have an account of the "conscience as the noonday clear"; and what statement of it could be more pellucid? In fact, in this compressed utterance, this koh-i-noor of thought—this mountain of light—you have nothing less than the

Judge and Assessor of the conscience, Himself telling you what conscience is. This word indeed might be said to be the essential epitome of the autobiography of the standard Conscience. It is the one Conscience in all the world that was always pure, explaining itself to consist in the absence of darkness. He tells us that if our souls would be good and honest and like Christ, we must not, so far as we can help it, let any part be dark.

My brethren, do you fully realise what a blessing it is to possess words like these? What would the world be without them? What is England likely to come to, if, from morbid scruples and from pretence of religious difficulty, she ceases to teach words like these to her children? Can you conceive anything—I was going (were there not such dangerous madness in it) to say—more *trifling* than for the sects to pretend that their conscience will not allow them to allow the State to give to English children words which all agree to be the only true account of conscience? And what, think you, is their reason for this refusal? You will hardly believe me when I tell you that their very reason is because He who spoke these words is Christ. So in fact that which should be a reason why the State should teach them to *everybody* is twisted round into a reason why the State should teach them to *nobody!*—so palpably may you see the cloven hoof in all this paralysis of legislation. A certain league, stumbling along its dark ways, led through its quagmires by no spirit of health, has been fain to quench what little light the State has hitherto caused to shine in the people's schools. May heaven "frustrate their knavish tricks," and "confound their politics."

Think, I say, what a blessing it is to have before our eyes, in our hands, in the fleshy tablets of our hearts, in the highest region of our memories, these very words spoken by the Light of the

World; to find falling upon our souls the beams of this true light; to have the Word of the living God thus made flesh, crystallized into human utterances, rendered in your mother-tongue, adapted to your comprehension, dwelling among you, so as for you to behold their glory, and to see how full they are of grace and truth. Look closely, and only see what it is to have a passage like this to contemplate to-day. Why, my dearly beloved in the Lord, you have the feelings which glowed in the heart of Christ; you have the thoughts which at the same moment took form in the brain of Christ; you have the very words in all their essence which shaped themselves on the blessed tongue and flowed forth on most gracious breath, from the lips of the Redeemer. You have sayings which none who can at all appreciate the highest science of life will dare to dispute. They must have been spoken by some one. If, looking at the Speaker, anyone can say that He is not the Christ; yet, looking only at the *words*, he must admit that none but the Christ could speak them. Those who recorded them were, if you are any judge of character, not the men to lie; and, *whoever* spoke them, He it is whom the world, whom you and I, want for our Saviour. Words like these, though we have but few of them, are the words on which the Church of God is founded and grounded. Whatever else is erected or crumbles in the ranges and changes of Time, the spirits who build themselves on such words as these never can fall.

Sometimes one feels almost nervous, so to speak, lest one should *lose* any of these accents of the Master; lest the hubbub of the world should chance to drown any of His syllables. One sometimes feels as if it were only safe to walk with bated breath and careful, silent steps, lest the noise of a hurried walk over the sacred ground, or the insolence of breathing over rudely should dull any of the whispered monitions of this Voice which has its echoes within us. In such a mood as this does it not seem to you a marvel how any man can dare to live and to go on living, as we see so many do, without ever thinking on such words, and without praying, and without caring for his conscience at all? Why, he so puts out the light he has, and has *all* parts dark. It is bad enough, God knows, and it is awfully perilous, if we have *any* part dark at any hour; but to have all parts dark at all hours, and thus to roam among black ruins of a life, it makes one tremble to talk of it.

Oh, unhappy fellow-creatures, if you omit to hold intercourse with your God, and with the light that lighteth every man that comes into the world —you lay aside, you forget, perhaps you extinguish that which marks you as a man. Or is it that you think that a man is a man merely in virtue of his being a wingless biped? A lower animal can also see, can hear, can feel, can design, can make signs, can find its food, and can build itself a home: but when in the ascending scale of beings you come to man, you find this difference: you find that *he* has an inner light, a conscience, a power of bringing before his mind the love, the presence, the protection of his unseen Father. Now what can be more clear than this: that if a man fails to use that power, in so far forth as he fails to do so, he lowers himself *ipso facto* to the condition and *status* of the beast? Pardon me, I am wrong, for the beast, like all other types, is perfect as far as it goes; a beast cannot fall away; there is a more dreadful name than the name of beast for that to which he the man thus lowers himself. He becomes what Christ calls a *devil*. " I have chosen you twelve, and one of you is a devil." Do you not see that if, by neglect or by any other mode, you kill your capacity of high love, you call forth in so doing your capacity of deep hate? You come to hate the happy light from which you fall. It good be not your good, ill becomes your good. As you cease to become capable of unearthly delight you grow in your faculty and facility of unearthly anguish. Ceasing to be a child of light, you become a child of darkness, and an inheritor of the kingdom of hell. A horror of great darkness falls upon your soul; you sit and grovel in the shadow of death, and your spirit is stained black by it. Instead of rising with Christ to sit in heavenly places, you fall and fall till you lie with the powers of darkness in the infernal places: "Quantum in caelum; tantum in Tartara."

Let us ponder further this photograph of conscience, this vivid picture of the inner kingdom, left for us on the canvas of Scripture by the Light of the world. Here is the evil eye and the dark life; there is the single eye and the bright life. What is this evil eye? It is set over against the single eye, which shows that the single eye is the good eye. To come into the detail of fact, the evil eye is a wandering eye: an eye which glances many useless and harmful ways; an eye which runs after and feasts upon, and madly fastens upon those things which God has forbidden because they are bad for us, and which conscience warns us against because they are ruinous.

It is on the beatific vision of God that we should ever be gazing. We should look in this one direction with an eye that therefore must be single. We should let our Father guide us with His eye. As, when a well-mannered child takes your wishes, listening lovingly to your orders that he may clearly know them and carefully fulfil them, he looks you in the face while you speak; so we should fix our eyes on the light of the countenance of Jesus. In this way, seeing Him face to face, we become changed from grace to grace, and from glory to glory. In His light we see light. His light shines through us, and transfigures us, till, *having no part dark*, we become meet for the inheritance of the saints who already are in light.

The evil eye, on the other hand, is the eye guided by low desire. The wretched man, having no fixed object of high divine regard, is the victim of a want idly vague, or else, which it becomes at last, madly intent; a want which has nothing to do with, but is the direct antagonist of duty, soon making all duty distasteful. He becomes the prey of all manner of wants, for they are a numerous family. They want everything, while none of their objects are really wanted at all, and all of them, if we had them, would but derange and encumber the life. He is torn and bewildered by feelings which spring not from the part which should be rising to eternal life, but from that which sinks to eternal death—earth to earth, ashes to ashes, and dust to dust; sad words, which are natural when spoken of the body, but horribly opposed to nature when spoken of the soul. He lets these feelings control his eye, his mental eye, or his bodily and carnal eye, or both; or each through the other.

He wants, for instance, to be what he thinks would be great; and so, not having or not using the divine power of conscience and of will to control this desire, he lets his eye, which God made and said was good, run away from God's Eye, till, from the loss of that light, it is turned into a dull and evil eye, and goes peering after those worldly things which may make him great in the world's eye. The world's eye is an evil eye, and it is of this that he catches the lurid colouring. He wants to be rich, and then, reckless of the divine means of industry and labour, looking off from God's treasures and the great riches of contented godliness, he pores with eager wistfulness upon the ways and means of avarice. His heart becomes stony, his staring eye grows glazed and hollow, his life is soon set and grey from want of love, because of this love of want; and he lays up treasure in hell. And so, aggravating the balance against him in the Bank of God, he proves himself, as all selfish and avaricious men do, a spendthrift on the largest and wildest scale. This comes of *that* kind of evil eye.

Take another kind of evil eye. The eye of his Heavenly Guide says, "Walk in the Spirit and thou shalt not fulfil the lusts of the flesh. To be carnally minded is death. Be pure of heart and see God." But the man, stifling this clear voice of conscience, lets his low longings take him in exactly the contrary direction. Losing, or never finding, the comfort, the blessing, and the supreme delight of the spiritual life, he comes not to believe in this high life at all. His body by habit comes to be felt by him to be a nearer and dearer part of him than his soul is, and thus, with contemptible contempt for God's light, he grows to look on things and persons with a decayed and murky eye. Thus his eye becomes wholly evil and his body wholly dark. His mind and conscience become downdrawn and defiled. His delicate and fine spirit is draggled in the filth and mire of sin. Just as a man who never uses a sense, loses that sense; so the man who does not walk in the Spirit *loses the power* of walking in the Spirit, and at last even seems to forget that he ever had a spirit to walk in! This is the case with that class of infidels who step forward into God's Sun, and say there is no God, simply because they do not see Him. With these the Psalmist dealt long ago:—"The fool hath said in his heart, there is no God."

There is a remarkable passage in one of the Greek poets—the famous drama of the Prometheus

Bound of Æschylus—of which the words of the prophet quoted by Jesus might almost be counted a Hebrew rendering. In those old and sacred stories, which were as their scriptures to Greece, there was one who, by the sacrifice of himself, had come, not indeed sent by their God but acting as his enemy, to impart to man useful arts and to bring fire from heaven. Prometheus was in fact a sign of the desire which that people had for our Saviour; the more so that he too, as the story goes, was despised and rejected of men, and a sign that was spoken against.

Now the poet makes this divine man say in his lamentation, that before his day men "saw, but saw vainly; heard and heeded not, but, like the forms and fancies which are seen in dreams they mingled up all things in confusion." Well: this is still the case, and always will be, with men who have the evil eye and the dark heart. So terrible a thing it is, not to have the eye single and the body full of light.

He who made the eye of the body made also the clear and pure and holy eye within. Do you think that He who made the eye of man, the paragon of animals, made it to be on a level with the fierce and wild eye of the common beast? Was that mechanism, always so beautiful in its order, connected by the paternal Artificer of Nature with the brain and heart of man simply that it might fetch and carry between the outer world and the inner heart foul and debasing fancies? Was it meant that it should contemplate the animal aspects of affection, rather than allow these to find their natural place and pleasure in their order and their time? that it should begin at the consummation, and altogether ignore the origin and growing of love? The eye of man has its true place and its rightful range; but if the Spirit, the Will, the Conscience—the Christ who is ready to dwell with us—does not make a covenant therewith, it madly leaves the law of God and man, a wandering star rushing wildly among others who circle, or should do so, in their own courses of duty ; and thus the ever-watchful enemy pours back through it black clouds of danger and misery into the heart. " When thine eye is evil," says the Master, " thy body also is full of darkness ; look therefore whether the light that is in thee be not darkness."

Now what does the Saviour say about the eye when it is single and the conscience when it is light? He says, " thy body also shall be full of light. If therefore thy whole body be full of light, having no part dark, it shall be wholly full of light, as when the lamp with its bright shining doth give thee light." *Having no part dark.* You see the stress which the Saviour lays on this,—that we allow no respect in which the conscience shall be dull. " Be ye perfect," says the same Voice again, " as your Father which is in Heaven is perfect," " and in Him," as the loved disciple says, " is no darkness at all." " Whosoever shall keep the whole law, and yet stumble in one point, he is become guilty of all." " He that is unjust in the least is unjust also in much." If there be but a little rift in the lute, it will by-and-by make mute all the music. One little flaw in the moulding of the lens will spoil the optic glass : one little flaw in the casting of the cannon will cause it to burst when you bring it to the battle. This close connection of the parts of our complex being confirms what we should expect from the Maker. Our moral frame is made as fearfully and wonderfully as our physical frame. Is there any clear-minded divinely-gifted inventor who would put into any machine a part which should not minister to the right working of the whole ? If there is a part which does not perform its work, is not the whole machine hampered, if not stopped, in its working? So, if one part be dark in the conscience—of which light and truth are the duty and the work—the light is spoiled, the truth is dimmed, and the soul is in the way for being damned. Clouds, as we have seen, gather over the spirit. As in some bad painting, the use of some ingredient, which was meant to give but a passing brightness and to enhance its immediate value, soon blackens and damages the whole. The delicate shades of right and wrong run into one another, and great mischief and misery is the infallible result.

Why is this? Is it not because conscience is a power of discerning right and wrong and commanding the right? Conscience is the battle-ground of religion. This seems a truism, but the forgetfulness of this is the source of all irreligion, and of all "religious differences." Most religious differences between good men are not only irreligious but non-religious—irrelevant, and about nothing at all. This will be seen as the Christian Churches simplify themselves into their original purity, and the singleness of their primitive eye.

If the will—that is, the master-part of the man—do not act, or act wrongly with reference to some besetting pleasure—if we say, "we may do at least this", "we may indulge in at least that", "to me in my special circumstances this cannot be wrong", "God would not deny me this great and natural satisfaction", "we cannot always stand upright", "I shall not surely die",—if, I say, we use this and suchlike language in our inmost souls with respect to any one thing—though of course I do not mean to include those real difficulties which practically do often arise in genuine cases of casuistry—yet, if this kind of self-excusing from duty becomes a habit with us, then the power of discerning right from wrong is in the way for being vitiated; the plague begins; rottenness speedily rankles in the core of the soul; you enter on the first stage of dissolution; you make a mad plunge into the dreadful dark. In that darkness pestilence loves to walk. If you go on so, the enemy will in the end put out the last faint flickering of your lamp of life, and that "flaming minister" of Heaven what light shall e'er relume? There is no salvation in any other, but in the Christ of the Conscience. Put out that light, and then you put out the light indeed. You stumble further and further off into the dark and boggy mountains of iniquity. You find yourself wandering in a land where there is no order. Nothing is more true than this, for the Master says so, that the love of inner darkness here will cast you into some outer darkness, both later on in this life, and in that life which is later than this, when all the changes of the world are over and done.

But let us leave this black and dreary picture— this terrible nightmare of sin. My soul turn from it—turn we again to survey the beauty and glory of light; let us bend our thoughts to that land of divine order where the true light shines. Let us think again of the pleasure of a conscience as the noon-day clear. Take the case of a man who awakens, ere it be too late, out of the darkness of this moral madness of which we have been speaking, and admits the light to play upon his life; of the man who arises and lets Christ give him light.

This light opens also, it may be, from a dawn, and coming on like the morning over the mountains, grows and spreads from a faint beginning. Look what befalls a converted man—for, you see, I am taking the case of one whose life has been broken in upon by admitted sin—not that happy case of one whose path from the day of his earliest life has been brightening ever like the shining light towards the day of his perfection; many cases of which we happily note and know. I am also now taking the case of a gradual, and not of a sudden conversion.—Though, lest sudden conversion should be thought unnatural, let me remind you, by way of giving you an authority for its possibility, that Shakespeare, who knew much that was in man, and never gave a false picture of human possibilities, recognises such a change. You remember how he makes the ambitious Cardinal eternally change with the change of his temporal fortunes, and that, in the space of a brief conversation with his faithful servant. To Wolsey the sudden loss of everything was the sudden gain of *more* than everything. But I am not, at this turn of my discourse, speaking of the case of a sudden, but of a gradual change.—Well, when first, I say, the man is converted, there are many dark regions of his character, hitherto unsuspected perhaps even by himself, which soon begin to disclose and to discover themselves. When the seed of the light of this new life alights upon the black and dark night of his heart, there begin the stirrings of dawn. Those bad thoughts and evil memories, which used to haunt him, show themselves scattering at the sunrise. The flocking shadows troop to the infernal jail, and all his dark intents slink away, and go to their own place. The secret design to enjoy what he knew to be wrong, or what now at least he recognises to be wrong, is crushed and annihilated. He begins to have a single eye to the service of his Master. Joseph's principle, "How *can* I do this great wickedness and sin against God?" comes and stands between his soul and sin. He gets more refined in his self-examination. Though when beneath it he scarcely perceived it at all, he perceives now the horror of that great darkness which covered him. As diseases are often the deadliest, so his darkness was in fact the thickest when he felt it least. It is only when the divine rays pour themselves among it that, in the moment of its growing rare and beginning to dissipate, it makes itself visible with all its gangs of criminal fancies. How many things has he been in the habit of doing which will not stand the strong light that is streaming down upon them now. He fancied perhaps that the chamber of his heart was fairly pure, but the heavenly sunbeam that slants in upon him from this rising light shows him how full he has been of dust and defilement. He turns this new power of light down upon the water drawn from the old tanks whence in former days he slaked his thirst, and he finds in this strict analysis that it was charged with loathsome matter, and that every draught was death.

How many things also he now sees to have been left undone—duties to his God, duties to his neighbour, duties to himself, which had never even presented themselves to him before. Persons to whom have never been fulfilled the great law of love—help and kindness, for lack of which those on whom he should have bestowed it have positively withered and died; words which should have been spoken in season, which, if spoken, would have been so good, *left unspoken;* deeds which should have been done in season, and which, if done, would have been so useful, *left undone;* seasons never to be recalled, golden occasions let slip never to return; life, in short, turned into a desert, which should have been the garden of the Lord.

Now, however, as we were saying, the light shines upon all this. God, of His infinite mercy, has commanded new light to shine out of that old darkness. The garden of the Lord may still be reclaimed from the waste that you have made it. This eternal light, I repeat, arises when a man, by the power of the renewing and uplifting Spirit, heaves himself from the dust in which he has grovelled and lifts his face to the sweet and pleasant light of the countenance of his Father—when he opens his soul to the bright beauty and simple glory of that highest conscience. Darkness now is no more put for light, nor light for darkness. The one is divided from the other by the same creative mercy which divided them in the world at first. This is God's hour and the power of light. This wise heart is lightened, and the man stumbles upon the dark mountains of misery and disorder no longer. He becomes more and more able to do what he knows to be right. His strength is as the strength of ten, now that his heart is pure. The Spirit of the Father and the Son takes of the character of Christ and shows it to him. Humble and satisfied, leaning on the arm of his unseen Beloved, in love with God and in love with man, he ministers saving health to all about him, and goes gaily on to his perfection. Stained as his whole being was by the shadow of death, to the fear of which he was before in bondage, he sits now clothed and in his right mind in the sunshine of life, does the truth of God, works the work of God, burns and shines, like the unconsumed bush, with the fire and light that fills him, and again comes to love, ever more and more, the happy light to which now he rises.

There was once, as I said in the beginning, a Conscience on the earth which never had one stain pass over its purity, and which, being the second Adam, and being not only perfect in His type, but also the perfect Type of Humanity, being in fact the God-Man and the Man-God, the Omega as well as the Alpha, the last as well as the first in the Alphabet of Being—not only never could fall, but could raise all the fallen. It was He who spoke the words of the text. He had no part dark; in Him was no darkness at all. His whole body was full of light. The disciples could not always see it. Their eyes were rarely single enough to note the vision of their King in His beauty. Their eyes were holden that they should not see Him as He was. Once however, it is recorded, three of them saw Him in a body of light. It was a sight which seems to give a high and beautiful literalness to the words of the Master. It was when He was seen to talk with the spirits of the Prophet and the Lawgiver on the high top of that mountain of consciousness—whether of Tabor or any other earthly mount—to which He updrew His chosen of the chosen. These told, when they came down from that third heaven of ecstacy, how He had been transfigured before them, and how His face did shine as the sun, and His very raiment was white as the light. Peter, who was one of them—whether in the body or out of the body probably he could not tell, any more than Paul could afterwards—Peter, dazed with wonder at this unexampled result of the influence of Spirit upon form, told how that he had hazarded some wild and carnal proposals; how that he had wished, not knowing what he said, to condition the unconditioned, and to stereotype immortality under mortal canvas; and how at that moment a bright cloud—for the very clouds of the Divinity are bright ones—had enveloped the group in its shadow, and how a voice out of the cloud had said, "This is My beloved Son, in whom I am well pleased: hear ye Him." They told the vision and repeated the Voice to no man, for this was the bidding of their Master, till He was risen from the dead. And when He *was* risen from the dead—what then?—what took place? Was the like phenomenon ever repeated? *It was.* For it is recorded by those who by no law of character could possibly either be deceived or deceive, so strong were they of mind and so good of heart—it is recorded that His unquenchable Spirit wore a form still more manifestly glorified, though in some sort their eyes were holden still. His whole body full of light, its material conditions lost and rendered ethereal by the power of the Spirit—for the Spirit so interpenetrated His form that at times at least it became impalpable—that form appeared to the Apostles, and to many holy souls; glided into the closed chamber, no door being able to bar out the ever-present Deity; made the hearts of those to whom, in the course of a walk, He drew nigh in sublime converse, burn within them from the mere contagion and the fiery baptism of His glory; and finally, in the act of blessing them, and promising never to leave them, was parted from their eyes and carried up in the cloud that received Him to that heaven in which He is with us to-day.

Do we profess to understand all this? Nothing could be more preposterous than to pretend we did, except to deny it because we do not. Nay, there is *one* thing more foolish—that is, to hope to persuade the man of evil eye and blind heart by any argument which you may place before him. You might as well ask some sightless man to delight in some delicate masterpiece of art. There are more things in heaven and earth, brethren, than are dreamed of in your mortal philosophies. If a philosophy is true in any sense, and if, as far as it goes, it has any colour of the divine, the best that can be said of it is that it is but the mortal body of one which when raised will become hereafter clothed with a body of glory. All human philosophies have notably fallen to the ground. The wisest of them contradict one another flatly on the points most affecting the heart of their theories. We need have no trouble about disproving them, for they discredit and disconcert each other; and are like those two wild beasts which, attacking the traveller, sprang, when he stepped aside, into reciprocal and mutual self-destruction. Sane men have given up all hypotheses but GOD. The Chair of Philosophy is vacant, and none can fill it but our *dolce maestro*—our divine Master. Thoughtful men love to give themselves to the pondering of phenomena, and enquiring into fact. Facts are an infallible revelation, and the study of these will bring men to acknowledge that Revelation is an infallible fact. Yet herein is a marvellous thing, that these recorded spiritual facts, and all the ongoing phenomena which cohere with them, have been left hitherto wholly in the haphazard hands of all kinds of ministers of religion, to whom it is not of prime importance to examine them at all; but have never yet been examined by those who claim to be the enamoured favourites of Thought. When this is done, and surely the time for it is come, what will be found? *This* will be found, that faith is not only a genuine human faculty, but that it is the highest of *all* human faculties, and that these our ministers of faith have for their statements a basis of fact as yet unfathomed by all the plummets of science. When the wonder of the Conception, of the Miracles, of the Resurrection, of the Ascension, come before the mind, all we can at present say is, "Lo! this then is what the New Man, the last Type of Man, the God-Man, can be, and can do." Indeed, how was it to be expected that we from our low type could form upon it any *a priori* judgment? To form an *a priori* judgment you must be an *a priori* being; which you are not; and therefore how can you form an *a priori* judgment? The old creature cannot judge of the new, any more than the dog can judge of either. It was to be looked for that the New Man should come in a new way, live and think and act and speak in a new way, die in a new way, and show us things that before lay hid. In this attitude before all these wonders the mind may rest, by no means claiming at once the power to understand them, and still less having the hardihood to reject them, but waiting in faith till the growing faculties of an honest science shall learn to handle them.

Highly interesting and delightful as these kinds of truth are to contemplate, especially, one would think, to people of an enquiring turn, they are not the most momentous to those who know in Whom they have believed, and who live by faith. *Them* they concern but in their moments of leisure, and such hours as may be free to them for pleasing speculation. Woe be to those who, on the other hand, refuse to admit a divine influence because they cannot explain it. They might as well decline to enjoy the warmth of the sunshine, because they cannot draw it down out of the empyrean and play at ball with the sun.

Meanwhile, dearly beloved in the Lord, as the lower world lags behind, unable to know and to note things only discernible by those who care to cultivate their spiritual capacities—meanwhile, I say, let us for ourselves take heed, in the presence of these divine enigmas of God's Universe, *not to lose the good of life.* Nobody can say what he may or may not yet become, if, being converted into a new creature in Christ Jesus, he mounts up into his Master's chariot, and lets Him bear him on by His side. As He was, so in a sense are we in this world. Let His spirit renew you from day to day and from hour and hour. Then shall you know if you follow on to know the Lord. The powers within you are even now putting forth new feelers, new limbs, new wings, to reach, grapple with, and soar to those infinite conditions which are for ever revealing themselves to your souls. Keep faith and a good conscience, from which those who err *must* make shipwreck, and you will find that your Father will give more grace—grace upon grace and glory upon glory. Eye hath not seen nor ear heard, neither have entered into the heart of man, the things which God hath prepared for them that love Him.

And how dare any mortal man dogmatise as to what change, "what dreams", what bliss may not come to those "friends" to whom God says "Come up higher"? What do men know about it who tarry among the baggage of life, the rocks and the incipient forms of dust, and leave the proper study of mankind, the facts of the spiritual life, unlooked to? If I want to know the earth's crust, I go to Lyell and to Page. If I want to know the laws of supply and demand, I go to Mill. If I want to know of the descent of man, I go to Darwin—but if I want to know of the Ascent of man, how to live and how to die, and how to rise again ; if in a word I want the Bread of Life, I go to CHRIST. To whom else should we go? He only has the words of eternal life. Cultivate the single eye, and then He who alone knows—no man having told it to Him, but He telling it to every man who comes into the world—the Sun of righteousness that gives light but borrows none—He, the Master of all humanity, the fulness of the Godhead bodily, He in whom we live, and move, and have our best being—HE tells you, that your whole body shall be full of light, that you shall be changed into His image from glory to glory, and attain that highest state to which the soul can aspire—if only you *have no part dark*. This may His mercy grant, unworthy as we are, to you, my brethren, and to me. Now to the King immortal, eternal, invisible, be all glory and dominion for ever and ever. Amen.

Wertheimer, Lea, & Co., Printers, Circus Place, London Wall.

ON THE DEATH OF BABES.

"Suffer the little children to come unto me."—MARK x. 14.

I HAVE chosen for our subject to-day the Death of Babes.

Those to whom I am bound by family love having, within a brief space, met with a second such loss, my own heart and mind have naturally dwelt much on this matter during the last few days. And therefore I should not only find it hard to throw myself for your profit into any other line of feeling and thought, but I thus feel the better prepared to admonish you in what light you should regard such a trouble, if ever it should come upon your own house.

And I offer you this contemplation with the less misgiving at the present time, for I am thankful to say that there is not, to the best of my knowledge, any one here to-day who has suffered such a calamity very lately, and thus what I may say will not, I trust, come so near to any heart as to give undue pain, while I hope it may come so near to all hearts as to do us eternal good.

If we look first at the case of the little ones themselves who pass away, we shall then better see what should be the feelings of those who are called to see them pass.

Let us think, as I said, of very little children; of those whom our Church bears on her heart when she says, " It is certain by God's Word that children which are baptized, dying before they commit actual sin, are undoubtedly saved:" a comfort which clearly refers to those who are not old enough to canvass their position in life so freely as to set at naught their Lord deliberately, and to rank themselves under Christ's enemy by refusing to remain any longer with His friends.

I presume this must be the main meaning of "actual sin," though the word being theological, and somewhat scholastic, is probably meant (and wisely, for the sake of avoiding controversy) to cover many meanings, and adapt itself to the dogmas of divers combatants. Sin of all sorts, God knows, is actual enough, in our popular sense of the word, if it be sin at all; and sin of some sort is manifestly bound up in the heart of every child. At least, no child comes forth of the human stock, as far as we can see, Christ excepted, in whom the highest nature holds from the beginning an unquestioned sway. We perceive imperfection in the earliest indications of the moral life. So soon as ever desire and conscience come into play, we find desire beginning to question, if not to silence, conscience. And as that temper, not being the highest, partakes of the low nature of sin, so every child born into the world must be more or less low and sinful. That one touch of the lower nature makes the whole world of babes and men sadly kin. It is comfortable to know that in a sense the children of Christian parents are holy. But, just as certainly as we know, on finding a defect in a breaking flower, that the same defect lay hidden in the bud before it began to break, so, where we find naughtiness in a child display itself when the character opens, we cannot but gather that the germs of it lay there before.

In a word, I am taking the case of those whom, in common with all other well-ordered and cared-for children, Christ had in due course gathered into His visible fold, and who have died before they have even had any chance or option to stray from it:—little lambs whom we have placed safe in the arms of Jesus, and who have been borne and carried by

Him to God's bosom before they became big enough and vulgar enough to struggle and spring out of those arms back into the bestial desert of the world. I speak of those, therefore, of whom we may safely feel, whatever may be said of others —of whom it is not my business as a Minister of our Church to speculate with you here to-day— that, as Christ has taken them from His fold below, He has folded them securely elsewhere, "beyond the reach of ruinous decay."

If the delicate but mysterious tie, wherewith the Maker chose to yoke its large spirit to those few handfuls of dust, has been snapped by the strength of another of His illegible laws, we may well believe, and it is part of our Christian faith to believe, that the Love, which allowed it to live in this antechamber of its being, will follow it through the doors of the Home that He opens, and will provide for it also in the next range of its life.

Oh strange and interesting destiny! oh marvellous difference between their precious souls and ours! They taken, we left. They carried off in triumph of bloodless victory before the fight with sin began; we left to win the same triumphant entrance after the burden and heat of the battle. They had, as we had, the crushing pangs and awful risk of birth—(for "the great pain and peril of childbirth" may probably be referred as much to ourselves as to our mothers); they had the agony of catching their first breath—doubtless as great, if not greater, than that of gasping for their last; but, as they never remembered the anguish of being born, so it is likely they will remember no more the anguish, if any, of passing away. And yet more surely will they forget all the sorrows and pains, wants and cries, of the little while that came between.

It has been said by Lord Brougham, one of the first authorities on Infant Schools—a tender branch of moral gardening which no generation had studied or dreamed of till our own, though all along our beautiful Burial Service has regarded babes as full brothers and full sisters of Christ—that we learn more, or at least receive more ideas during the first two years of our time than in all the rest of our years put together. Perhaps it might be added that during that early period children also suffer more. Think of the bitter, envious frosts and chilly winds, the nipping, eager airs that bite and blow upon their tender bodies; the witless ignorance of those who are generally about them; the want of imagination which so often spoils, and sometimes kills them with mistaken kindness; the crashing of loud sounds and heavy buffets, not to say of fierce and unnatural looks and words, upon organs infinitely delicate and wholly unfitted for impact; the roughness of those who should be most gentle; the convulsions and nervous storms associated with mere growth, combined all along with the incapacity of plainly expressing their wants and telling what is the matter with them. But as all these would have been forgotten by them, had they lived on earth, is it likely that any trace of them will be remembered now that they are living in Heaven? If birth and death have been forgotten, all those sorrows, far less critical, of the brief interval may well be forgotten also; nay, most of these common pains of life by dying early they escape altogether. Except, indeed, in this respect of capacity of pain, our babes seem all along well nigh to have been equal to "their angels."

The case of the death of Holy Innocents seems verily to be a marvel—yet what is there in life which is not a marvel? How few things there are which we can regard in any other light than that of unintelligent, though not unreasonable, wonder. Still, few things seem more marvellous in the rough aspect than that a little child should be allowed to suffer pain and die. Here is a little bud, a tender nursling of the spring, in the fairest way for flower, fragrance, and fruit, nipped by the world's unkindly weather before a single leaf unfolds itself. Here is a little barque, freighted with costly wares for the markets of earth and heaven, bound for eternity, launched into life, but wrecked at the very harbour-mouth. A work nobly simple, yet beautifully complex, with God's fresh breath of life inspiring its every look, and the power of the sweetest nature swaying its every movement; lo! it drops from His hand, as it might seem, in the very act of His holding it up to show its beauty to the world. It falls to pieces in an hour. The high art of its creation is negatived in a moment; its lovely mechanism falls off into dust; all its myriad contrivances for life—no one of which any man, since the world began, can imitate with the slightest effect, no, nor even rightly understand—in a few days are crumbled into mould, and as if they never had been at all. In fine, a work designed for duties of seventy or eighty, or perhaps a hundred years, capable of beautiful deeds, and of filling happy places in the State—in the church of the family, and in the Family of the Church— is destroyed, as it might seem, by some slight accident, before any one of those duties has been met; and, to outward view, annihilated as though it had never been meant for anything whatsoever in the world.

The little one, moreover, was planted in the midst of circumstances remarkably adapted to its life. All things seemed to expect it, and to be prepared to supply it. The air had elements of breath and nurture for it; songs and sounds ready to amuse and instruct it. The earth and sky had a thousand shapes and colours wherewith to delight it, and make its coming life dear and enjoyable to it; and, though in all these there is made a blank when it is gone, yet gone it is, and the blank is made. Add to this, the world was full of ideas for its mind and scope for its spirit. There were companions and teachers ready in due course to take it lovingly into their classes and their company; bright games and pleasant school-rooms waiting for it with kindly welcome; but it comes not. Above all, those to whom it was more especially given had a large room ready furnished for it in their hearts, and bosoms full of love wherewith to nourish and to cherish it, of which the warm cheer of the comfortable home was but a faint symbol and a rude outward image. Yet, as I say, in all this there is made a pitiless blank; yea, to the yearning hearts of those that love it, as all did that knew it, that blank is infinite, though as far as humanity goes, the babe was almost infinitesimal. All things seem to have been made as vainly for the child as the child for them. Here was a child, and there were the prepared circumstances for the child, obviously made for each other, set over against one another (ἕν πρὸς ἕν), and yet both perish without fulfilling what looked so like the very end of their being. All seems to fall through and come to nothing, as if there were not, nor ever had been, any end or aim, purpose or intention, or any reason at all in the complex circumstances, any more than in the intricate machinery of all that creation.

This may seem the more marvellous to those who live in days like these, even than it can have seemed to those who lived in the days of our fathers, before Science had been empowered by God to watch so closely His workings in Nature. In these days, when labour, with excessive subdivision injurious to the mental capacity of the workers, bends itself with both hands and intent eyes over the most trivial objects; when gigantic or unremitting efforts are set afoot to bring about or to bring to light effects which are slight, or which are transitory; when these results, be they in the improvement of an instrument, or in adding a trait to an animal or a flower, become at once universally known and publicly canvassed; when vast learning is brought to bear on the microscopic dissection of some almost invisible insect; when men not only weigh the sun in the heavens, but decompose the motes in the air, we in our days, I say, naturally think more of a human body, however small, if not more of the human soul that houses therein, and are disposed to pay it more reverent respect than men did in the times that are past.

Not but what David, the mighty monarch, the slayer of giants, the scatterer of armed hosts, the sweet Psalmist of Israel and of Christendom, and in the lineage of the babe of Bethlehem, alarmed his courtiers by the shock which convulsed his tender nature when his baby was only taken ill. But then David was a great man and very wise. He saw things as they are, and was not under the mastery of conventionalities which turn the greatest marvels stale.

The fact, as I was saying, that we now know more of what a human body is, might make it seem even a more monstrous thing that such a mechanism could lightly be allowed to perish. And, therefore, it seems to the first thought as though, in the dying of a child, some unseen power had simply been at play, and a very cruel play; building up all this astonishing fabric of beauty and of love merely in order to pull it down again; setting up bright and holy hopes in order but to throw them over; and making human love with a view, regardless of our best feelings, to breaking it again before our eyes.

So it may be thought, I say, at the first blush of the matter; and so it must have more or less been always thought in dark times; and so, in fact, it must be thought still by dark, unhappy hearts, who know not and believe not all that we, dear brethren, believe and know.

Up to this point we have been thinking and speaking as heathens might speak and as heathens think. Now let us draw the curtains, unfold the shutters, raise the blinds, open wide the windows, let in the light of heaven, and give your dark and dismal fancies a breath of the pure and wholesome air. Now what a different aspect comes over the musty chamber of the heart. Till now the soul had made herself a charnel-house, and sat with leaden eyes sulking in her ignorance. But now what a new glory falls on the whole place where abides the faithful Spirit! Her murky, miserable imaginations, and her dank distresses evaporate in the sunbeams of heaven. The shadows of the Tomb flee apace. From under appearances the most hopeless, what blessed hopes reveal themselves — full of immortality. The view of the cave of despair sinks down and dissolves, while to the sounds of heaven there rises through its ghastly details the City which hath foundations, whose Builder and Maker is God, the New Jerusalem, the river of the water of life, and scenes of pleasures so enchanting, that no dreams of an old Elysium, no Happy Isles of fancy can picture a world so fair. A divine interpretation has unravelled the most entangled difficulties of the heart.

With what altered feelings do we now stand beside that little marble form, smiling as in the rapture of repose.

As those two unearthly beings in white apparel sat, the one at the head and the other at the feet, where the body of Jesus had lain, so those three angelic Ideas, Faith, and Hope, and Love, wait by the side of the mourners.

There, with calm brow, and resolute, submissive

lips, is the angel of Faith. She tells us that God alone knows the end from the beginning; that we cannot follow even a short piece of the thread of human affairs; that it was He who made the child; that He makes nothing in vain; that He does all things well; that therefore it was well that this sweet immortal being sprang from His bosom; that He is absolutely wise; that therefore what has befallen must be for the best. Faith also gives us full assurance that if, after having shown it to the world for a moment, the Father draws it *to* Himself at the first, it is only that the world may not for ever draw it *from* Himself at the last; that, if we fancy it is not so, it is only that our dark minds are throwing over the face of the matter our own confusion, taking away its true colour and all its likeness to life—for that here we see but one side of life, and that the dark one; that the little one whom we weep for is only being taken over from the dark side of life to the bright one; that it has but gone to realise its fortune as a child of light.

Then Hope takes up the strain and uses the like language. Her upward eye is bright with the prospect of immortal destiny. If in our despair we point to all those high and vast faculties of the vanished life, and all those happy, earthly circumstances in which those powers and capabilities might so usefully and pleasantly have found their field and their play, she bids us remember this:—that if those earthly visible circumstances pass, of which we think so much, those infinite powers remain of which we know so little; that no eternal germ can die; that, as for that long list of happy duties and prepared enjoyments which we had ignorantly hoped it might enter on below—what were they but so many clear prophecies, what are they but so many comforting symbols of a longer list, nay, an infinite sum of still nobler employments and far deeper enjoyments elsewhere? that, however the things which are made but to pass are shaken from the soul as it bursts from its husky chrysalis, the soul, being a thing immortal as God Himself, is not among the things which can be shaken, and, therefore, why should we fear for that?

Hope reminds us, moreover, that God over all, blessed for ever, is not so poor a Designer, that the Maker of mind is not Himself of such stunted capacity and so straitened in His imagination, as that the whole of His scheme could be comprised in the part which we can see, or limited by the little that we can know; that behind and beyond, at the disposal of the babe whom we have lost, lies the infinite future of an imperishable career; that in His world, which is so wide, the spirit, so largely and nobly made, is gone to inherit larger and nobler regions of immeasurable growth, and to find a far freer and fuller fruition of the glorious Godhead of Him that made it—fuller and freer than the fairest prospects of this lower life could even feebly indicate, much less fully furnish; that if sorrow has endured for one short night, and a night shorter than wont, of which no trace will soon remain behind, joy has already come to it in the morning of Heaven and the sweet summer day that is before it; that, though the mourners bear its holy dust through the village street, the little foundling, laid on the threshold of the Church, has been taken to a long, eternal home; that, in short, the mere thought that it was mortal was merely a mortal thought: and much more, in kindred strain, the ministering angel Hope has to tell.

And I spoke of another angelic Idea, and that was Love. Love also, the greatest and sweetest of the Christian graces, waits with you beside the cot in which you have laid for its last sleep the cold white beauty of the little one that you seem to have lost. No less full of immortality than Hope was, no less trustful than Faith was, comes Love to your side, with comfort, which is soul-reaching and bosom-searching, breathing warm from her lips—comes to say to you everything which Faith or Hope may perchance have left unsaid. Love repeats all in yet more rich and glowing colours, and with holy contempt smiles down in your heart any lingering thought which, with unholy brooding, could possibly fancy that all was not for the best. This angel of Grace tells us again that God is the child's First Father, and also *our* Father, and that God is Love, and that this being so, how can anything be amiss?

Does not Love remind you that, since He is, without bound or limit, wise, and kind, and true, therefore nothing in His government can in any way be wrong, or cruel, or false; that it would indeed have been false and cruel and mistaken in us, had we been able and had we chosen to take any other way than His; that, if it has been His good pleasure that His child and yours, in the language of earth and time, should die—it is His better pleasure that, in the language of Eternity and Heaven, it should live; that losing its life to *you*, it has found it still in Him; that thus, in a word, in His pleasure is life; that in that Bosom of the Father to which it has gone back, it will find comforts a thousand-fold more comfortable than in any of your houses and lands, or any of the chequered circumstances of what the world calls fortune; that, if, having created it, as it seemed, for the chances and blessings of humanity, He withdrew it, while yet it was safe, from the changes and disasters of humanity, what was this, in fact, but a signal mark of His favour and His love? that this indeed is a lot for which, as you know, millions in the Judgment-day would give all the world, had the case been theirs, contrasting it with their desperate and desolate wish that they had never been born. Was it not well worth those few hours or days, or even months of sickness or weakness, or even pain, all of which are so soon forgotten that they become as though they had never been, to have its immortal foot planted for that brief space, as the condition and warrant for its Eternity, on these shores of Time; for has it not thus gained the invaluable step-stone by which it may pass from this shadowy region of flitting embryos up to the solid ground of eternal activities? Why, says Love, should you murmur that it has gained the greatest step a soul can take in the promotion of its everlasting career?

And many such-like consolations, only far fuller and richer, sweeter, and more explicit than ever I could name to you, the Spirit of Love can minister to your listening soul.

So now we should be at no loss to understand how Christian parents feel when they lose a babe. Do not Faith and Hope and Love abide by them and tell them how the matter stands? So that there is no room—I do not say for tears, since Jesus wept—but I do say there is no room for those tears which come from the deepest source of all. No, you must keep your bitterest tears and your profoundest anguish, not for those who have died as babes to live with God, but who have lived in sin and *left* their God. Weep not for those whom Christ has taken into His ark, whom we have offered to Him at the font, and who have not lived long enough in the world to give the world their preference; souls that, like the star of the morning, are hidden in the light of the Sun of Righteousness ere they have risen for more than a little arc over the horizon of Time. When Christian parents, as befits them, are filled and inter-penetrated with these hopes and convictions, have we not known, have we not seen how they can show themselves to be miracles of resignation and peace, though first one child was not, and then another was not, for God took them; and though they were tempted to say with impatience, "All these things are against me"? I myself have known them, aye, and I know them now—though, such is their humanity, that their hearts are wrung with anguish deeper than most of us are capable of—though their natural affections are set to a far higher key than in the stunted and undeveloped hearts of mere worldlings would have been possible—though they have seen and felt more of the sweet intensity of the love of kind than is even conceivable to souls unrenewed in the spirit of their mind—I have known them, I say, in the heroism of their confidence hold aloft in their arms their dying babes, and hand them back one after another in successive acts of faith, like wave-offerings, as into the very arms of the Good Shepherd, that He might in their very sight gather their children back· again into the Bosom from which they received them at first.

Dear brethren, I have said what I have in order that if any of you, in days gone by, but with sorrows that perhaps will linger by you for long, have lost your little ones, you may learn, if you have not learned it before, the lesson which your Father fain would teach you, and even now may be able to say, "The Lord gave, and the Lord hath taken away: blessed be the name of the Lord."

I have said these things, moreover, in order that all of you who are parents of babes may lay them up in your hearts. Not that I mean to do so unwise and unchristian a thing as to suggest grief to you before the time—grief which, let us hope and pray, never may come to you; nor that I would have you anxious, God forbid, about the morrow of your little ones. But I have spoken thus, in order that you may master this portion of the chart of life against the day when such a storm may overtake you, and come down perhaps suddenly upon your souls. I would have you view aright the dealings of your God, wherever and whatever those dealings may be, at a time when you know that He may be found, lest in so great water-floods of sorrow you should not feel able rightly to come nigh unto Him.

Lay up, therefore, the remembrance of these truths in the calmness of your prosperity, so that, if such a day do come, you may not be tempted to regard it as wholly evil, but that you may know how to feel and how not to feel, how to act and how not to act; how, in short, to repose in the love of your own Heavenly Father, and say fully and at once " Thy will be done."

Above all I would urge you to take all pains—though where can you find greater pleasure?—so to feed those lambs whom the Good Shepherd has given you, that they never may wander from His fold. Take care lest the days come, for those days would be evil indeed, in which you could even passionately wish that they had been gathered into that fold in heaven, before they had been old enough to stray from it on the earth.

For is it not indeed possible, that *sometimes* at least, there may be a sad but merciful reason why our infants die? Is it not possible—I had almost said probable—that the All-seeing Eye, looking before and after, knowing the weakness of principle or the want of principle in us parents, and gauging the inevitable results of the combinations of our circumstances and our sins, may, of His Fatherly love, well shrink from exposing the little ones to the rough calamities which He foresees that they would encounter by our example or our neglect, and so, tempering the wind to His lambs, draws them back earlier than wont into the shelter of His invisible fold? Who shall say that this is unlikely?

Thus you clearly note that it is a matter of very touching moment that you for your parts take heed so to strengthen your principles, so to consolidate yourselves with God, that in your case no such melancholy reason should come into play why Heaven should, in anger with you and in love for them, snatch your children away from you before their time. If Jesus with threefold earnestness said to Peter, in reference to the little ones, in every sense, of His rising Church, "Feed My lambs," so surely, not with less but greater earnestness, He says the same to you, O parents, through His minister to-day, "Feed My lambs, your own lambs"—those little ones whom we rightly regard as the brothers and sisters of "the Lamb of God."

A word in conclusion for us all. We have all been received at the font by Jesus, buried with Him in baptism, and lifted by Him in due form into the courteous position of the new life. Most of us are now little ones no more. The symbolic water soon dried on our brows; but the Cross which was made there abides as the token of our service and the sign of our hopes. We have learned to speak, to move, to think, and to act. We are in the full activity of our trial-time. The Spirit, that like a dove rested on Jesus, and the holy angels—are they not leaning over us with love—aye, it may be, leaning with fear—to watch whether we still are little children in our hearts? "Except ye be converted, and become as little children," says Christ, "ye cannot enter into the kingdom of heaven." Let us, then, however long our souls may have been launched, and though they be running now with crowded canvas in the mid-ocean of life, let us keep our Christ on board with us; that so, when we come to die, be it soon or late, we may immediately find ourselves at the haven where we would be. Let us with guileless and implicit obedience always do and always abide God's good will, and, while we live the lives and fulfil the works of men, cherish the spirit of the child. May it never be said of any of us, as of the first traitor of his Lord, "It were better for that man that he had not been born"; or, being born, that he had died a child.

Oh! may God of His infinite mercy gather, not only our children, but ourselves into His happy Home at the last. If He sees it to be for the best, may our dear children grow up, and grow into Christ in all things; and may they live to close in due course their parents' eyes; but always so, that, live as long as they may, pass as soon as they may, they may still be all "undoubtedly saved." Thus may it come to pass that, as our several households break up on earth, they may be forming anew in heaven. Let us not only suffer our children to come, but so bring them and draw them to Jesus, and so try to keep them by His side, that it may be ours to say on the last day, that great day of the Feast of Heaven, that Marriage-Supper of the Lamb, "Behold me and the children whom Thou hast given me."

In re
ROME *versus* ENGLAND.

(Preached in Arundel in 1873, and needed everywhere now.)

PREFACE.

Any readers who may feel aggrieved by this Sermon should remember that it was preached to an audience exclusively of Protestants. To the critical reader I would apologise for the style by stating that it was written *currente calamo* during part of a night following a day of hard work, a few hours before it was preached. The references made to the priesthood refer, I cannot too strongly observe, not to anything in their private life, of which I know nothing, but solely to their religious functions, which I maintain are alien to the genius of the English People. Once, when a young man, I went with a friend to one of their rites. When we came out of the place, with its darkness, its incense, the mysterious movements and general mystification, into the sweet sunny air of God's heaven, I said "How do you feel after this?"—for we had entered in a very solemn mood. He drew a long breath and said "To tell you the truth, I feel much as Jonah must have felt when he was cast up out of the whale's belly." It was a remark of which, I own, I felt the force, as entirely expressing my own sensations; and I believe it expresses the sensations of all rational Englishmen who, after witnessing the modes of worship which they seek to foist upon us, are not too sad to smile— supposing, that is to say, they have not already become demoralised by our Anglican mimicries of these Romish mummeries.

Persons who must be either indifferent, or dull of perception, or Romanists at heart, may pretend to decry language such as this as "too plain," as "setting people by the ears," &c. But we all know what this means. Except *somebody* speaks out in the several neighbourhoods where the Enemy is at work, how can the people be *put upon their guard* ? The fact is, the friends of Rome *hate* to see us put on our guard—of course they do !—and this is why they call putting us on our guard "setting us by the ears." We are not ignorant of their devices.

The text is a brief, but full, complete, and authoritative denial of Mgr. Capel's Anti-Christian statement that men are to find rest for their souls in any alleged external certainty, such as is held forth by the Romish fiction. It is easy to see why they hate the light, keep the Scriptures in their back-closets, and use in their rites a language dead and not "understanded of the people."

"He that believeth on the Son of God hath the witness in himself."—1 JOHN V. 10.

THIS passage describes the state of the soul of the man who allows the SPIRIT of the FATHER and JESUS to create him anew.

You will find this drawn out more fully by St. Paul (Rom. VIII. 14). "As many as are led by the Spirit of God, they are the Sons of God, for ye have not received the Spirit of bondage again to fear, but ye have received the Spirit of adoption, whereby we cry 'Abba, Father.' The Spirit itself beareth witness with our spirit that we are the children of God : and if children, then heirs, heirs of God, and joint heirs with Christ." That is the *status*, and that the temper, of us plain Protestant-Christians.

Again, St. Paul says (Gal. IV. 3) "When we were children, we were in bondage under the elements,"—the rudiments, the Alphabet—" of the world." That is, before Christ came and lived and died and rose, we, even the best part of human society, were under the training of children, and under Old-Testament ideas, ideas of Priesthood, sacrifice, and ceremonial law. But when the fulness of the time was come, all these things were changed. " Behold I make all things new." " God sent forth His Son, made of a woman, made under the law, to redeem them that were under the law, that we might receive the adoption of sons; and, because ye are sons, God hath sent forth the Spirit of His Son into your hearts, crying, 'Abba Father.' Wherefore thou art no more a slave, but a son ; and if a son, then an heir of God through Christ."

"Now" he goes on to plead, "after ye have known God, or rather are known of God, how turn ye back to the beggarly elements, to which ye desire again to be in bondage? Ye observe days and months and times and years : I am afraid of you", says the minister of Christ, "lest I have bestowed upon you labour in vain." And these beggarly elements are much the same as those to which the same Apostle refers in the 4th Chapter of the 1st Epistle to Timothy, when he warns him against what in fact were the beginnings of the Papacy. "Now," he says, "the Spirit speaketh expressly, that in the latter times some shall depart from the faith, giving heed to seducing spirits, and doctrines of devils, speaking lies in hypocrisy, having their consciences seared with a hot iron, forbidding to marry, and commanding to abstain from meats", &c.; in fact, bringing in again all the bondage and childish trumpery of those very superstitions which the priests of Rome and their most eloquent advocates are seeking to impose upon us in this neighbourhood at this time.

For take notice that, to bring you in this good old English town under the dark follies and degrading tyranny under which you lay before your national martyrs died in the cause of Reformation, is the end and object of this whole business. And it is the solemn duty of your minister, even for the hour, to guard you against it.

Now I should be profoundly hurt if I were to hurt anybody by what I say. I would not hurt any conscientious person for the world ; but I say that advance on the part of the enemies of England must be met by public warning such as I now give you. Let it be remembered that we here are of the Reformed Church, whatever other ties we may have beyond these walls, and it is our business to guard ourselves against danger. We probably most of us have Roman Catholic friends ; for my part, I have many such whom I deeply regard ; and you, in this place, must be bound up with many such in divers relations ; but all that is neither here nor there. The truth, however painful personally, must be spoken when it becomes the duty of the preacher, whether regular or occasional, to warn the people. And if ever there was a time when it was necessary to warn the people, it is now, when such efforts—I do not say from at home, but from alien quarters, are made to disturb you.

Well, as I was saying, the words of St. Paul apply to these times no less than to those. Can you not see, for I can, the finger of the great Apostle, pointing to-day to that pile of stone-work, which, beautiful as it is, is in large part a temple of Idols ?—Can you not see him, for I can, pointing to Archbishop this, and to Monsignor that—a robbery of English names and a sly introduction of Italian names, which I for my part hold to be an unpardonable impertinence—can you not hear him giving you solemn warning, ere you hang with rapt attention on that eloquence of falsehood, to which my plain language of truth must be but poor ?

"Yes," says Paul, "these are the very men of whom the spirit speaketh expressly," when he says, "in the latter times there shall come seducing spirits who will try, by appealing to your weakness and your fears, to make you forget that *the witness must be within you*, and so to drag you back to the beggarly elements to which only pagans are in bondage, and from which your fathers faced the fires and the racks of Rome in order once for all to set you free."

What would Wickliffe say?—what would Ridley and Latimer say, whom Rome burnt in that Oxford ditch, were they to find they had stood in their fiery shirts for the English people in vain? Yet here are the same kind of men as those who burned them, come back again to trouble you. They are the same, every inch of them. They cannot change if they would. Is it not their pride and boast to be the same? Do they not *tell* you they move by laws which are irrevocable? Do not their customs,* their bearing, their unmanly garb, their stealthy serpent-like un-English ways—the mischief they make in families—the disobedience which they inculcate on your children—the foulness of their confessional—the stupidity of their wafer-worship—the mumbling of their prayers in an unknown tongue—the insolence with which they

---

* Be it here again noted, that I am not speaking of the men personally,—not taunting (God forbid) those numerous men, *naturally* vigorous, fine-hearted, and intellectual, who have allowed themselves to be driven by circumstances, or drawn by infatuation, to drown their noblest faculties and throw away their dearest rights;—but I speak here and all along, of that killing system which needs must merge their humanity, and which arraying them as mutes or as harlequins, isolates them from human sympathies, and withdraws their special powers from the ranks of the growing State. I do not apologise for making public remarks on the eccentricity of public costume. Dress is open to comment, whether in a church or in a fashion-book.

trample under foot the plain judgment of common-sense people—the craft of their creeping into houses and leading captive silly women and the weakest of men—does not the dead-set they make, which no one can help observing, at great fortunes and young inexperienced persons who possess them, and who would be good, useful citizens without them—in a word, does not every trait which you find in them prove them to be now the same as your fathers found them to be of old? and does not every child see that these same men, if only they could get power enough in this land, so far as in them lay, would set up the stake and set fire to the faggot again—aye, and would even think that in doing so they were doing God service, and would call it kindness to you and me in the end?—nay, they would find a pious satisfaction in drowning with the chanting of their Latin litanies the groans of Englishmen's tortures, and the wails of English-women's agonies.*

---

* If all this seems heated or over-strong, as they would doubtless have you believe, you have only to remember the Court of the Inquisition. That Court sat, at least till lately, in its dark chamber at the Vatican. It was described to myself by an eminent Roman citizen in '59, who had himself been dragged before it and worried by it for weeks for merely having had in his possession a picture of a certain historical personage. It is still waiting to do its worst wherever scope may be given. Civilly speaking, it may be now held in check by the new freedom of Italy; but it is a couchant dragon, only "biding its time." It was only the other day that the organs of Rome spoke with ominous fanaticism of the "spiritual sword"—not the sword wielded by the enlightened Christian State, but the same old sword of the dark and deaf Priesthood. If they retort and tell you that Elizabeth also, in turn, made her bloody sacrifices, you may tell them that this was the work of an irritated people; this was done in self-defence and retaliation, according to the tone and temper of the times; *but the State*, which did this, *has now become a tolerant State;* while the Church of Rome still maintains this power of the Spiritual Sword, which is sharper than the civil one; and that *Church has not changed, and cannot change.*

Does anyone say this is an overdrawn picture? God grant that the logic of events may not prove to you its truth. Don't let their precious balms break your head: don't let them wheedle you into fancying they must in our days be harmless. There are many ways, moreover, of stifling freedom and life, short of death. The least part of the evil would be the stake and the rack—all that is accidental; the worst would be that *the Truth must perish from the land*. Perhaps you say, good easy man,—"these enlightened times would not permit of such dark barbarities, and would not allow freedom to be slain." But what are two or three centuries to a Church whose principle it is *never to admit one real ray of new light?* Remember, the Pharisees and the Priests of the Catholic party of Christ's day were personally, as many of these are, respectable men enough,—for, bear in mind all along, I repeat that this is not personal to the man, but only truth spoken of the *system*.—Those Pharisees held the doctrines of the Old Testament; they were devout, they made long prayers, they adhered to the synagogue, they even believed in the resurrection;—*but*, take note, *their* doctrine too was to *admit no new light!* Christ came and brought light to life through His Gospel, and how did they treat Him? Did they not harden their hearts—as these men do when it is a question of mercy? Did they not close their eyes fast and tight against the light He brought—just as these men do? Did they not fasten Him to that stake on Calvary? and did they not kill HIM? They did; and these men would have done the like, had they lived in those days. The men who represented them in the sixteenth century did the same to your fathers,—and these men to-day,—*to whom change, as I have shown, is impossible*,—will do the same now to you and your children, if you let them have their way again, and if, with too credulous ear, you list the songs and music of their enchantments—those enchantments which they will pour into your minds when they dedicate their temple to that grotesque fiction which they call their god.*

---

* I say that the view given of God by "father" Dalgairns *is* a grotesque and pagan fiction. *The god of the mass is not the Christian's God.* I do not say that there are not, for I know there are, many, very many holy souls in the Church of Rome who live above all this, and who share our common Christianity : such men as Dr. Newman and Dr. Manning, for whom I have, personally, a profound regard. It is not of this common, this public, this inner-life Christianity that I am now speaking. I am speaking of what are the *distinguishing characteristics* of Rome, and of the public teaching of these living anachronisms; and when a professed teacher of Christianity stands up and tells me that God requires local habitations (!) and that Christ dwells locally in a certain wafer, in certain spots, and in certain Temples made with hands (!!) —why, then I am entitled to give him, if only on the authority of St. Stephen—the first martyr—of Wickliffe, of Huss, of Ridley, in short of the great Protestants of the early Church—the flattest and most unequivocal contradiction. If you will turn to Acts vii., 47—58, you will find these words :—

"But Solomon built him an house. Howbeit the Most High dwelleth *not* in temples made with hands ; as saith the Prophet, Heaven is my throne, and earth is my footstool ; what house will ye build me ? saith the Lord : or what is the place of my rest ? Hath not my hand made all these things? Ye stiffnecked and uncircumcised in heart and ears, ye do always resist the holy Ghost ; as your fathers did, so do ye. Which of the prophets have not your fathers persecuted? and they have slain them which shewed before of the coming of the Just One ; of whom ye have been now the betrayers and murderers : who have received the law by the disposition of angels, and have not kept it. When they heard these things, they were cut to the heart, and they gnashed on him with their teeth. But he, being full of the Holy Ghost, looked up steadfastly into Heaven, and saw the glory of God, and Jesus standing on the right hand of God, and said, Behold, I see the Heavens opened, and the Son of Man standing on the right hand of God. Then they cried out with a loud voice, and stopped their ears, and ran upon him with one accord, and cast him out of the city, and stoned him ; and the witnesses laid down their clothes at a young man's feet whose name was Saul."

Now I ask, what do these men mean by speaking of God

This is an early day in the history of Catholic Emancipation. Forty years have hardly elapsed,—hardly more than one generation has gone by since, in the high and noble, but characteristically incautious temper of toleration, you tolerated the Church that is intolerant. Don't you see that in that act, by not making Rome an exception, you dealt a deadly blow to your very principle of toleration? It was the folly of "mere good nature," but it was *suicidal*. It had been wise in that day to say to the Papacy "No: you serve a foreign power, you are not genuine subjects of this realm; you admit no freedom to those whom you can inveigle; you have at command boundless resources, you are a dangerous lot; we have learnt enough of you in our history; you deny us the right of private judgment; you are perilous tyrants to have to do with; you hate the light; you slew our best prophets and you have not repented of it; nay, you show by your principles that, if you could, you would slay them again; we have had enough of you; we will keep you down as much as our free principles will admit; we cherish toleration for the tolerant—but *not for you*." I say this language in 1829 would have been wise and safe, but *this chance was lost*. You let in the enemies of England like a flood, and what is the consequence? England, which is the freest of all countries, is now spotted over with the disease of their monasteries and their nunneries; you hear everywhere the hum of their mummeries; the wealth of this land is swept into their coffers; the young nobility of this country kiss the feet of

---

in Christ wanting a local abode and a home in "a temple made with hands"? It is nothing short of the abnegation of Christianity! *To chancel Christ is to cancel Christ.* It is the language not of the converted Paul, but of the Priest-led and unconverted Saul. These men would be under the logical necessity of murdering Stephen and Paul, and all such over again! If anybody fails to see this, I can only say we must all pity his intelligence.

their Pope: and that old man whom they regard as their godhead bodily—and whose health may Heaven at this time restore!—only the other day lifted his finger and gave the sign to his adherents in the House of our Parliament, and turned out an English Government! *The Pope was master of England at that moment.* He stopped the machine of Victoria's kingdom and threw the realm into confusion. Why? because he would not bate a jot of his demands, and because *he knew his power.* None, except thinking men, could have imagined, when he ascended the Papal throne, that Pius IX. ever could do this; and yet he did it. Let none therefore hug himself in the delusion that we are safe from Papal domination. I tell you their influence eats as doth a canker. The poison of Rome courses through the natural gates and alleys of the body politic, and deadens the wholesome working of national life. They who, by an astonishing misnomer and extraordinary perversion of terms, have been allowed to name themselves the Society of Jesus, have been well called "a sword whose hilt is at Rome, and whose point is everywhere"; and that sword has its point at this moment flickering like the tongue of a cobra at every turn in the towns, villages, and cities of England. They mean to return their own majorities—witness their machinations among the agricultural voters—they mean to make your laws for you; they will have one day, as they grow bolder, a professed Prime Minister of their own; they mean to have the Cabinet Catholic—and then you will be at their mercy, and God help you! *Then* you will see what they will do with poor credulous, tolerant England.* We

---

* What in the ultimate issue—of which they constantly express the strongest hopes—do they mean to do with the Queen's prerogative in spiritual matters?—that is in *all* matters, for in the Irish debate their Bishops claimed the multiplication table as a spiritual matter.

thought we should do well in letting our worthy honest Dissenters — plain, simple, English folk — have their rights of conscience ; and that of course *was* well and was in keeping with the progress of the times, and we could in some sort deal with Dissent on the "give and take" principle ; but at that same door of toleration in there rushed, I say, such a flood of intolerance that we shall, I fear, be no longer masters of our fate ! Our very freedom has admitted a cancer into its vitals. The constitution of this noble and ancient and reformed country is being eaten away by it. We thought by a simple operation at our Reformation a few centuries ago to cut it out and have done with it, but it had got into the blood ; and here again we have the mischief blazing out more fiercely than before, and your town, my neighbours, seems from circumstances to be one of the centres of its malignity.

When I look at that magnificent structure which, without offence, I may say has been reared under priestly control — an edifice for which the best epithet I can find is that it is "imposing," — when I see its vast shameless beauty dwarfing the fine old Castle as if in contempt for the very victim of their seduction — just as the Church in their hands would dwarf the State itself — when I see this ancient church of yours, half in ruins, mocked and docked of its fair proportions and robbed of its very chancel — which they seem to want, by a legal quibble, to keep for their dust-bin — I think of what one of your own poets once said when he came in his travels upon some such structure in poor priest-ridden and ruined Spain :—

> "There, too, the Babylonian——hath built
> A dome, where flaunts she in such glorious sheen,
> That men forget the blood which she hath spilt,
> And bow the knee to pomp that loves to varnish guilt."

But I have said enough to warn you. There should have been another voice here to warn you ;

but he, having seen Arundel in better times, has been taken from the evil to come. Still, methinks he being dead yet speaks to you. There are no voices so solemn as voices from the tomb; and when, in such kindly masses, you gathered the other day about his grave, I thought I perceived a spirit which showed that his teaching was likely, not to be forgotten but to live amongst you still. I do not wish here to reinforce the eulogy which has been so well made already, but I cannot help saying thus much: nor will it be in vain that for 30 years he taught you, and your fathers, and your children, the lessons, pure and simple, of the free Christianity of Englishmen—lessons which no imposing structure, no gorgeous ceremonial, no eloquent rhetoric of strange preachers will, I think, ever tempt *you* to forget. I have no sort of hesitation in speaking thus, seeing that Rome makes no hesitation in sending down her most crafty emissaries to unsettle you all from the faith of your fathers.

To close then with the teaching of your lost pastor, and your living minister (whom I would fain see your pastor for good)—with the teaching of the Spirit and the lesson of the text. The kingdom, remember, is *not without you, but within you.* No church, however pretentious, can redeem your soul—it may let that alone for ever. It cost more to do that, for it cost even the precious blood of the crucified and risen Christ. As He lives, you by His Spirit must live also. Nobody else, however presumptuous be the promises of a priesthood, can do your religion for you, or give you another Gospel. I believe the reason why so many slide back into that mire, is because they find it easy and comfortable to have their religion done for them—but *it won't answer.* It is the blunder of ignorance and vice. In God we live and move. In Christ we find access to God and forgiveness of sin. So keep your private judgment and common sense on these matters—or you will be led by this Will-o'-the-Wisp of Rome into quagmires in which your belief in Christ will be swamped, and the *witness within you* will be lost for ever.

I heard M. Guizot say to a large English assembly, at the restoration of Yarmouth church, in 1848 —when France was suffering one of those ghastly paroxysms of madness to which all along the priesthood have goaded her—I heard that fugitive statesman say on that occasion, by way of final advice to his audience, " Keep your faith ; keep your laws ; keep the traditions of your ancestors; but, above all, *keep your faith*." Yes: prove all things ; hold fast that which is good ; quench not, resist not the Spirit of your Master. Let that Spirit dwell within you which was also in Christ Jesus. Let us all, in our thoughts, words, and deeds, bear witness to ourselves, to our families, and to our neighbours, that, according to the teaching of our own beloved Church, we are the plain straightforward followers of Jesus, our own beloved and only MASTER. One is our MASTER, even Christ, and all the souls who receive as "the witness within them " the renewing element of the SPIRIT that proceeds from the FATHER and JESUS, are brethren—in whatever Church on earth they may choose to rank themselves.

"THE FAST WHICH GOD HATH CHOSEN."

"Is not this the fast that I have chosen?"—ISAIAH lviii. 6.

THE principle of fasting is one which has always been, and must always be, acknowledged by good people. And where persons are really religious, the direct practice of it has been kept up by them as their wisdom and judgment has directed. Not but what I cannot help noting that, while some good people seem to make religion to consist mainly in outward observances, a number perhaps still greater make as though religion lay in running such observances down!

The principle of fasting is, however, obviously not of Christian origin. I mean that, even short of being Christians, persons must maintain and carry out this principle if they do not wish to be lost. For what is it but that self-government which holds together everyone who does not allow himself to go to pieces? No one is meant to become loose and to perish, to become dissolute and to die.

The animal whom we call "man," like other animals, is composed in large part of desires; but in *him* there stands among these in his make and composition the power to rule them. A common beast is also a beautiful composition of desires and of what we call *instinct*. In an ox or an ass instinct, which is an unerring sort of common sense, tells it when in the enjoyment of any pleasure it has had enough. And as Christ brings man to perfection, Man also will rise to the possession of powers answering to instinct; so that he will naturally and infallibly, while unconsciously, keep all his desires and emotions in balance. Love thus becomes an unerring light, and joy its own security. You do God's will without being aware of it. Jesus describes this high state of soul when He makes the righteous say, in delighted surprise at His approbation of their conduct, and at His lifting their poor fellow creatures to a level in this matter with Himself—"Lord, when saw we Thee sick or in prison, and visited Thee?"

But at present, and in most people, this power which we possess is seldom sufficiently formed to be called instinct, but is still called *reason;* which, even before blooming into instinct, is the highest form of our intelligence. In Man, I say, reason, or judgment, stands up and orders the life. This is a god-like capability. And if it "fust in us unused" the desires run riot in us, and the best part of us becomes decayed.

You see, of course, how it works. If not, I pray you take note with me. If you look into yourselves, you probably know that, were you to do what you like, rather than what is good and right—were you to let this and that vague desire have way—you would soon make yourself intolerable to others, and after awhile to yourself. Indeed that way lies madness. And any person, female or male, who moves in good, by which I mean orderly society, and desires to be a good member of it, and not to be an object of reproach to his neighbours, is called upon to keep in constant exercise this principle which lies at the root of fasting. For while our nature and imagination, if we have any, are apt to conjure up at every turn phantasies of enjoyments, not perhaps all wrong in themselves, and often physically open to our choice, we are bound on such occasions, when we are fain to turn to the right hand or to the left, to hear, and listen to, a voice behind us, which says "Thou shalt not"—"This is the way, walk thou in it." I mean, at every turn we must all curb ourselves and hold ourselves in with the bit and bridle of prayerful resolution, when it comes into our heads to do things which we know we ought not. Take any desire you please and look at it by itself, and you will easily note, that each of these in turn, when indulged freely and without check—some of them if indulged in at all—have the immediate effect of clashing with your duty to God and your neighbour, and bringing you to shame and contempt, if not punishment before the tribunals of man below and God above. For whatever clashes with your duty to your neighbour clashes by the same token with your duty towards your God, and *vice versâ;* and Christ has come, not to do away with one jot or tittle of the moral law, but to lift it and take it up with Him to the Mount of His holiness, and transfigure it with His newness of light.

I need not go through the whole catalogue of desires; *that* you can do for yourselves. But take a few. The desire of eating too much, or too often, if given way to, sooner or later makes a person ill, sadly deranges the functions, and in time so damages the organism and constitution that he dies: and even short of this it makes a person lazy and destroys his usefulness, not to say is apt in some cases to get him into debt. The reason must say, "Control thyself, if thou be a person given to appetite." The same may be said about drinking. And this is the more important, because, whereas too much food and meat makes you lazy and useless—a superfluity which alone would make several honest labouring men healthful and useful—too much *drink* excites the blood and affects the brain, and makes you harmful. It is especially true of *drink*—"that way lies madness." People when found about the streets in this dangerous condition are taken up and locked up, and that is well. But late legislation has facilitated the obtaining of inflammable liquids for use in private houses. Now it requires the greatest care to use these wisely. It is said that there is less of public-house drinking than there used to be, but more of private house drinking. Now if the State protects the public streets, every man, if he be not an enemy to God and man, will protect his own house, which, as we proudly say, is our castle; and drink is "the very devil" to get into a house. I say this first about all houses rich and poor. Even if a man can afford it and does not himself become ruined by it in fortune—he must still take care that his own soul and body, and the souls and bodies of his friends and his household be not ruined by it. He must exercise at all times the principle of self-government in this as well as in all other matters. He must be temperate, if he would be saved; and if he finds the temptation too much for him, he must not touch at all the thing which has to him become unclean. This holds true of those who are wealthy and able to pay for drink, and who can obtain it without in a financial sense ruining their families.

But what are we to say of those who *cannot*, and who have to starve or overwork their wives and their families in order to get it? If such a man do not govern himself, do not check this desire, do not keep his foot from crossing the threshold of drink, what are we to say of him? What are we to think? If the State assumes to care for any helpless women and children, here indeed are objects for its solicitude. The wife of a drunken husband is a hundred times worse than a widow, and his children a thousand times worse than orphans. If the children were orphans and the wife a widow, then the parish would step in, and charity would hasten to their relief. But here is a case where the parish can give no help at all—for, say the guardians and neighbours, the man receives his fair wage as other people do, and we cannot spend the money of rate-payers, many of whom are themselves living a life of struggle, to give these drinking men more. Yet, when the poor wife and bairns can get no food or fuel or clothes with it, of what good is that wage to *them?* The family has the credit of having the means of life—and therefore nothing reaches them from elsewhere; for charity itself is afraid of the man. You can give no money there, except by stealth, lest that also be wasted in the debasing passion for this infernal poison, and lest matters be thus not mended but made worse. So the scoundrel, instead of doing his part as a man, and as an Englishman, instead of supporting by his honest labour and his regular wage the poor, dependent, helpless partner of his house, and the dear blameless children whom God has given them—positively stands at his threshold —not to keep the wolf off, but as himself the cruel wolf that keeps the help of other people's kindness off! I say it is time that such men were tackled effectually by the State. Law should lay its strong hand on these men, and not allow them any longer to play the petty tyrant over their hungry wives, their cold hearth, and their haggard, beggared bairns. It is hard to say where madness and badness run into one another—but if such a bad man be not also a madman, who then is mad? and whose family more piteously pleads for the protection of Society? How much of this and of other deep misery would be saved if only the Nation were leagued to learn to be more provident, and therefore more sober, in its youth.

To most of these it is too late to talk of self-discipline; and as for dwelling with such persons on Christian fasting, it would indeed be to cast pearls before swine; for the whole idea presupposes a platform of morals and a level of life, of which they in their low-lived wretchedness know nothing. Yet, let me say to rich and poor alike, this condition of misery and hostility to society is the end to which, from all points of the moral compass, that course leads which is pursued by the person who has not that principle of self-restraint and of self-government, which should characterise him as a man. He is in the way for altogether losing his manliness. His reason, not being employed to govern his desires, shrivels up and runs to waste in him, just as the brain softens, when its alimentary ducts, the little vessels that nourish it, are clogged. He becomes lower than the beasts, for the beasts enjoy that divine gift of instinct to keep them straight, and to make them leave off when they have taken enough, which is "as good as a feast."

How plainly then does it behove us to call to our aid the Spirit of God and of Jesus to preserve and elevate in us this power of self-control, which, as I have shown, lies at the bottom of all Lenten observance. I might exhibit to you many companion pictures, if I were to take you with me round this gallery of perdition. I might make it clear to you for instance how, for want of this principle of self-control, the wandering eye drives the gazer mad; makes him the enemy of the gentle, the tyrant of the weak, the corrupter of the children of the people, turning him into that selfish coward who takes advantage of those who want bread and have no honest men to win it for them, no strong arm to keep such enemies at bay—for want I say of this manly use of reason, and the principle of self-control. And I strongly advise you young men who know of any one that for his own pleasure would thus tread down your sweet flowers, to take all fair means of making him remember it. To take one more of these pictures : look how men become misers, or thieves, if they let the desire of gain become rampant within them—"covetous men whom God abhorreth."

Well, I have been dwelling, you see, all along on lower ground. Common reason, itself a gift of God, should keep us all from all these mischiefs and disasters. The principle of self-control should of itself, I repeat, be enough. A man even without Christ, as Paul says in the first chapter of the Epistle to the Romans, should perceive that invisible truth, namely, the eternal power and Godhead of his Maker ; should by reflection note in himself the image of his Father, and remember the fact that he possesses this voice of conscience, and this power of self-management. He should observe the necessity of withholding himself from this and that indulgence, and should put in practice, so far as need be, the principle at least of fasting. Even his common sense and mother-wit should tell him that if he do not, he is very like to be lost, perhaps suddenly, at an instant when least he looks for it. Such characters, to take the forcible image supplied by the Jewish prophet, are like those ill-built walls, which, before the mortar becomes set, bad mortar to begin with, bulge out here and there, and totter to their decay; and at last, when some stronger breeze blows against them, come down with a run. It is as when the ocean gets under the defences of our poor watering-place—a lesson which we learn to our cost. When the floods ascend, down come the breakwaters. Instead of their breaking down the water, the water breaks down them.

Life is always against the current of a stream, or at any rate it is so at present, I suppose, with the most of us. But there *are* happy cases in which a man can step over the table land and strike upon that course which shall bear him down in the direction of the islands of the blest. There are some who allow Christ to lift them over the watershed, and to drop their boat into that river that flows down to the shores of bliss, into those streams that make glad the city of God. So that, whereas with others it is hard to resist the lower desires, with them their very desires are high, and their very impulses and tendencies are such as may well be fostered, gladly encouraged, and by all means promoted. To be good and true, and to govern themselves becomes to them no longer a difficult task, but quite a faculty of easiness; and rectitude, as aforesaid, becomes instinctive. And this state of theirs is what we all should aim at. Let none grudge such their freedom, nor ignore the facts of their renewed nature. These persons know whether they need to fast, or whether they are so conscious of having the bridegroom with them always, that their thankful heart gives them a perpetual feast. And, for the rest, they are in the habit of eating their bread and drinking their wholesome beverage, whatever it may be, with singleness of heart from January to December, from Christmas round to Christmas again, praising and blessing God, keeping the feast of salvation from the hour of waking round again to the hour of sleep, from the hour of baptism, or at least of conversion, to the hour when God shall say to them "Friends, come up higher."

Such good people on the one hand always feast, and on the other always fast. There would be something incongruous and ridiculous to lay it upon such a soul to take a morsel less of this, or a morsel less of that, or fish rather than flesh, over which in the license of Eden God has given us due dominion. To such every day is a Lord's day, and therefore every day is a feast; and because every day is the Lord's, so also every day is a day on which reason and charity will hold absolute, yea, instinctive sway over every action of their life. To such a soul all he eats and drinks is sacramental, and of this the stated and occasional "Lord's suppers" are but a renewed and sacred sign. I say, on the one hand, let ordinary honest folk take note of such and allow for them, and see where they stand towards God, and not try to vex their minds and drag them down to bind them to observances which such persons must regard as childish, and at which they can but kindly smile. Let not you and me grudge such wise and grown-up children of the King their immunity from these modes of duty, which we, for our humbler part, may find useful, if not essential, for ourselves.

Nor must *they*, on the other hand, from the serenity of their region of conquest, dispute the wisdom of the Church which helps its weaker children by all ways to win the crown. Our English Church does not profess to be perfect in all her members; she only aims at making all her members perfect. While perfect in her ideals, as her Heavenly Father is perfect, she finds it in accordance with her Lord's will to gather her children together, and not to treat them as outsiders to begin with. She remembers that Christ said His Church was a net which gathered of every kind. Like a wise mother, she does not cast her children off because they have not yet become so good as she hopes to make them. She takes them all, I say, into her baptismal net; she hopes that those of them who now are bad will repent and be converted, and not, at last, have to be cast away. She does not begin, as most of the sects do, by regarding her children as aliens from her commonwealth, seeing that her Lord has told her not so to do. She does not in this eternal matter exercise her feeble, fallible judgment. She does not deem it right to plunge into the wheat-field, and trample down good ears in order to root up too hastily what she may fancy to be ill weeds :—for this is in effect what those communities do, who aim to keep no members among them except the perfect. The only difference is this—a course no less unnatural and undivine—that *they* plunge in and try to pluck up the wheat and to place it in the barn before the harvest is ripe, and before the Lord of the harvest Himself shall come to do so. Thus, while seeming to keep the letter, they in fact break the spirit of the Book. They do err, not knowing the Scriptures nor the power of God. While our Church allows, and gladly, her genuine and more cultivated children to assemble themselves, and pray, and take counsel, and make what melody of heart or voice they may please—still she remembers that her mission is not merely, nor so much, to pass in secluded communion bright and happy days herself, good as such days may be, but rather to help all those that need her help. And this is why she makes a general injunction that the season of Lent be more especially a season of self-government, and, where need is—yea even for our brethren and companions' sake—a season of taking less of that animal food which goes mainly to feed the animal.

I say, at this season in particular, for all about us, and in so far as we are children of Nature, we may say within us also, there is a bursting power and a forth-welling exuberance of the lower life. The black soil which seemed vacant, but for our memory of what grew there before and of all that lies hidden below it, is already beginning to teem up with its milky blooms, and to break into colour about our feet. The fruit trees begin to burgeon and swell, and soon over the woods that drape your Downs the russet fabric of their winter robe will be shot with the delicate fashion of the spring. Every thing is on the move. That living maid, the spirit of

Nature, will soon show that in these long months it was not dead that she was, but only that she was sleeping. Soon, shaking off the signs of her slumber, she will arise; and, drawing her green skirts in her train, will walk the earth and sweep through plain and over hill, glorious in the freshness of her gaiety, and overpowering the spirits of men with her annual newness of pleasure And this is why those of us who are wise take especial heed at this time of the year, that not only the lower life, not only the animal region of our being, not only the desireful part, but also the higher life shall in due proportion grow.

I know not whether it be found as a matter of general experience that the Spring is a season in which the spiritual life, no less than the bodily life, is conscious of such impulses and such hidden emotions of change. But the fact that God is One would lead us to expect so. The spirit has its springs, we know; but whether habitually and at all times they tally and coincide with the spring-time of Nature, is among the questions which, however interesting, have not yet, to my knowledge, received due attention. Scientific men have observed the signs of the insects and the apes, with a view apparently in some cases of lowering our view of ourselves by trying to show where we come from; but have left the traits of the new creature in Christ Jesus, which is what our race all along is coming to, to be examined by men of insight into such regions of research. It has long seemed a pity to me, that such men should not step up, vindicate the authority, and more systematically note, so far as may be, the facts of their own splendid realm, in which moves the Science of sciences.

But what I was going to say, and the last thing I shall say, is this :—that the reason why fasting is practised by wise persons, and persons who may believe that they require it and that it will do them good, is, not from any antique and grotesque superstition, but that the soil of their soul may not be overgrown with those ill weeds which grow apace; nor possessed and poisoned by the rank luxuriance of the springing up of wrong desires; but may show forth better those virtues, those graces, and those glories of character, which beseem the joyous Spring-time of our Christian Church, and which are the best flowers in the garden of God.

THE GOODWOOD WEEK.

By the Rev. W. B. PHILPOT, M.A., Vicar of South Bersted, Bognor.

Sermon Preached at South Bersted on Sunday, August 2, 1885.

"Even so run that ye may attain."—1 Cor. ix. 24.

THE minds of those of you who take any interest in what the masses do, have been in all probability more or less occupied with the events of the week.

Now it is not part of my special business, that I know of, here and now to go at length into questions touching the national pleasures of the English people — any more than St. Paul, or Apollos in their Epistles discussed the wisdom or the folly of the amusements of Greece. I simply take the week as it comes round, and try to use it, as St. Paul used events somewhat similar. For St. Paul, having been a year and a-half at Corinth, no doubt witnessed those great games of the Isthmus. He must have seen the sacred Stadium with its seats of white marble (a grand stand indeed!) rising on that far-famed Saronic Lawn below the citadel, like the foundation of a temple, with Athens gleaming in the distance—a more sublime and moving spectacle than we can show here in England, where our horse-games are certainly not, as in Greece, professedly religious. He had beheld those solemn athletics which to the Greeks were half their culture—for, except among the Hebrews, the spirit of man was lying fallow as yet.

a

He had seen the friends of the candidates watching the struggle with breathless interest, not from any anxiety as to the loss or gain of a few hundred or thousand pounds; but knowing, as they did, that the name of the victor would be rung forth in Pindaric ode, and his effigy placed in the line of statues whose glittering vista led to the Temple of the Gods. Paul had seen the judges sitting in state at the end of the course, as at some solemn assize—clear of all financial excitement, but inspired with religious emotion—holding the small cool wreath of simple pine leaves, to be placed on the brow of the man who should win. St. Paul's mind—and who knows whether he had not among those young charioteers some candidates for the cup of salvation? —St. Paul's mind seems to have been at least as full of this racing event as the mind of any of us can be who may have witnessed in the last week the madding crowd's less noble strife, and the low excitement of "the ring," surging about the wooden stand and wooden benches of the most refined course we have, beneath the abiding beauties of the hill-sides and the passing beauties of the Lawn. The preacher might, I say, be charged with treading out of his province, if he assumed, beyond obvious limit, to arbitrate what sports are permissible to a Christian people and what are not:—though indeed it is the Christ-Spirit which must eventually shape and fashion all national interests and amusements, and this of horse-racing among them, if it should then survive. But looking at matters as they stand, and in the view of common sense, there are at such times many wheels of fair amusement and honest recreation—not to say livelihood—for many classes of the people, revolving one within another; and there are, moreover, executive officers to check disorder, detect iniquity, and stay all palpable causes of offence. In all great gatherings there are those who abuse them, as well as those who use them; and as the country becomes more trained and better trained, so greed, and selfishness, and haphazard modes of money-making will become less rampant and obtrusive; the crowd will become less unchristian; and, just as other public spectacles have cast off most of the scandals which formerly made them offensive, and which got them an ill name—a name which in most religious circles has clung to them longer than is reasonable—so it may fairly be expected that scenes such as that of the last few days will clarify themselves in due course and in like manner. The Drama, which might be used, and sometimes is used, for moral and even Christian culture, is indeed in large part given over to the Enemy, till Christian poets shall arise, willing and able under more favourable circumstances to throw themselves into its stirring and magnificent agency; while, unlike the Drama, the race-ground can hardly ever be used for anything better than a wholesome mode of recreation, in witnessing, with very human interest, that dominion over the fleet and beautiful beasts of the field, which was granted to us in the great game certificate of Eden.

The question as to what sports help rather than hurt the highest life, is always one for fair discussion. Still I hold it for the present to be a distinct part of a Christian minister's duty to protest, in the name of the Christian congregation, against the tyranny of all falsehood in religion, and herein against that falsehood which assumes to say of this or that social gathering, " Lo here, and lo there is Satan, and nothing but Satan"; for that is a kingdom which, like the kingdom of Christ, cometh not with observation, and is not always without us so much as within us. Satan pushes himself into most places, as well as into places of pleasure. If indeed any honest and sensible person, owing to any special reason (best, or only, known to himself), feels that this place or that scatters his mind instead of bracing it, disturbs and pollutes his spirit, instead of giving it wholesome satisfaction — why then he will not himself frequent such gatherings. But it is obviously as wrong and dangerous for any man to say of his neighbours that they are bad because they go to one place, as to say that they are good because they go to another. This too frequent practice leads to all manner of false and uncharitable estimates. It spoils wholesome consciences. It is a mistake full of peril and needless offence against Christian freedom. So here let us leave this vexed, and vexing, question of sports.

St. Paul, at any rate, brought for us, as we see by the text, some wholesome food from the races to which he went :—" Know ye not," he says, " that they which run in a race run all, but one receiveth the prize?" And to that one, oh ye men of Corinth, he says, I would lead your thoughts. Let this one man who wins his race be an ensample to you, remembering how much greater is your reward than that pine-leaf garland of the games, how ever great and however human be the honour that is bound up with it; and a main difference, mark you, between this Christian race and all others, is that here every man may be the winner. Note, he says of those runners, what self-denying pains are taken by each man who means to win. Such too, he adds, is my own practice. I, Paul, am not less eager, nor less severe with myself, than is that winning runner of whom I speak. And the enemy with which I contend is my own body, that bears in it marks of its hard service, the proof of my self-denial. Thus much for St. Paul's view of racing. Again, the like lesson was gathered from the like occasion by the writer of the Epistle to the Hebrews :—" Seeing," he says, " we also are compassed about with so great a cloud of witnesses—greater and nobler by far than those who range themselves on the marble steps upon the grand Isthmian stand—let us lay aside every weight, and the sin which clings like a close garment about us, and let us run with patience the race that lies before us, looking unto Jesus, the Author and Perfecter of our faith, the Assessor of God, the Adjudger of the prize—who, for the joy that was set before Him, endured the Cross, despising shame, and hath sat down at the right hand of the throne of God." So let us, my Sussex neighbours, by like grace of God, try with Paul and Apollos to stamp upon ourselves that lesson which is taught by all human contests :— " Even so run that ye may attain." My brethren, as there is a looking which is an overlooking, a seeking which is not searching, so there is a going which is but loitering, and a running which is not racing. Why is it that we admire (as who does not?) so splendid an animal, compact of blood and fire, as the winner of a great race like one of those lately run at Goodwood? It is because, under the magical handling of a perfect steed that knows his rider, both man and horse adapt themselves to their work, and mean what they are driving at? Whatever pleasure or excitement may fill the minds of those who are but looking on, man and horse mean business, and know what they are doing.

What long care, what close attention to studied and understood conditions, what infinite caution, what lavish expenditure, what absolute perfection in training, what concentration of effort! Why, do you think yon horse and man would have won that cup, if they had run their race as most of you Christians run yours? Not a chance. "So run that ye may attain." Heaven help us, what sorry running most of us make in our race of life for the crown of glory.

I half suspect many of us do not quite know that there *is* a race, and do not grasp the fact that there is a crown. What? do you suppose that while the lower life has its prizes, the higher life has none? Have you your set prizes for wrestling, for leaping, for racing, for shooting, as at Wimbledon and the like—and has the *spirit* of man nothing before it to aim at, nothing to gain? Have you in this country your mind prizes, your crowns of intellect, your reward of brains—dusty organs which so soon fade and fail, crumble and perish, or turn into atoms to feed other forms—and is there no prize for the immortal spirit, made in the image of God, which cannot decay, but which goes back into the unseen Personality of its Source, and lives there for ever, lives in the self-renewing charm of its ever-rising and forth-rolling powers? The idea that there is no such prize for the soul of man would be preposterous in the extreme. And if you can think that God has got no prize for you, all I can say is, that the Adversary, the great Swindler that haunts this race-course of life, must have effectually relieved you of your best senses and be gambling you out of your immortal fortune. Nay, does it not stand to reason that the prizes of the spirit are out-and-out the highest and the finest there are? The fortunate owner of the winning horse may well say to his friends at the close of this contest on the downs, "Rejoice with me, for I have gained the cup which I sought." But I tell you that the man, be he rich or be he poor, who either by some happy find that rewards his search, or, like St. Paul, at the close of a long and hard career of self-training, can hold fast in both hands the cup of salvation, and claim it as his own—*that* man is your prize-winner if you will. Lay hold of Christ and you lay hold of nothing less than life eternal. You have for an inner indefeasible possession the richest prize there is, and the one prize which, inter-penetrating all other prizes, gives them all the value they have. Match me, if you can, in any other region of being, the comfort and the satisfaction which St. Paul felt when he said "I have fought the good fight, I have finished my course, I have kept the faith. Henceforth there is laid up for me a crown of righteousness, which the Lord, the righteous judge, shall give me at that day; and not to me only, but to all them" on the coasts of the far isles, to all the Bersted souls that love Him to come to them and to appear to them, and to show Himself to their hearts. There indeed, in St. Paul, was a man for you in the moment of his triumph.

What is it, oh ye people, that bewitches you and holds you back from racing forwards to the arms of your Father? There is nothing worth having, if you have not Christ formed in your heart, the hope of glory. Having Him, you have all things. If you cherish not that spiritual element in your life, your soul will putrefy and go to the bad, breeding all manner of noisome and creeping habits of thought, the beginnings and foretaste of hell. All your possessions and earnings, winnings and prizes, are like unmeaning noughts, empty cyphers without that one integer figure before them, which, the moment it stands there, gives them the force of tens, of hundreds, of thousands, and of millions. It is a shallow, a vulgar, and a selfish satisfaction, which makes a man happy merely in the being more successful than his neighbours, and in receiving from them honours, mingled more or less with jealousy and ill-blood, and only by a trick of conventionality thought by any body at all to be at all better than nothing. But let a man once be " in Christ Jesus," in that condition of the new creature into which the Christ-Spirit alone can bring him, and then all things assume at once a higher tone and a grander significance. Try it, and you will then taste and see how gracious the Lord is. Christ comes to you bringing His reward with Him, and then for the first time you " give the world assurance of a man." Virtue is its own reward, and the Christ-Spirit, stamping the soul with the highest virtue, brings with Him the highest reward and the most splendid prize that Heaven can give or man can take. Well then, " Even so run that ye may attain."

Paul had prizes enough, if without Christ he had cared for them or thought them of value. He says " If any other man thinks that he has, outside of Christ, enough to trust to and be proud of, I more;" and then he recounts his fictitious, his adventitious, and worldly claims to honour ; and they certainly make up a list which should satisfy a man, if any lower thing can; the more so as he ends all by saying that, from the lower aspect of life, he has been a blameless man. "But," he adds, "what things were a gain to me—race, family, extraction, culture, yea, and a good conscience itself—all these things I count loss for Christ. Nay, moreover, I do not consider that I have yet, before I die, laid hold of that prize; but this one thing I do, forgetting those things which are behind, and reaching forth unto those things which are before, I press towards the mark for the prize of the high calling of God in Christ Jesus."

Yes, *there* is the prize of life; it is to have the life hid with Christ in God, and to become *new men in the New Man*. If you do not grow to be new creatures in Christ Jesus, renewed in the spirit of your mind by the implanting of the seed of the Christ-Spirit—for that regeneration in the higher region answers to all generation in the region below—if you do not become new creatures, what is left for you? what but *this*? Why, *you remain old creatures*, old-fashioned, worn out, and sinking creatures; for you attach yourselves to a type which is effete and ready to perish, to be laid aside like an old garment, and to be accounted among the fossils of the Universe—a mere curiosity of the most good-for-nothing antiquity. The pre-Christian man, mark my words, will in future days become a rare type in the land, and only so far interesting. Men of intellect, mere intellect which is not the highest, have the foolhardiness from time to time, perching themselves in their special cloudland, to deny and rail at God—first to deny God, and then in the same breath to rail at Him whom they deny!—as if they sprang wholly from the dust, and had no breath of God in them at all, even to set their wicked tongues upon the wag:—an account of themselves, however, to which it may well be granted that they give no little plausibility. Thus these men, fain to oust themselves from their high personality, and clinging to lower forms of being, yet reputed to be somebodies, scatter round them many unripe thoughts, bitter ashes of apples of Sodom, which make those that taste them mentally and spiritually mad. And there are many who come and eat of these crude fancies because they are glad to be told there is no God. And why are they glad? Mainly *because they desire to sin.* They know that God—the Source of all society, and who has taught society, made in His image, for its own self-preservation to *hate* sin—will not permit people to enjoy themselves at their neighbours' expense, as these bad men want to do. And so they catch at the straws held up by any and every fool who with an air of gravity says that he has added up the Almighty, weighed the Deity in the hollow of his hand, and finds forsooth that He comes to nought!

But they will not long have this delusion to hug themselves in—for Science, which is no fool, will not say there is no God, but will say the same thing as our Jesus says. The whole round world is sooner or later coming to discover that *the New Man is the true man*, and that those who would be saved from the destruction that awaits old and effete types, and which will sweep all but the chosen type away, must in all sober verity arise and let Christ give them light—thus by God's selection and their own surviving as the only fit souls there are. When human society so arises and comes to Christ, the race of life will be easier for all. Man will prove himself a vaster being. Earth will be a nobler sphere; all pleasures will find their field; and there will be nothing left to vex the happy ear, either blasphemous on the one hand, or fanatical on the other. It is to this crown and consummation that humanity, I say, is forth-reaching. Take care *you* are not left behind. "Even so run that ye may attain."

Well, I will keep you no more from breathing the divine summer-evening air, and from praising God upon His pleasant shore; and therefore let me close by praying that you and I may not after all be beaten in this race of life—and by ascribing all honour, power, majesty, and dominion to Him who reigns and will reign for ever and ever. Amen.

ON A MISSION WEEK.

THE Mission-week has come and gone. It has swept over us like some fertilising rain-cloud, that comes upon a thirsty and thankful soil; and we trust time will show this ancient Borough to be the better for all the fatness it has been dropping. Benjamin Franklin is said to have once attracted a thunderstorm over Paris; and we are bound to thank our liberal-minded Vicar for having brought this bright cloud, with all its voices, to overshadow Boston.

What vast growths of mind, or at least what changes of history the world has witnessed, since the gallant Missioner *Mayflower* sailed forth with that "seed of men," which was to shoot up into the mighty Transatlantic race, who regard Boston with such filial devotion. Whatever their divarications of politics and creed, it was to Boston-stump that their piety gathered them to plant their Cotton Chapel beneath its sacred shadow; and all the men of the old Boston as well as of the new are proud of the association. But if this be so even with those whose Faith, transplanted into a soil that fosters gigantic growths, is assuming an infinity of forms—much more do we, the people of the mother-place, not yet so shattered asunder as they, retain of sheer necessity an affectionate claim upon this noble, beautiful and venerable landmark and seamark, whose chimes play over us the holy hymns that enliven our labour and solemnise our leisure. The fact is, we are given to crowd beneath its fretted roofs and long-drawn aisles upon all great occasions. Men, now white-haired, can remember being carried on their fathers' shoulders among the masses that thronged to the Funeral Service of that darling of the English people, whose death deprived them of a Princess, at the hour when she was giving them hopes of a Prince. Again, we recall how dense it was with mourners, when our beloved Queen was widowed of Albert the Good.

But all who can recount such solemnities aver that on no former occasion were the hearers so closely packed as on the evening of Sunday last. And what was it that brought us together? It was no national event, no public calamity. What went we forth to see? and what went we forth to hear?

We are glad to feel it was no narrow spirit which was at work. The hearts of our people, Churchmen and Nonconformists alike, have been moved, as the trees of the wood are moved with the wind. This has been no party movement. It is as honourable alike to one as to the other. The latter have for the nonce merged their antipathies, as the former for the nonce—*esto perpetuum*—have widened their sympathies. It may fairly be regarded as a kindly act of respect to the feelings, and of consideration to the freer manners of our Chapel worshippers, that the wonted rigidity of Church forms was in a marked degree relaxed; and our varied readers may well inquire, why, if the Church has all this while been capable of this elasticity in their behalf, they have been constrained to seek it elsewhere? But let us leave that question for the future to solve. It is not so much the spirit of the national Church of England, as the in-dwelling spirit of the universal Church *in* England, Who, coming up like a flood, swells, sweeps over, and effaces all our lowlier landmarks. As in an inundation the face of the country is laid under water, so that no man can say which field is his own or where he may find it, thus it was with this vast sea of spiritual life which last week overwhelmed the population. Nobody asked who was of Church, who was of Wesley, who was an Independent, who was a Baptist; but all said, "This is God's beloved Son: hear Him." While this solemn tide flooded and filled the streets, the lanes, the alleys and courtyards of the town, skilful fishermen of the Master lost no time in doing His gracious bidding and letting down their nets for a draft. And if we judge rightly, the draft was something miraculous. Those stalwart fishermen, beneath the approving smile of Him who stood there, could hardly draw the net ashore because of the multitude of souls.

Well: the time of emotion—for we will not say excitement—is past and the time of trial has come. We trust to see our Town more pure, more just, and more sober for all the good words which last week have been resounding. We hope to see our churches and our chapels more full of devout and earnest worshippers; and we shall be disappointed if we do not find many fresh faces of those who have come to learn the sweetness of religion and the blessedness of the service of Christ. These are the fruits that we may fairly look for, and we earnestly pray that this bread cast on the waters may be found in these after-days and in the after-years. We trust that the maidens of the Factory, the men of the Railway, the hands of the Foundry—those exemplary men of iron, who esteemed the Word of God so much more than their necessary food that they gave up half their dinner-hour to hear it—may have become so possessed of the New Life, that all with whom they have to do may take knowledge of them that they have been with—and are remaining with—JESUS.

WERTHEIMER, LEA & Co., Printers, Circus Place, London Wall

THE LAST MESSAGE OF THE PRESIDENT.

*" That their hearts might be comforted, being knit together in love."—*Col. ii. 2.

IN these days, when a great event happens in the world, the intelligent inhabitants of the world, generally speaking, assist. For we are not altogether as our fathers were, nor as we ourselves were in earlier days. It becomes more clear that we belong to the higher and wider order of being. Man as a race grows more quick and powerful. Hence there is more fellow-feeling in mankind. Whatever may be the case with individual men, "the world is more and more", and mankind at large is coming to realise its unity. The kingdoms and states of the earth are in some senses more United States—more "knit together in love" than ever before. Just as persons, who have been kept apart, dislike each other in their reciprocal ignorance, but begin to like each other better as they know one another more, so it is with peoples: except with those who form a sort of outer-court civilisation, or who have no civilisation at all; and even these are being swept without their will into the dance of common interest. The heathen are becoming more manifestly the inheritance of the Son of Man. The divine music of God's Will is with low swell winding itself into the furthest circles of humanity, and those populations who now sit sullen and remote in the corners of the banquet-hall will in their turn start up, will hand-in-hand swing themselves into the movements of higher forms of being, and will be ordered by the Divine Spirit into gracious ways of life.

Nothing is more pleasant than to watch the modes by which the Truth makes men free, and knits them together in love, except it be to note the fact that it is so, and to cherish the hope that it will be so more and more. When that organ was in building, with what interest did we watch the advancing work. We saw its stops, its pipes, its keys, its source of air, and all its parts gathering and growing into power of sweetest sound. The beautiful instrument was at last made; its patient potentialities were ready to break from their dumb material conditions; and now all that we hoped for has come to pass. We hear "the very pulse of the machine," as it renders forth melodious and full discourse at the touch of the musician, accompanying, leading, and heightening the hymn of the choir and the praises of the congregation. In like manner this is what the Spirit of God is doing with the world. Humanity is God's great organ. He is building it up so as to sound forth in His own good time the music that He composes, and the hymn that He has for it. Already He brings some of its stops into play.

To drop metaphor, look what He is doing even now in the world. Here are mighty peoples far apart in respect of space. Owing to some mistake a century ago in Imperial rule—the undue pressure of a tax upon an article of general consumption—our American Colonies broke off into flat rebellion against our Crown; and in a war, which was a war between brothers, they rent themselves rudely away from us. They abjured our very modes of government. They set up a State, and then a system of States, wholly alien to the ancient modes of this side of the globe. And yet, while the vindicators of their own freedom, some

States held the dark-coloured races in that slavery which the more advanced of our European States had long abandoned. Not many years ago they fought another civil war over this, and the result was that slavery disappeared from among them. This, too, was a great step in the Kingdom of Christ. That also cost the life of a President. Now look again how the champions of Christendom prevail; and that at a moment when least expected, and by a means which of all others seemed the most unlikely. Up to July the 2nd there were terrible quarrels among the leading men of the States; quarrels about principle, conflicts involving the very organism of the constitution; disputes in which each would have it that the others were traitors and enemies to the Republic. The very purity and honesty of politics, whatever there was, seemed likely to be lost in this national pyæmia. For a very poison of place-hunting seemed to be rioting in the veins of that vast community. Most men sought their own and not also others' good. So noisome a leprosy of selfishness was coursing through the natural gates and alleys of the body politic. Indeed, it became sadly clear to thoughtful men that a day was at hand when the States would be united no more.

At this juncture a man had been prepared by Providence, and happily chosen for President, such as I need not try to describe to you. Have not all your daily journals made you familiar with his rise, his progress, his virtues, his works, his struggles, his in-born God-given energy, and the crownless Throne to which his right ambition led him? At this very crisis—when such a man seemed to short-sighted mortals essential to the triumph of his cause, the welfare of his country, and the staying of that virus in the nation's blood—a half-mad assassin, inflamed and bewildered by brooding over imaginary wrongs, driven into the worst and last insanity of crime—caught, it is too probable, by the contagion of European Nihilism—sprang from that miscellaneous population; and on the 2nd of July, in an unguarded hour, when his victim was least suspicious of danger, discharged shots at the President, which on Monday last, alas! proved to have been deadly.

Now mark the results; mark how beneath all political passions, while men seemed given over to wild hatred and indiscriminate selfishness, this crime has knit together the whole American people in a unity of horror and of love, by which all those wounds of the United States have been drawn together and healed. So that, whatever course they may now take, it is most unlikely that the principles of their murdered President will be forgotten or displaced. Already President Arthur, beside that mangled corpse, has solemnly and religiously promised that it shall be so. Nor would he on any other condition be tolerated by that great Republic. That which perhaps not even a Garfield could have done by his life, has been thus done by his death—as by some Samson who in his fall drags down with superhuman strength the temple of a Dagon. The self-sacrifice and the purity of his character are striking themselves into his fellow countrymen much in the same way on the national scale, as the self-sacrifice of the Master of all humanity is, on the world-wide and time-long scale, saving by degrees all society and all humanity. So marvellously does God bring good out of evil. By so obvious a law in the working of His heavenly leaven does He use crime itself as an instrument for arresting crime, and for the promotion of the saving health of a people.

With what affectionate feelings these States have been standing at their President's long death-bed during these eleven weeks of his suffering, united in a sense in which they never were united before!

Such was his manly nature, his splendid endurance, and such, let me add the faith and courage of his noble wife, that never before in the history of mankind have any people had the opportunity of learning so great a lesson from their Ruler. Never was a President's message more effective. We had in some sort a like experience when our own beloved Prince Consort, and then our Prince of Wales lay between life and death, between death and life. Nor has England forgotten the interest, the sympathy, and the gratitude which then she learned. By the mercy of God, that experience ended, in the latter case, in recovery and thanksgiving.

But the lesson across the water has been deepened by death; and our own Royal Widow, and our Prince and Princess have been the first to voice their sorrow to that desolate home, and to those fifty millions of fraternal people, along the new nerves of language which underlie the deep. Her heart has been moved and the heart of the Anglo-Saxon people as the trees of the wood are moved by the wind. Another act has been done by our Queen, a little one in itself, but yet one which America will remember as a great one. Her Majesty wished a wreath of flowers to be offered from Her own gracious hand as a token to the living and an honour to the dead. What a tender and delicate act it was! The thousands who hastened and crowded to weep with those representative travellers on that long journey of death and honour, over plain and hill, beheld the wreath of Victoria resting on the bier. If any other ever was, that *immortelle* will be immortal. The memory of the fragrance of those funeral flowers, which has been wafted through that land, will methinks, prove sweeter than villainous saltpetre and all the fumes of war. From those blossoms will be distilled a dew from which will breathe all the kind-

ness of England when She who sent them is gone
—gone, which heaven for the world's sake delay—
to the everlasting kingdom. Never went a sweeter
message from a Queen.

Let us take this occasion to dwell together for a
few moments on this beautiful idea of humane unity
amidst human variety. With the exception of
France and Switzerland there is no other Republic
in Europe. Even the new nations which have
arisen in modern history have held to the ancient
type, and have either chosen to themselves kings,
or allowed kings to be chosen for them. But just
as over yonder all the internal differences of that
one nation, which more especially suffers, have been
laid aside and forgotten, and, in the presence of
that horrible crime and in the death-chamber of
that great man, have been laid aside and made of
no account, so it is with all the principal nations
on this side of the world. All the members of
Christendom suffer with them. Though the Ruling
Houses of Europe who wield these old nationali-
ties abhor from their hearts, and dread beyond
measure the very idea of a Republic—though they
feel and know that all the elements of danger
among their own subjects lie in this very direction
—yet there are hardly any of them, however despotic,
however attached to their own ideas of statecraft,
but in this hour have a kindly word to send to
the sorrowing States. They and their people with
them, by State messages, by incessant writings in
all their journals, of whatever shade of politics,
have been, so to speak, all of them American in
their sorrow for Garfield, in pure regard for this
great, simple, honest Ruler, and in sympathy with
his nation; and that, I repeat, although he was
the choice of a Republic. The ancient Churches
of the world have prayed for him—without asking
what was the meaning of a Campbellian. So sweetly
has Christianity stolen a march upon orthodoxy!

Science, we thankfully own, is a gift of God. It is He that teacheth men knowledge. How could men know anything, how could men contrive anything, were it not for that indwelling power of the Divinity which guides us into *all* truth? We commonly indeed regard the achievements of science—notably of this new science of electricity—as ministering to the national needs of commerce and the communications of business-men. But see how God can vindicate science as His own chosen vaunt-courier for the highest welfare of His beloved creatures. Note how He uses it to promote the Kingdom of Jesus — that kingdom which is righteousness, kindness, and peace. There is something, I had almost said, of a divine pleasantry in the manner in which the great Magician of the Universe can take those same wires—which commonly flash to and fro nothing more important than the rise and fall of stocks, or the intrigues of " corners "—and use them for His own sublime ends: to silence enmities, to check political passions, to bring into action the kindliest emotions, to allay prejudices, to bind together distant and alien nations, to express the best feelings of kings and peoples, to unite all in abhorrence of crime and in love of honesty and truth—in a word, to prove Himself in His own hour and way the Ground-Landlord of the globe, and the one immanent Influence in the human race. See how kindly Heaven can catch mankind in this network of science. Far as the West is from the East, look how He can make His lightnings give shine unto the world, from the East even to the West, to comfort the hearts of humanity—as if Time itself already were no more.

We ourselves in our Sussex village form but a very little part of the English nation—but we do form a part ; and, I doubt not, you have all taken your part, and felt your part, through this sad crisis ; so that what I have said has been, I am well convinced, an expression (though I know too feebly put forth) of what we must all feel at one of the most remarkable events which have come into the round of our experience. The Dead March of our voluntaries rolling from our organ to-day, and the bell tolling from our spire to-morrow will voice our share in this mighty sorrow with which the planet is now trembling all over. Let us all pray that the mourners may be comforted, especially that Lady who has set so noble an example to the wives of the world. Let us pray that the American people—our brethren and kinsfolk—may by this great trial be sobered and steadied in their great experiment of modern history, in the endeavour to live in their chosen form of government for the good, not of a part, but of the whole community, and for the glory of God. Let us pray that our European peoples, and our own beloved England, and herein more especially our Queen and Royal family, may be guarded from the like dangers, and that we may be bound together in love for our living Sovereign as they are for their departed President.

And while we pray for the unity of peoples, for the averting of wars, and for the growth of the Kingdom of Christ in this nation and in the world at large, let us first and foremost see to it that our own natures be all brought under the same gracious influence, and that we pass through our "little while" on earth with our own inner elements of spiritual rebellion reduced to order by the mastering and unifying love of our dear self-sacrificing Redeemer. For to each of us, as well as to His own people, this is the last message of the lost President.

Wertheimer, Lea, & Co., Printers, Circus Place, London Wall.

A LESSON FROM ARCHBISHOP TAIT.

Sermon Preached at South Bersted on Sunday, December 9th, 1882.

"In all thy ways acknowledge Him, and He shall direct thy paths."—Prov. iii. 6.

THIS would be remarked upon by anybody as a manifest word of God, even if it were not known to come from the Bible. It has about it the ring of the Spirit, who proceeds from the Father. And when Christ also came from the Father, dowered with that Spirit in unmeasured abundance—when Christ became the world's Life, the world's Truth, the world's Way—then the text was lifted in its meaning. For when we make Christ all our Way, then we find and acknowledge God to be in Him as the Guide of our lives—God in Christ reconciling us to Himself: and this is to secure for ourselves the best, nay, the only safe Way. In the Apostolic Church, Christianity was called, by excellence, "The Way."

This word of God I am the more glad to give you, for it was given to me, brought home to me, and, as I hope, implanted in me by the man whom I am more especially bound to honour as having helped me to the most comprehensive of all blessings, namely, my life-tenure of being—"without whose life I had not been." We learn by tradition that the Apostle St. John, when he became very aged, and when the younger generations would cluster around him to gather from his lips the sayings of the Lord, used to be fond of repeating to them the sweet words of the Master's new commandment, and would say again and again "Little children, love one another." And so—if it be not accounted too filial to be reminded of that other by this one—this aged disciple (whom I freely quote to you, dear brethren, because ye know him and pay him kindly regard, and often hear him from this spot, and will, I trust, sometimes, if it cannot be often, hear him again), has long been in the kindly habit of saying to many, especially to the young, the words of this text: "In all thy ways acknowledge Him, and He shall direct thy paths." It was but the other day, while walking among some young plants which he was tending, that he told me the following story. He once went into a shop, and was about to transact some little piece of dealing with the grave and kindly man who stood at his receipt of custom. The man looked at him, and held out his hand, moved manifestly by some solemn and affectionate memory. "You probably do not remember me, sir?" he said. My father confessed with regret that he could not recall his features at the moment. "Once," said the tradesman, "you were conversing with my mother, I was her only son, and she was a widow. I was standing at her side. Before you went away, you laid your right hand on my head and said, 'My little boy, let me give you a great text, and never forget it. It is this: 'In all thy ways acknowledge God, and He will direct thy paths.' Sir," he said, "by the blessing of God on your words, that text laid hold upon me. It came down into my heart from your lips as from heaven. So I have tried always to remember to acknowledge God; and I am thankful to say that my ways, in so far as I have done so, have always been directed by Him. I have been prospered in my business, and now I teach those words diligently to my own children." This was pleasant to the old man's ears and heart, and he thanked God, and took courage still to repeat our text. In some talk which he once had with our Bersted children in the school-room, he said, " My dear children, let me give you a text; and he gave them this same one; and when last he came to me, I set him in their midst again, and he said, "Now what was the text which I gave you?" There was a general answer, " In all thy ways acknowledge God, and He shall direct thy paths." The master had taken wise and kindly pains to impress it on their memories, and to have it ready for him when he came again; and I need not say, my venerable father was highly delighted.

Now I take this for my text to-day, because it is the text which above all, from childhood up, was acted upon by our late beloved Archbishop, whose hour came on Sunday last to depart from this world to his Father. We could not know, when we desired your prayers for him, as usual, that they had already been answered in God's best way, and that for some hours He had taken him to Himself. Thus God showed that, in the words of the father of history, it was "better for men to die than to live"; that, in the words of St. Paul, " to depart and be with Christ" was "far better." To us it would have seemed that it was better for him to live than to die. In the course of a letter which I received, shortly before his own departure, from the late beloved Arthur Stanley, his dear friend, I remember he said, " The most valuable life I know is that of the Archbishop of Canterbury." He had indeed grasped so well the needs of the Church of England and of the Church of Christ in England; he was so broad—which made some few narrow people misunderstand and dislike him—so large-minded, so large-hearted, so conciliatory and loving to all Christian Churches, and to all Christian souls; he saw so clearly what, amidst all failing and error, was genuine and true, that he proved himself as a Father in God even to those who, for one reason or another, in this tangled age, did not regard him as their Primate. I saw some of those on Friday morning among us in his darkened rooms, and beside his open tomb. So that in point of fact he had rendered himself leader, in one sense, to the Church in the Nation. In all his ways as an Archbishop he had acknowledged God, and, in this as in all stages of his career, God had directed his high and dominant path; so that his most reverend voice was listened to with more than usual heed in the chief councils of the land.

It was so at last because it had been so from the first. This is not the place to record to you his life, or pourtray for you the details of his character. Are not these given you in the book of the Chronicles of the doings of the English Church and the British people? And your daily journals, which have in such matters, as in so many others, grown to be very valuable and interesting, have gone through the doings and sufferings of his life and of his last hours for your private reflection and edification. But let me, so far as the time permits, select for you some of those more marked paths which the God, whom he acknowledged so truly, directed so clearly.

In the first place, he was an example to our youth. The memorable incidents of this early period have not yet been fully set forth, as doubtless they will be; but it is clear that he had made the most of his pious teaching, and already acknowledged at his first schools the God of industry and duty. He went up to Oxford with his principles fixed, and his mind ready to drink in the best wisdom of the place. We Rugby schoolboys, who knew so well his deep manly voice, his strong Northern pronunciation, and his courteous address, can well imagine the firm tone and modest manner in which, when the famous Head of his famous college said, "What has brought you to Oxford, Mr. Tait?" he made answer, " To improve myself and to make friends." With him, to improve himself meant no selfish ambition. It was at once to tell his Superior that he meant "to put his talents to the exchangers," so that he might hear at the close of his career at college that "Well done" which now, from God and his country, he has heard at the close of the career of his life. With him "to make friends" did not mean merely to secure to himself the support of the great among men, the rich, the powerful, or the grand, but it meant this :—that he trusted to merit the approbation of the wisest and the best; that he hoped to join the divine phalanx of those among his betters and his fellows, who were acknowledging God in all their ways, and whose ways, according to the promise of the text, God would direct in the advancing of His Heavenly Kingdom.

Well, his ways were made so direct from the first, that he gained the highest honours of Oxford, and soon became one of the leading Tutors and teachers of the University. And when he found that some—who were carrying thought, or rather sentiment, before them—were (as he considered nor wrongly considered) trifling with the great truths of the Reformation, he was among the first to put down his foot and say, "Hitherto ye may go, but no farther." Thus he did his first public act as a leader of men. In this he acknowledged the God of our English Faith, and God directed his ways.

He was chosen soon after to be a leader of boys. Our great Arnold had passed from among us in the midst of life on the 12th of June, 1847. When we re-assembled after the summer vacation, we found Mr. Tait appointed as our new master. I can well remember (though I do not wish here to introduce more than duly my own personal reminiscences) how soon his manifest honesty secured the confidence of the Sixth Form of Rugby. Methinks

I can now hear his clear but humble voice when he gave out his first text from Arnold's pulpit. It was this : " My grace is sufficient for thee. My strength is made perfect in weakness." It was the keynote of that acknowledgment of God which he made in all his Rugby ways; and through all those ways his paths were acknowledged by his God.

He acknowledged the same direction when he opened out into domestic happiness. All Rugby boys of the time can recall how there came to his side that sweet and kindly soul, who, with her deep religion and saintly ways, ripened with him and helped him to ripen—for they acknowledged God together; that Catharine, whose life and character he lived to tell forth long afterwards for the example of the households of the nation. Sickness and suffering then came over him : we all thought it was then to be even to death. But God had wider paths in which still to direct him. God's loving-kindness was yet to make him great. He had already sent forth many scholars, some of whom were to become great and to pour forth powerful influence in their day and generation; but the work was judged too heavy for him, and he was sent to be Dean of Carlisle.

There he at once plunged, as soon as ever his health was re-established, into work—far different, but still in the single-eyed acknowledgment of the great path-Director. It was there, among His visits to the courts and alleys of the city that, in the inscrutable dealings of God, He brought back, it is supposed, to his own hearth that deadly fever, which swept five little girls from their parents on earth up to their Parent in heaven. In this dire calamity they both acknowledged God—and see how He directed their path.

It was a trouble in which all who heard of it felt with him profoundly. The Queen, who has so tender a heart, was moved towards him, and her Royal attention was drawn to his singular merits. The See of London fell vacant. Who was a fitter man than this gifted person who both in prosperity and adversity had shown his masterly powers in important spheres already, and whose path had been directed in the public acknowledgment of his God? Lord Palmerston, who made so many good Bishops, appointed him—as it has always been understood, by Her Majesty's personal choice —to the splendid opportunities of the Bishopric of London.

London had grown beyond all influence of the Church. Many millions were as sheep having no shepherd. Whatever his eminent predecessor had done, Archibald Campbell Tait felt that more distinct efforts were called for on a larger scale. All the good works which he found in progress he maintained, and many more he set afoot. Among these was the more direct establishment of "the Bishop of London's Fund." He acknowledged God herein by the building of a great number of churches, and by bringing the ministration of the Gospel within reach of hundreds of thousands of souls who before had not so much as heard whether there was any Church of England or any Holy Ghost to influence their lives. Could God have more clearly directed his path than to prosper him in this, which, under the government of its present Bishop, has increased to be a still wider means of grace to the Metropolis, that great heart of Great Britain?

His work there he had done so well, and in that important sphere he had acknowledged God so thoroughly, that the same gracious Queen, who had noted and rewarded his work before, repaid it still further now by appointing him to the highest post which it lay in her power to bestow upon a Churchman; and when the venerable

Archbishop Longley was removed by death, he was raised to the Primacy.

He had said when he stood before the head of his college, "I have come to improve myself and to make friends." He then little thought of this good work which God, acknowledged in all His ways, had prepared for him to walk in; or of the friends he was destined to make. In this also God directed his path and the path of the Queen and her advisers. All along God's loving-kindness was making him great—great as Christ's minister, and as ours. There also, as everyone knows, he was the right man in the right place. He who had acknowledged God as the young Oxford student, as the responsible Tutor, as the Master of five hundred of the youth of England, as the working Dean of a Northern City, as the Father-in-God of the greatest and most busy Capital in the world, was now called to acknowledge Him as the Primate of the Church of his Nation. And he did so.

Thrown upon a strange and conflicting time, when "free thought," that singular misnomer, in the form often of Atheism, was rearing its many heads; when the Church of England was on her trial; when within were fightings, when without were fears —when all the waters of Religion and Irreligion were at the height of tempest—this Pilot, in the humble and firm acknowledgment of God, sat resolutely at the helm; and, God directing his path, guided the Christianity of Great Britain through all the waves and storms that broke over it.

Personally and domestically he, like the Captain of his salvation, was not to be made perfect except through suffering. This Christian Nestor was called, not only himself to undergo many illnesses, but to see taken from him his only son, whom he was bringing up in the like acknowledgment of the same God, "a youth of rare ministerial promise." He bore to lose him; and, ever bent on turning all events of his life to good example, so far was he from repining at the ways of God, however painful to flesh and blood, that he set himself to put together, for the study of all English families, the written story of those whom he had lost—the wife and the only son—between whose fallen bodies we saw on Friday last his own laid to rest.

How he bore his last illness you well know. I read to you on Sunday last part of a letter written by his beloved friend and Suffragan Bishop Parry; here is another written from beside his bed of death. They tell us that he was "calmly and patiently watching on this side the river for the coming of the Messenger of the King—longing to grasp the many loving hands reached forth to him from the other bank." We could not here know that already the joyous meeting had taken place—on that Advent Sunday on which he expected it—the day which he had always kept as that of the passing away of his beloved wife into the better land. Thus he had the blessing of "an expected end."

On Friday last the whole nation by its representatives was assembled round his tomb, in hope for him of a joyful resurrection.

Dear brethren, he had taught us all how to live, and he has now taught us how to die.

Could I, whom he sent among you, have given you a better illustration of my aged father's great text—"In all thy ways acknowledge God, and He shall direct thy paths"? May our last end be like his. May our paths through the great waters of life be alike directed by the same Heavenly Father to the same Haven.

WERTHEIMER, LEA & Co., Printers, Circus Place, London Wall.

A SERMON

PREACHED AT SOUTH BERSTED

BY THE

Rev. W. B. PHILPOT, M.A.,

VICAR OF SOUTH BERSTED, BOGNOR.

(*Reprinted from the "Church of England Pulpit."*)

LONDON:
"CHURCH OF ENGLAND PULPIT" OFFICE,
160, FLEET STREET, E.C.

1881.

ALL SAINTS' DAY.

"Such honour have all His saints."—Ps. cxlix. 9.

I WILL ask you, brethren beloved in the Lord, to heighten the tone of your feelings, to add proper dignity to the sense of your position, and to lift your lives, by dwelling on those great thoughts, which by the order of the year are brought before us to-day: for are we not called upon to celebrate the Day of All the Saints?

How can it be imagined that any of you can be wholly unmoved by so great a consideration as this? Think with me only for a little space this morning on the delightful advantage of belonging to so great a Company.

Take some of the ideas with which, as life passes, we are some of us wont, it may be, to make ourselves more familiar.

You count it a grand thing in its way, if you can reckon a long line of lofty ancestry. You hold it to be a high honour, as the world counts honour, to belong to a family that bears the name and wears the arms of some historic hero, handed down through generations of the brave; and, if you do not disgrace the name, much more if you grace it, this may well be deemed by you a very signal honour. You take a just pride in forming one of the complement of a great ship, or in belonging to some famous corps. You are conscious of a thrill of deep emotion and high self-sacrifice, if you march to battle under colours scorched and rent in victorious onsets, through which your regiment has triumphantly borne them. You regard all such fellowship as great, and you are penetrated with a sense of genuine manhood, when you call up to your minds in what communion you are moving.

You look upon it again as a fine thing, and so it is, to stand as an honoured name on the roll-call of some great public school; or on the books of some ancient college or institution of high repute. You are not insensible to a certain *esprit-de-corps* —if I knew any English expression for this I would use it—when you are attached to some princely firm of unimpeachable mercantile credit; or if you, as your fathers before you, have a holding in the rent-roll of some ancestral tenantry—and many other such companies I might name:—and *that*, although these, however great they now may be, are most of them, as we know too well, subject, in the course of human affairs, to sweeping and disgraceful changes; nay, although all of them, sooner or later, are sure to perish and be forgotten.

You are proud, I say, nor wholly without reason, if you belong to any one of such bodies as I have named. To an honourable mind, a mind bent, not so much on gaining and bearing away private credit from the company to which he may belong, as upon doing his part to maintain the dignity which he inherits or the honour which he shares, and to shed upon it still brighter lustre—to such a mind the feeling to which I allude is a natural and a wholesome one. Yea, though it may seem to involve the paradox of a becoming selfishness, that feeling, when drawn out towards our mother-country, is at the root of patriotism itself, which is beyond controversy all but the most manly principle there is, and only short of the highest that we know. But what are we to say of this body of persons in whose company I call you to-day to remember that you are enrolled? The Army of the Living God? The Regiment which is Christ's

Own? The Club, the Firm, the Family of the Holy and undivided Trinity? In a word, the Communion of All the Saints?

Think not that I am now speaking in the clouds, or that I have got among unreal natures; for I beg you to mark that I am telling you of the most actual, the most honourable, the most worshipful of all mortal or immortal Corporations. What are we to say of our belonging to such a company, limited in a sense in respect of our own private and personal responsibility, but unlimited in the credit that it imparts to us, the splendour that it pours on us, and the glory which it promises to reveal, in the holders of its shares and of its debenture-stock, both here and when this world is done?

And yet, as for the *word* "saint," the Adversary, among his thousand devices, has, by a piece of mastercraft, managed, strange to say, in some weak and worldly minds to cast a certain ghastly slur upon it; so that it has even become on loose lips a term of mockery; as though it befitted only the long drawn grimace of the false religionist, or the nasal whine of the canting hypocrite; as though it were a title wherewith to brand either the fictions of a knave, or the drivellings of a fool; as though in short this highest name in all humanity were a grotesque appellation of mere poltroonery, and were not at all descriptive of a man!

It is possible, indeed, that some false men, because they were *no* saints, have sometimes, in their own unhappy case, given colour for such an abuse of this great word; but it has, I repeat, been a prime device of the Devil, and we are not ignorant of it, to call such people saints at all. It did not answer his dark purpose that these should be called by their proper names of hypocrites and knaves; for then possibly for very shame they would themselves have dropped their knaveries and hypocrisies, and the whole body of *real* saints (to whom for interested motives, they had attached themselves) would so have stood clear and unattainted by their reproach; and that would ill have suited the object of one whom our Divine Friend calls "an Enemy." It matched better, you see, his fell design to drag down, if he could contrive to do so, all the saints to the level of these false brethren by turning the very word "saint" itself into a term of reproach, and a brand and token of contempt. It would not have carried out the aim of the power of darkness to leave the splendid title of "Saint" to be the unsullied addition of the people of God. But nevertheless—nay, all the more—in the Heraldry of the Church of Christ, in the office of the Church of England, it remains to you a name untarnished by time; and thus, in pious memory and buoyant hope, we thankfully acknowledge to-day that we belong, unworthy as we are, to the Communion of Saints.

Do I say *we* claim to belong to it? Aye, *we*—however humble, however young, however small and of no reputation, we may be—yet, I tell you, *we* belong to that Guild, and have a vested stake in its best blessings. "Such honour have all His Saints."

Tell that puny boy, so soon as ever he is able to apprehend anything of the blessing of being one among a happy number—and that is after all about the utmost range of all that the wisest of us can as yet take in—tell that little frail child, girl or boy, whose intellect is the dullest in the school, who stands the last in the class, but who is *doing his best* to please his parents, his master, his minister, and his God—tell him or tell her, for you will tell them truly, that he is wearing upon his brow the cross of his Redeemer's Order, and the seal of the Living God; that he is held in great account where alone it greatly imports that he should be accounted of; tell them that the Church of God and of England regard them as members of Christ, as children of God, and inheritors of the Kingdom of Heaven. Tell your sweet children that they each have a whole share and a perfect part in the honours of the Day of All the Saints.

Yes indeed, you may say, good children who are brought to Christ, we *know* share this honour; for has not Christ Himself said " Of such is the Kingdom of Heaven"?

Nay, but what honest Christian does not share it likewise? Or is it that this is an honour for Emperors, Kings, and the rich? Is it indeed, that for statesmen, philosophers, poets, the teachers of men, the leaders of science, and for authorities in theology, reserved seats are kept at this Feast of all the Saints? For them certainly this is an open honour, and the highest which they can aim at or hope ever to attain—an honour, before which all honour that may come to them from men pales and fades in the comparison. Though with the cable of earthly eminence it may be found to be hard to thread the needle's eye of the gate of heaven, yet when—by the help of Him with whom all things are possible—men can once manage to thread this divine needle, then temporal greatness is no more an obstacle to shut you out from the portals of Paradise than it is a passport to let you into them.

The title for admission, the qualification for membership in this world-wide Society is drawn up and couched in terms so broad, so high, so deep, so grand, that all the many tests which men have sought out to replace it, are mean and pitiful indeed.

The fact of being made at first in the image of God, and then becoming a new creature in Christ Jesus—this is the watchword, this the wedding-garment which passes you into that Banquet Hall, where the King holds high festival for all His Saints. Yes, you good Christian souls, who, amidst all the struggles and vicissitudes of your varied fortunes, over all the ups and downs of your daily life, go forth to your work, and your labour till the evening—you who guide or carry out the courses and duties of the natural year—who, by grace of God, cause the earth to bring forth her increase and supply the world with bread—you, before whose steady eye and firm hand the plough, by horse or steam, clears the ground, and the seed falls into it—before whose steady stroke the woods bend and the great trees fall—yea, even you, by whose weather-beaten parish-paid work the very roads on which we go to and fro become harder and higher, and fitter for the uses of traffic and travel—you, by whose graceful skill these hedges that "honour the holy bounds of property" come to look so trim and cared for, while the waste waters of the well-drained uplands keep only the courses you make for them—yes, you, I say, every one of you, with your wives and children, have a cover laid for you at this High Festival of all the Saints.

Let us try for a few moments to contemplate and realise this Company, both in itself, and by way of contrast with another company, a company which is set over against this as its awful correlative and its corresponding term in the ratios of Eternity. And to this end how can we do better than take our keynote from that ancestral hymn which your children and your choir just now so sweetly sang?

For what sang they? "We praise Thee, O God, we acknowledge Thee to be the Lord. All the Earth doth worship Thee, the Father everlasting." Who are they that thus lift up their praises? *We and all the earth.* There you have one branch of the Company, and it is the branch of it best known to us as yet. We mount higher in recounting the grades and orders of the Saints. "To Thee all angels cry aloud, the heavens and all the powers therein." Break up the heavens again, and scan those ranks of which we can now but dimly forthimage the being and shadow out their offices, knowing, as we do, their very names but faintly, and but as falling echoes of some world of which men once indeed, it would seem, knew somewhat more than now—if indeed, before Christ came, this by some mysterious foretaste so could be.

There are the Cherubim with their light of lofty knowledge, and the Seraphim, with the burning glow of their immortal love. Having thus soared to the highest we can hear of, and caught what names can be named in heaven—though still only of such beings as star the verge of the vision of things not fully to be conceived nor lawfully to be uttered —that galaxy of undeciphered light, whose rays have not yet reached us—leaving these, the Hymn, as though its wings were out-wearied with ascent, hovers down to earth again—at least to those earthly memories which are her personal treasure gone before and laid up in Heaven by the Church.

"Heaven and earth are full of the Majesty of Thy Glory. The glorious company of the Apostles praise Thee. The goodly fellowship of the Prophets praise Thee. The noble Army of Martyrs praise Thee"—as though in all these the praises of heaven and earth were blended, making up full concord to the angelic symphony—their memories left on the earth, their spirits made perfect in Heaven.

And lest any of you be left out in the cold, omitted or forgotten, this hymn, in its Catholic sweep, wakes up to join in its praises, "the holy Church throughout *all the world;*" which is to say, throughout not this planet only, but if in any other realm, or region, star or asteroid there be any created souls, redeemed or unfallen, any lives capable of hymns, belonging to the domain of God.

Now I pray you to take note that all this is in the words, not of one man's vague fancy, but of the soberest, wisest, most cautious Church there is—a Church from which some have been runagates because forsooth the language of our public worship seemed inadequate to the warmth of their private conceptions! Such are the breathings of our *Te Deum*, sent up through long ages, held to by the Church of God while many dark and foolish ways clave to her, but reverently preserved by her still, when, on her resurrection to a wiser and nobler life, she cast the worser part of her old superstitions to the winds.

I have thus given you—not, I repeat, in my own language, but in the best I could anywhere find—the catalogue and programme of the personages who, in this supreme Legion of Heaven's own Honour, make up the goodly array of the Communion of all the Saints. Great God! can it, I ask, be possible that any of us here to-day will be indifferent as to whether we belong, or do not belong, to such a Society as this? Have you any ambition in you? Here, indeed, is a range for it—the best crown to which the only right ambition leads. Have you any gift of imagination? Here, if anywhere, is a legitimate scope for it. Have you any taste for divinity? any spiritual intellect for pondering with pious calculation on the fitnesses of eternal verities? any music in your soul for unravelling the harmonies of the purest Truth? Here is an infinite field for all the highest powers you have, in which to find their purpose and their play. Have you anything of our human faculty of Faith, by which you may revel with delight in the regions of lofty instinct, and infallible intuition of the things which are higher than proof? Have you, lastly, any genuine capacity of immortal Love, so as to enjoy with pure eye the sight of God, and those visions of supernal and eternal beauty, and so as to find an expressive relish in the practice of loving-kindness? Well: here is a range below, prophetic of infinite ranges above; *here*, I say, in the Communion of all the Saints—for the Master says: "Inasmuch as ye are kind to one of the least of these My brethren, one of the least of all the Saints, ye do it unto Me." This is the path by which alone you can "rise in the world," if indeed your aim be that—the only world, believe me, worth your rising in. If not—mark my words—you must *sink* in the world—down, down, down—for time and for eternity—sink in this world, sink in *that* world.

For I spoke of another company. It is the communion of all the sinners! A day is coming which will be the counterpart of this. That will be "All Sinners' Day": for all power in heaven and earth is given to the President of our Society, to Him who is, and already in all civilised societies is acknowledged to be, the Judge of all mankind. The King will say to His servants, "Gather out of My Kingdom all things that offend, and them that do iniquity: there shall be the weeping and gnashing of teeth." A terrible converse to this day of All the Saints will be that day of all the sinners; for "Cast the bad away" are the words of the Master. "Bind him hand and foot and cast him into outer darkness," says He who casts out none that come to Him. My brethren, glance through the things which were told to St. John, and you will find some awful revelations about that fiery communion of the damned. Is not everything that makes life miserable—*sin?* Is not everything that makes life happy—*Christian goodness?* In that great refining process, by which sin will be purged away and the salt of the earth left pure, it is clear that those who take their part with the bad will leave the good happier by their absence; and will themselves be made more wretched by the absence of all in them and around them that was good. For the reason why the bad are not as yet wholly wretched is only that there are roots of goodness in them still; and because a merciful, long-suffering Father prolongs to them the power of choice, and holds out to them a hope that they may yet make that choice aright. Moreover, at least in a nation like this, sinners cannot choose but enjoy the surrounding gleams of the very communion for which they affect contempt. But a day is coming when the "sweet Master" and only Saviour will, perforce and by all the necessary laws of moral judgment, bid the ministers of divine penalty to "Cast the bad away." What becomes of *them* it concerns us not, on this bright festival of ours, further to ask; but let us take heed to ourselves lest, haply, a promise being left of entering into His rest, any one of you should seem to have come short of it. In the words of him who wrote to the Hebrews, "Seeing we are compassed about with so great a cloud of witnesses, lay aside every weight, and the sin that doth so easily beset us"—for *that* surely it is which debars men from the sweet and bright companionship of the Saints, and plunges them into that bitter, black, and tragical society of the lost—" looking unto Jesus, the Author and Perfecter, the Alpha and Omega of our Faith "—who, " being dowered with the scorn of scorn, the hate of hate, the love of love"—"for the joy that was set before Him endured the Cross, despising shame, and hath sat down at the right hand of the Throne of God "—that right hand where His people shall reign with Him when the world is over and past. *" Such honour have all His saints."*

WERTHEIMER, LEA & CO., Printers, Circus Place, London Wall.

HYMN FOR ALL SAINTS' DAY.

Praise Him, world without beginning,
  First that left our Father's hand,
Primal souls unsoiled by sinning,
  Ere the younger Earth was manned;
Ye the full-come kingdom share,
Praise Him, all ye Saints that were.

Praise Him, world that now is going
  Wrapt in dusty raiment still;
Purer than we dream of, glowing
  Like the snows on early hill:—
True the vision, though afar—
Praise Him, all ye Saints that are.

Praise Him, world with judgment ending,
  Praise Him, ye that shall be born;
Clouds of souls henceforth ascending
  Ever till the general morn;—
Wider, wiser Church I see:—
Praise Him, all ye Saints to be.

Way, and truth, and life discerning
  Are they few whom Christ has saved?
Christ an answer now returning
  Points to these His love has laved:—
Oh that as Time's river rolls
All the Saints were all the souls!

Now the Son delivers over
  The domain He died to bring
To the Universal Lover,
  Highest subject of the King:—
Now the kingdom flows serene
As though sin had never been.
              So mote it be.

HARVEST HYMN.

Lord, in grateful adoration
  Lo, we bend before Thy face;
Landlord of the great Creation,
  Grant, we pray Thee, grace for grace.

Rain and sun Thou duly gavest,
  Seed to sow, and heart to till;
Now again our life Thou savest—
  Miracles of mercy still.

Twice the thousands hungered round Thee
  Hearing what Thy love would say;
Little had they, but they found Thee
  Loth to send them faint away.

So Thou bid'st the willing season
  Take the scanty seed we throw,
And, unread by mortal reason,
  Feed our hungry thousands now.

Harvest passing, summer ending,
  Sin o'ercome, and sorrow braved,
Grant, we pray before Thee bending,
  We and ours at last be saved.
                    Amen.

ERRATA.

Page 2 (mid.).—*For* back-water *read* back water.
Page 15 (bottom).—*For* Ænead *read* Æneid.
Page 5 (Sermon iii., line 10).—*After* finished, full stop.
Page 15 (line 11).—*For* hae *read* had.
Page 15 (line 12).—*For* thd *read* the.
Page 18 (Sermon v., line 4 from bottom).—*Supply* into parts of which.
Page 18 (Sermon viii., last line but one).—*Delete* comma *after* wrong.
Page 6 (Sermon xvi., top).—*For* knaveries and hypocrisies *read* cloak of saintship.

ΕΠΙΦΟΡΕΜΑΤΑ.

THE WAFER-GOD
"HOCUS POCUS" AGAIN.

[The Preacher at the opening of a Romish "Cathedral" at Arundel had spoken of God requiring "a local habitation," and "Christ's Home" being in the Wafer on the Altar.

The following formed part of a sermon in the neighbourhood for the next Sunday.]

"Woman, believe me, the hour cometh when ye shall neither in this mountain, nor yet at Jerusalem, worship the Father. Ye worship ye know not what : we know what we worship. * * The hour cometh, and now is, when the true worshippers shall worship the Father in Spirit and in Truth, for the Father seeketh such to worship Him. God is a Spirit, and they that worship Him must worship Him in Spirit and in Truth."—ST. JOHN IV. 21.

* * * * *

AND when I find this "father" talk of God—the unseen Father of men and the Source of Life—requiring a local habitation on an altar :—and when I find that "Monsignor" telling you there is no certainty to be found anywhere but here—pointing, as he speaks, like some mediæval wizard with an inimitable gravity to the magic circle of his mystic rites—I ask, are we, ministers of this common-sense reformed nation, whom not the Pope of Rome but the Queen of England has sent to help you to heaven after the teaching of Christ and by the paths of your fathers—are we, I wonder, expected to sit through all this patient and tongue-tied? Is plainness of language on the part of the enemies of light to be not only tolerated but commended, while the like plainness on our part is to be reprobated as intolerant, or regarded as a breach of reserve? Away with such trifling, for it has no place when your dearest—nay your immortal interests are at stake! This English reserve of ours within certain limits is wholesome; —nay, when the breach of it would make sad the heart of one whom God hath not made sad, or when it would make an undue advance upon the convictions of tolerant souls, then it is just and admirable; but in matters like these, when you have to deal with an ungentlemanly Church which will not let you speak with it on even terms but which coolly damns you when you differ—why, in the presence of such men as these, you may bend, and scrape, and apologise, and hold your tongue, and shift out of the way before their shouldering and down-trampling advances, till some fine day you find yourself, and your Church, and your Nation, tumbling backwards down that precipice over which they are struggling to push you. Do you flatter yourselves that *they* care to pay any attention to your convictions, your remonstrances, or this misplaced delicacy of your reserve? No: their manner is to carry things with a high hand, and bear down before them everything sacred, everything gentle, everything delicate in woman or in man, if only it seem to be against the interests of the church of the priests; so *let plain speaking be the order of the day.* Methinks, my neighbours, you will expect and demand that your minister for the moment, whoever he may be—even though he be so feeble an one as myself—if he have aught to say, should say it to you now; and you will bid us use no mincing or uncertain tones either, about the saying of it.

Does the Monsignor prate of certainty and say "Lo, here is certainty," to be found only in the "secret chambers" of Rome? "Lo, here is Christ in this piece of bread;" or "Lo, there He is on that so-called altar?" What christian lover of wisdom, nay what cultivated child, would speak in this way? By what grasp can you lay hold of such "airy nothingness" as this is, so as to argue with it? Who can grapple with these lies which Rome's imagination keeps bodying forth, when her only answer is that it is the Church herself who tells them? The man himself says he does not understand it. Indeed how *can* anyone be certain about a thing when he knows he does not understand what it is that he says he is certain about! The fact is, that all which they say on the " Real Presence " is—I do not say like a *dead* language, but like a language which never was alive :—like nothing so much as gibberish in an extravaganza, or the croaking of the frogs in the ancient comedy. The comfort which good men think they find in it would be found in infinitely greater purity and with more sane satisfaction by direct communication with the Spirit of the Father and the Son, who after all must be at the bottom of all the true comfort there is.

This taunt against our alleged divisions is by this time a threadbare and a vulgar one, and hardly worth our serious notice ; yet, as it is the best with which their quiver of poisoned arrows can furnish them, it is more worth our notice, I suppose, than most of the things they trouble us with. Let us ask them, *what are* our divisions ? Why, what are they but the very forms of our unity? they are the signs of our national life. Divergence, within certain limits, is an essential sign of individual, social, and political vitality. What are these divisions but the free-play of our British natures in the course of our several and special modes of spiritual development? Like the varied beauty of our island, —the mountains of Scotland, the hills of Derby, the meadows of Wilts, and the downs of Sussex,— is not this better than the dull, burning sands of the uniform Sahara, which is regular in nothing but in the absence of life? Are not our divisions demanded by the very conditions of our freedom ? If the truth makes free, our freedom correlatively must make us true,—and if, as Rome does, we were to pretend that we all thought the same, when we do not and cannot do so, we should be liars like unto them. For what unity of thought is there when in their whole communion no single man of them dares to think? It is a contradiction in terms. The only unity of thought which they have lies in not thinking at all! and that is not—and cannot be—a unity of *thought*. That is not a human unity. It is not a unity worth having in a progressive nation like this. It may do very well for Spain— but it will not do for us. That is but the unity of a herd of swine running down they know not whither, possessed by the spirits which Christ is casting out of Paganism. Oh! lamentable spectacle, to see a whole community, which might have done the work of the kingdom of God so well, throwing away all its noblest chances, and possessed by all the spirits that are fighting against freedom and man! But as for what are called our "divisions,"—are they not permitted wisely by the Church and by the State? Could we do more wisely than allow them, even if we could help so doing? These are but the growing pains of humanity. What can be a more natural preparation for the coming of that Church of the Future, wherein each man, woman, and child, according to special make, shall be allowed without fear to grow up unto Christ in all things, and in which our modes of thought shall have cast off these fetters fastened upon us by Rome in the darker past, and shall have burst once for all the swaddling bands which now stunt and deform spirits that are meant to grow? For, mark you, it is mainly the remnants of Rome in us which refuse to combine with the elements of our freedom—it is mainly the Latin mischief yet lingering in our constitution which gives us these internal disorders, and causes us to seem to be divided.

And yet they are for ever harping upon this "want

of unity." "Look," say they, "at your divisions! Look at your high church, and look at your low, and look at your broad." Well—*look at them*, and be thankful for the blessings of them all. I do not admit, indeed, the correctness of those terms—for there is lowness in much that is called high, and a highness in much that is called low; and broadness is wisdom, when it does not mean indifference. But take the names which these slaves of Rome venture thus to throw in your free English faces, and regard them, if you will, as applied to the spiritual building and to all these freely-springing side-chapels of the Church of Christ in England. If you want any building to be beautiful in its proportions, it must surely rise up on high; if you want any building to be safe, it must surely in a certain measure go down low; if you want a building to be capacious and not one of those imposing structures which have nothing but shop-front, and which a stronger breeze would blow over, it must in all conscience be broad; and in our Church when you ask for these characters, you may thank God, that in some true sense you have them all.

But if a Church boasts that it is neither high nor low nor broad, in the name of goodness what, I ask, is it? I will tell you what it is. I will tell you what the Church of Rome is. It's a *deep* Church—a *very deep* Church; and its depth and its danger and its subtilty are not to be fathomed. It was an ominous thing, by the way, that in building this Cathedral of theirs they could find no foundation. They had to go down almost to Tartarus, as you all remember well, before they got one, and whether they found one after all in those crumbling and shifty sands, I know not. But we know what the Master says of all houses or Churches "built on the sand." The floods shall come on them and they shall fall, and "great will be the fall thereof."

But the Monsignor says it is to be "a centre of fire to all this neighbourhood." Now Heaven save us from the fires of Rome! Our fathers have left us too many records of what those fires were at Smithfield. I myself, for instance, am told that I can claim as an ancestor that Archdeacon of Winchester whom Bishop Bonner, of London—the "Archbishop of Westminster" of his day—on the 18th of December, 1555, in the 44th year of his age, sent from his custody to the stake. This was but three centuries ago; and him, for one among hundreds, they taught what Rome means when her preachers tell us of her *fires*. You may read his examination and letters in any book of the Martyrs. May the Lord deliver us from such fires as Rome kindled for our fathers, and which, if she dared, she would fain kindle again for ourselves! If they tell you, as they will, that Protestants did the same, tell them that *our* Church has learned mercy, but that *theirs* must always be what it was. She may not, perhaps, ever be *able* to burn us again, but depend upon it she will go as near it as she can; for, like the she-wolf that nursed her pagan founders, she knows nothing of mercy. She ravins as much as ever after all the votaries of freedom and of truth. Does she speak of our "finding certainty in her"? Yes, there *is* certainty, but it is this:—that as the Kingdom of Christ prevails, she is certain to be doomed and damned, and all those with her who knowingly drink of the cup of her falsehoods and her sins. And since those of us who wish and who may find it convenient to-day, purpose presently to partake of our own simple and truthful form of the Sacrament, let us contrast with that for a moment the monstrous and grotesque claim which Rome makes, that God has, as their preacher said the other day, "a local habitation on the altar," and that Christ is given by her priests "a home in the bread."

What! is it possible, I ask, that at this time of the world's day a man should venture to get up in a Christian country and tell you that God requires a local habitation in an earthly temple? Did Rome never read, or does she forget, all that Stephen, the first martyr, said? I don't wonder she should not care to remember that leaf of history, and that she should hide the Bible from the people: but let me read it to you, as it stands, or with such implied variations as our own times and case demand. "Men, brethren, and fathers," said Stephen, "hearken,"—and he then traced in the lucid tone of a historian the annals of Jewry till he came to the era of Solomon. "Solomon," he said, "built God a house. Howbeit," he went on to say—in a very broad, unorthodox, and, as Rome would say a very profane manner, considering that this great Reformer was speaking of no less a place than the Temple of Jerusalem, and of the House which, till then, had, in the infancy of the Faith, been regarded as holy—" Howbeit the Most High dwelleth *not* in temples made with hands—as saith the Prophet, 'Heaven is my throne; Earth is my footstool; what house will ye build me, or what is the place of my rest? hath not my hand made all these things?'" And then the speaker broke off into a strain of magnificent and inspired invective, which might—*mutatis mutandis* (though there is but little to change)—have been addressed to these very men who mangle Christ's sacred body again by the profane use they put it to—a strain of indignation which would that your preachers could command to-day!—" Ye stiffnecked and uncircumcised in heart and ears, ye do always resist the Holy Ghost, and the light of Reformation which God sends you: as your fathers did, so do ye. Which of the prophets have not your fathers persecuted?" He would say, were he here to-day— for he was not for mincing matters, nor did he hesitate to speak strongly when authority was teaching men wrongly—no, not even though, like some Samson, he brought ruin down on his own mortal head when he wrenched from their sockets the pillars of their prejudices—he would say, were he here to-day, " Does not the blood of the Ridleys and the Latimers, of the Wickliffes and Hoopers, cry aloud from the Oxford ditches? They have slain them who maintained the truth as it is in Jesus the Just One—of whom ye are now the betrayers, and, in spirit at least, the murderers ; who have received light by the teaching of your national prophets and have not kept it, but like regenades have gone back again, though washed with the rest of England in the blood of our martyrs, to wallow in the mire of your paganism." When Stephen had said words such as these to that council—while they looked steadfastly at him, and saw his face as it had been the face of an angel —what did that Papal Council do ? When they heard these things they were cut to the heart and they gnashed on him with their teeth—just as these Romish prelates under Queen Mary gnashed their teeth against those whom they burned to ashes at Smithfield. But he, Stephen—a poor deacon, and but a humble minister of the alms of the Christian community,—being full of the Holy Ghost looked up steadfastly into Heaven and saw the glory of God, and Jesus—not with the outer eye or in a morsel of bread on an altar, but with the soul's eye,—saw Jesus standing on the right hand of God, and said " Behold I see the Heaven opened and—not Mary, nor any saint—but Himself, the Son of Mary and of God, standing on the right hand of God." Then those Romanists of the time cried out with a loud voice and stopped their ears, just as these priests do when there is any reason or reformation in the wind—being men who (whatever they may be in private life, which they seem to drown in their superstitions), hate to be reformed as a Church—and they ran upon him with one accord, and cast him out of the city, and stoned him—blinding his divine vision, and quenching those eyes that heaven's light made so beautiful, with the dust and bruises of their murderous onslaught. " They stoned Stephen," says St. Luke, " calling upon God and saying ' Lord Jesus, receive my spirit ' " ; and he kneeled down till their stones overthrew him as he knelt, and cried with a loud voice, ' Lord, lay not this sin to their charge,' and when he had said this he fell asleep." And *why was all this*, I ask? Why, indeed? I will tell you why. It was because he had just said that the Lord "dwelt *not* in temples made with hands." And yet at the consecration of that temple over there on Tuesday last a man, purporting to be a minister of that Jesus Himself whom Stephen appealed to when he said this, gets up and tells us that God *does* require a place made with hands, and that " Christ's home *is* on the Church's altar." What, I ask, can be ranker blasphemy than that? No; let us break bread, and, people and all, take the cup which He blessed; in pious remembrance of our Lord and Master Jesus, and let us ever more and more fashion our lives by the guidance of His in-dwelling Spirit.

Now to God the Father, God the Son, and God the Holy Ghost, be all honour and glory for ever and ever.—Amen.

SUBSTANCE OF AN ADDRESS DELIVERED BEFORE THE CONFERENCE OF THE EVANGELIC ALLIANCE AT BERLIN, 1857,

(and then printed by the desire of Chevalier Bunsen, who at that Conference was again embraced by the King on the steps of the Palace of Potsdam).

MY brethren beloved in the Lord,

* * *

In Religion, no less than in our Royal Houses, we would welcome your alliance. May the marriage ere long be solemnized, if indeed this be not part of the ceremony, between German and English theology. You have given us our stock, our language, our Reformation, and, you see, we come to you now for another boon. Unhappily for a long time the theology of your country was such as to make some of our simple hearts afraid of the very sound of it, especially those to whom hardly anything but the sound was known. But now let us hope it will be different. It has already begun to be so. We have learnt scholarship from your scholars, and our own is the sounder; a scholarship which is being turned, we trust, to good account as one of the most useful handmaids to our Christianity. So also I hope we shall learn some divinity from your divines;—not indeed from those ἄθεοι θεόλογοι who seek to banish from their divinity the Spirit of the Divine Being;—for how could we hope to learn any divinity from them? *Ex nihilo nihil fit*—but from such noble workers as I could name. We shall none of us probably admit all their views, nor need we admit any, except by the force of truth; but we are most assuredly bound carefully and thankfully to weigh well what they tell us. For what else are they doing but putting out for the use of the Church, as faithful servants, whatever diverse talents and opportunities God gives them severally for that special end? Let men beware lest haply, in the endeavour to stop such men's mouths, they be not found fighting against the Head of the Church. These are the best champions of our common faith, philologists and philosophers while humble-hearted Christians. These are our best defenders against the follies of Rome, because too manly to fondle any kindred and counter-follies in Protestanism. The days are past when ignorance can be regarded by sane men as the mother of devotion and the neccessary companion of piety. These are the men who must help us to gird on our armour and to keep it bright.

And is not Truth urged upon us by Paul as the first piece of the whole armour of God? We have to fight not so much with flesh and blood—though sometimes even with these—but with men, some of them, of princely intelligence and boundless resources; men of whom, if we could gain them to the Lord's side, we might feel much as Hannibal felt, when he beheld on the field of Cannæ the soldiers of Rome lying each on his back with his death-wound in his breast—that with such men in our ranks we could the sooner bring the kingdoms of the world into subjection to our Master. Alas! however, they fight and fall under the banners of the Prince of the darkness of this world.

But we, my friends, must fight as children of the light. We who profess to be of the light—what need have we to borrow the weapons of darkness? And in fighting this fight of rational faith we must see to it not only who are our enemies, but what in them is hostile and what is not. So mixed is the character of all things human, that, while laying about us among our very foes, we must take good heed lest we deal unkind and hurtful blows to some honest friend, or some friendly principle, and inflict wounds hard to be healed, wounds which may fester and rankle on to the end of time. We must do battle, I say, in the light. Not, God forbid, in the light of carnal wisdom—a light equal to darkness—but under the colours of Him who is the Light that God sent for us into the world, even that Personal Truth in whom is no darkness at all. We must never blind ourselves to any fraction of the Truth. Are not Faith and Reason alike the gifts of God? Faith is but Reason in her attitude of love; Reason is but Faith in her moments of reflection. Or, Reason is as Faith's younger sister, and if rent from her side she soon must die, while Faith herself is left alone to drag on a life that is but half a life, being one made up of contradictions and tears. So, with open eyes and faithful minds, we must desire the truth, and hate, first in ourselves and then in others, everything which makes against it; and then the good Spirit of God will guide us into all our best desires, as the times come when He sees we can bear their fulfilment. Only, in all our contests, outward and inward, we must take care to keep our ears open to the lightest whisper of that voice behind us. We must not go on in advance beyond the guidance of that voice. There are many things which we had better not think of now. We shall, if we endure to the end, have powers and leisure to enter upon many speculations, when our Heavenly Father shall let us walk in a happy Eternity beside the river of the water of life; and so let us lay aside such contemplations till then.

For the present, be not afraid. Indeed we are bound in God's name to examine those matters, and above all those documents which concern our present Salvation, and which God has permitted as channels through which His divine streams should run. Had God given us those precious leaves ready bound, in finished order, in our own several languages, with no need for translations and manuscripts, with no risk of being tampered with by foolish or designing men; had He chosen to guide the grammar of the writers as well as to fill them with His Spirit; had He intended to instruct us thereby in history and science; had He intended more than—to give us all our souls need;—had He in short, after the manner of Jupiter, flung down a Book for us to worship, the case would be different, and we durst not then touch one single arrangement, one sentence, one vowel-point.

And it is impossible to understand on what principle, though it is easy enough to see with what feeling, some can proceed, who dare meddle with one single letter, holding what they do; or who, allowing any the slightest alteration even in manuscripts, can hold a different view of Biblical criticism from those which I am maintaining. In the former case they are bound to be the adorers of every fool, every thief, every liar who has intentionally or unintentionally in the course of many centuries added to or taken from the pure Word of God: in the latter they are bound to use every means that God has mercifully given us of finding out what He has said to us and what He has not.

And can we not well afford, my brethren, if we have real faith on Him of Whom the Scriptures testify, and if we are satisfied, in the words of the Church of England, that "they contain all things necessary to Salvation"—can we not well afford to hold up to the sunbeams of the judgment of an enlightened Christian every opinion about their form and garb? It is but an ill compliment to the God of Truth to think that He cannot help us to fight His own battles without getting our falsehoods to help Him. A weak believer is timid in proportion to the weakness of his belief. No two facts are irreconcilable. If *we* cannot reconcile them, we may be sure that God can. All truths are in harmony, and the practised ear of the man of spiritual and mental acumen will soon detect a note out of tune. Most differences arise from the fact that no ear is fully cultivated; that no one can catch precisely all that the various voices of God are saying, but that some do so more clearly than others, while those others will not allow it.

Therefore, in ever-deepening humility and ever-expanding power of prayer, we must prove all things, refuse the evil and choose and hold fast the good, wheresoever it may be found, remembering that we can learn even from those whom we may, rightly or wrongly, regard as our enemies. Men too often cling to what they have been accustomed to, because, though an old folly, they regard it as an old friend; sometimes amiably, always weakly, and usually because too idle to think. How unlike the wisdom that is from above, which is "first pure,"—clear-headed, clean-handed, clean-hearted. The spirit of love when alone is folly; the spirit of power when alone is sin :—but vhen these golden twists are intertwined with the spirit of a sound mind they form that threefold cord which is not easily broken, and which is the best bond that can hold Christ's Church together. Irrationalism is as grave a heresy as rationalism. To let that "godlike reason fust in us unused" is much the same sin as to refuse in any of our sayings and doings to admit the interpenetrating influence of that Divine Λόγος, which, as Coleridge has well said, is Reason in its highest form of self affirmation. He graciously deigns to make our personality His Temple, and it is one of the highest forms of irreverence, and a sure road to ruin, in any way to ignore Him.

And in these our struggles with Romanism, rationalism, irrationalism, infidelity, or by whatever name we may designate the enemies of Christ and

His Church—in whatever form we may find the vices of our depraved and corrupted nature—you may depend upon it that it is bad generalship, fatal tactics, and certain to end in our confusion, to allow ourselves miserably to be beaten back from point to point. Should we not rather, with the best men in our several Churches, under God, for our common leaders, rather reconnoitre fearlessly and speedily what ground is tenable and what is not. I speak of opinion only—not of that which is, thank God, beyond opinion. And should we not, with the elastic step of those who know, not only *what* they believe, but in WHOM they believe, march forward, seize, and occupy such a solid and certain position among the swamps and morasses which lie around that Living Rock, that we may be able not only to make a stand there for the moment, but to keep it for ever. If *we* do not do this, it will most surely be done by our children. But meanwhile, let it be remembered, we are recruiting the ranks of the infidel by swarms of deserters, who, inveigled by a thousand allurements, are tempted to run away from ground which they are pleased to think may be all unsafe because they see some of it to be so, and from a Cause which, not having the like precious faith, they foolishly expect to fall. Thus every person, in proportion to his influence, who maintains as essential to the Church of Christ what must in the event be abandoned, may have laid at his door the ruin of the souls of men.

Oh what a blessing it is that we have that for which Socrates in the Phædrus of Plato sadly but not unhopefully longed; when he said, in reasoning so well on immortality, that we needed surely some raft on which to cross the ocean of life; except he added,—or rather the Spirit of God added within his honest heart—except God were to send from Heaven some θεῖος λόγος. For what else could that θεῖος λόγος be but this very divine Word who, as John tells us, did in the fulness of time come forth from the bosom of the Father—He in Whom we believe and whom we love, and in whose name we are all met together in this Church to-day.

To conclude: be sure that we English shall remember with fervent affection these signal days spent among you.

For is not this, after the divine manner of Scripture, which is limited to no single fulfilment, another realisation of the prophecy of Joel? Have we not heard and felt, in thoughts which have breathed and words which have burned, the language of which those tongues of fire were but the symbols and the signs? Have we not heard men speak as the Spirit gave them utterance, in other tongues than those of the hard unloving world, each in his own language, the wonderful works of God? Have we not heard in those loud and deep Amens, with which that language has been greeted, the very rushing mighty wind of that same Divine Spirit of Christ?—May that Spirit send us back to our several homes across plain, river, and sea, like those Christians of old, with our minds and hearts more enlightened and warmed, to be more than before centres and sources of light and heat in whatever circles, large or small, in city or in country, God has allotted to us the fields of our work.

PART OF AN ADDRESS TO MEMBERS OF A LITERARY INSTITUTE.

* * * *

DOES the loving intercourse with knowledge which a fine mind enjoys in the silence of our reading-room ever suggest a mistrust in the God who guides him thus? Does a miserable fancy ever obtrude itself that your life is being lost because you have not the leisure or the means to walk more freely in this pleasant world of thought which our library opens up to you? Do you, in short, ever feel hardly treated by the Most High in not having been allowed to become by profession a student or a minister? Such a thought *may* arise, and it is quite in accordance with the purport of this evening if I stop for a moment to examine such a case. Should there be only one such among us, it is highly becoming that from this chair I should offer to that one man a solution of his misgivings. For if religious discussions are excluded by our laws, there is no law to exclude, while there are many to enforce, such cautions as may preserve any of our members from becoming irreligious. If reading our books and becoming enamoured of these stores of knowledge works in any young man so grievous a harm as to make him unhappy towards his Heavenly Father—I mean if this taste of a student's delight makes any one discontented in his calling—it is our duty to try and help that brother over this difficulty. Well—the best I can do is to offer you one or two considerations. Indeed we might shut up the whole argument in two sentences. For any man of common observation knows that *no one of us has any business to expect that all his circumstances should be happy*. And also *every man of Christian principle knows that God loves him*.

It is the old adage of square men in round holes and round men in square. If a round man has the disposal of himself, he must take care in the first instance to avoid that rectangular aperture; and if a man be rectangular, he will not be blameless if he thrust himself into a circular one; and being in, each will do wisely to change himself, if he fairly can. But I speak now of a man, who, with an aptitude for a learned profession, and with a native power of pushing the bounds of knowledge, finds himself in an unalterable manner doomed to manual work, necessitated to live among uncongenial materials, and to earn his bread by toil which is distasteful to him.

The fact is, society abounds with persons in the like case, and it fills all considerate men with infinite pity to behold them. There are many men in other walks than yours, whose life seems to them blighted, because they have been forced into a line which is alien to their composition. There are men endowed, for instance, with vast powers of historical research—some of us have known them even at Oxford—men born to grasp the root-ideas of nationality, men capable of bringing about by their wisdom the harmonies of states and races, men adapted by the kindly mixing of their elements to work out in society the very order of Providence and nature: yet, such is their evident destiny, that their lives seem as good as lost both to themselves and to their times. They might, either as statesmen, as politicians, as historians, as bishops, or as poets, help on with clear insight, magic administration, or potent utterance, the very Kingdom for which we all daily pray and daily strive;—yet, by some slight mistake, some little oversight, some selfish blindness, or some sin, perhaps on somebody else's part, their lines have fallen in places unpleasant to themselves, and, to all appearance, injurious to the world. Perhaps that man of angelic temperament, every lineament of whose face speaks world-wide power, and beams with intelligent sympathy, is doomed to grime his soul in sifting parchments to which there is no clue, and to wear his delicate' mind in tracking trickeries and raking up iniquities to which there is neither bottom nor bound. Is there not many a lawyer wasting fine brains in gaining, or keeping together, lands—for whom? For one who would be far happier on its roads; strong-built, muscular, and highly adapted for breaking parochial stones, but wholly unfit to manage the property which that noble mind is burying itself in dusty deeds to gain for' him—deeds of the dead hand, which perhaps were evil.

There are thousands of such instances of men who find themselves with no taste whatever for their calling, yet without any power whatever to extricate themselves. You may know parsons who should be lawyers, lawyers who should be country-gentlemen, doctors who should be butchers, butchers who should be financiers, farmers who should be historians, kings who should be farmers, and so forth, in an infinite series: and, what is more immediately to our present point, some of you yourselves may be young tradesmen who would rather be anything than what you are—if, that is, you had but the arrangement of society. The phenomena of human life, however, are much like those of the atmosphere; and we shall most likely not know rightly how to arrange these laws of the state, before we find ourselves able to cope successfully with the eccentricities of the sky. A gentleman-farmer once complained to one of his Irish labourers that the weather was not to his mind. "Och," said Pat, "your honour wouldn't mend the matter if you had the sun in one hand and a wather-pot in the other." Neither would our tinkering of the social kettle end in its holding water, if even we could contract for the job. In fact society is very much what its own blunders have made it. It is indeed the duty of every statesman to do for his country what Admiral Fitzroy is doing for the sailors—to learn, I mean, the laws of danger and to set up drums of caution; and in the next election you must choose the men who will do this best. But upon the whole, the best thing that any man can do who thinks that he finds himself out of place, is to remember that *he is beloved of God*, and that this *life is comparatively short*. If any man be unhappy in his place, let him reflect how many would be happy to be in the place that he is wishing to be out of; and let him pity the thousands who have no place that they can call their own. If any man murmur at having missed the blessedness of finding his work, let him with all solemnity bethink himself how many sweet souls, whom we can ill spare, are taken away without finding a work at all. But to you and to them, the grand blessing is, that by whatever way you go, you may, if only you learn to say "Thy will be done," live in the world, and then leave it, reconciled to your Father and your God.

And there is one last counsel on this head which I cannot but give. I give it, not in the way of religion—for by the strange contortions of modern necessity that ground is one on which I must not go too far, lest it involve me in a breach of rules which I above all am bound to obey;—but I introduce what I have to say as a *historical lesson*. Remember, my young friends, remember, I pray you, who was once apprenticed in the hot workshop of human life. Jesus was in a plight more hapless than the most unhappy of us. He, by all His powers—to say nothing of His Godhead, birth and heritage—by all His powers, I say, shown forth in His words, words open for anybody to read—He was fitted to sway the conclaves of mankind; yet, when there stood before His consciousness that mighty opening, what did He say? "*Get thee behind me*, thou enemy of man, and let me finish the work, with all its misery, which my heavenly Father hath given me to do. *Get thee behind me, Satan.*" And so He worked by day and prayed by night, first a carpenter, and then a missionary in the streets and lanes of that woebegone people. The foxes had holes, and the birds of the air had nests, but the Son of Man had not where to lay His head. He busied His great hands about poor folk, with all their little ailments; unbent himself from all mere human conceptions of greatness; chose the greatness of patient ministry, and without unseemly hurry postponed His genius to find its field in that long hereafter, in which we love to believe that He is waiting to draw us nearer to Himself. Thus it was that the devil left Him and the angels came.

I said when I began, that it was my duty to offer you some words of good omen, and therefore with that Name, which is above every name, I close what I had to say; and I will now ask my brother-in-law and old school-fellow, Professor Conington, to begin the lectures of our winter session, by reading to you Tennyson's new poem of "Enoch Arden."

WERTHEIMER, LEA & Co., Printers, Circus Place, London Wall.

CLAUDIA.

WHAT time the State of Rome began to grow,
'Twas told by the report of oracle,
That she could only flower to Empery
If in the girdle of her walls there came
The goddess of Pessinus. Whereupon
They sent their noblest on an embassage
To crave her marble form from Phrygia
(Whereof Pessinus was a little town):—
"Cousins," said these, "were they, of the whole blood,
"Sprung of the lordliest of the Phrygian lords,
"Æneas." Upon this that kindly folk
Let go their goddess. So with heedful joy
They laid her gently in the sunny lap
Of a fair ship to bring her home to Rome.
But when in course they came to Tiber mouth,
It seemed the pure divinity that lay
Immarbled there was heavy and displeased
By reason of some wrong, they knew not what.
Howe'er it was, the conscious ship stood still
And that, although the West implored her sail,
And the importunate waves, running apace,
On their white shoulders would have lifted her.
They haled, they strained—the stoutest arms in Rome
Tugged, till one said the very prow of her
Would part—and yet she stirred never an inch.

It chanced, if chance it was, the selfsame day
There was a maid of Vesta's nunnery,
Claudia by name, sweet as a violet,
Whom some lewd fellows of the baser sort
In low-tongued babble, gloating on some lie—
Some garbage in the sewage of their slums—
First low, then loud, charged with a deed of shame.
Of this she rightly recked not, till she found
That, like a swollen drain, they hurried her
To that Tarpeian rock, from whose high crag
They hurled frail Vestals. Then she rose and spake,
While all the ribald folk fell back from her—
"What I have done—why you, oh men, do this—

"I know not. Pessinuntia be my judge."
Then all the people said "Let her be judged
By Pessinuntia." So they led her down
To where the ship stood fast at Tiber-mouth.
And here she loosed the band that girded her
'Neath the fair place of snowy hemispheres
Unsullied ever by a print of sin—
And held it streaming forth and fluttering
All in the air of heaven, and straightway said
In hearing of them all, goddess and men,
Praying aloud—"Oh mother of the gods,
To whom my heart is known if innocent,
If guilty, known ; if I be found by thee
To be as one of thine—come on to Rome."
And then she wound her girdle in a noose,
And catching loosely the gay prow thereby
Held it aloft with airy finger-tip,
Like one that tices more than one that draws.
Before her sash could lose its light festoon
Lo what befell ; for that obedient craft—
Much like a swan that hastens to be fed,
When some sweet child holds bread upon the bank—
Came after her so willing, that the waves
Of that dread stream, which swallowed Silvia,
With merry music round about the prow
Danced up in curvy founts with silvery crest,
Pleased to the ground to make a way for her.
This was because the goddess who was there
Knew what she knew ; and what she knew was this :—
That that young vestal was as white in soul
As she was beautiful to look upon.
Then all the people came about the maid
Rejoicing with a tumult of delight,
And all made holiday the whole day long
Hailing the fair oracular augury
Of Empery with Pessinuntia.

SECOND THOUSAND.

AN
UNSPOKEN SPEECH,

MADE TO THE

Chichester Diocesan Conference,

AND TO ALL WHOM IT MAY NOW CONCERN, ON THE
ROAD HOME FROM

HORSHAM, OCTOBER, 1882,

BEING MAINLY THOUGHTS, IN SEQUENCE OF THE
LEADING NOTE GIVEN BY THE CONDUCTOR
OF OUR DIOCESE, UPON

The Salvation Army,

AND THE RELATION THERETO OF

OUR NATIONAL CHURCH;

BY THE

REV. WILLIAM B. PHILPOT,

BOGNOR, SUSSEX.

Author of "A Pocket of Pebbles;" "Selections from the above," made by
Bryce & Son, Glasgow, for their Miniature Series; Vol. of Sermons, reprinted
from "Church of England Pulpit," and others, including "Law, the Forerunner of the Gospel," preached in Westminster Abbey on the occasion of
the Opening of the New Law Courts (in the Press); &c., &c.

---

*"The Lord prosper you: we wish you good luck in the Name
of the Lord."*

PRICE TWOPENCE

PRINTED BY H. W. MARDON,
THE WEST SUSSEX STATIONERY AND GENERAL STORES.

THE SALVATION ARMY.

My Lord Bishop, my Lords, and Gentlemen, clerical and lay, and all ye sober Churchmen whom this may reach, give eye, I humbly pray you, to my speech—

Apart from all that can, or ever may, be regarded by any one as being wild, eccentric, or fanatical in this movement, which gives itself the aggressive name of "The Salvation Army," the fact which must strike every reflecting mind is this :—that up from the people themselves, and wholly apart from their parochial organization, there has come and is coming a præter-ecclesiastical, a subter-sectarian, nay a superhuman flood of new spiritual life. This is due neither to the Church, nor to opposition to the Church. It is a new, but yet an old phenomenon. The old, old story, but in a more popular version, and in a cheaper edition.

All great religious movements have, as histories bear witness, sprung from the masses of the people. It was so first of all with the preaching of the Lord Himself. The Church of that nation stood aloof in disdain and hate; and, while the common people heard Jesus gladly, she said "This people that knoweth not the law—be d——d." And so that venerable Established Church with zealous deliberation, in the name of Religion, and to maintain its ritual, crucified the Preacher, saying "His Blood be on us and on our children."

It was the same in the days of the Reformation. The Lord gave the word: great was the multitude of the preachers. Popes with their Bishops did flee and were discomfited, and they of the household, with many who were not of the household, divided the spoil—but not till all the leaders of that movement, whom she could catch, had been burnt alive by that old Romish Church, whose millstone of Infallibility is drowning her in the depth of her unrepented, irrevocable Past.

Again, the Reformed Church settled upon her pillows and composed herself to slumber. But some (they were her own ministers it is true) alive with the fire of the Holy Ghost, lit anew the souls of the people. The common people through the length and breadth of the land heard the Wesleys gladly. But what did the Church do? She turned them out of her communion, and, like the heathen magistrates, forbade these new apostles to preach in her fabrics. If a Church, as well as a man, can commit the sin against the Holy Ghost, the Church of this country did so then: nor has it been forgiven her. She will suffer the penalty of it to the end of time, and perhaps the like temper will be her ultimate ruin. Yet let us be thankful that no mad claim to Infallibility shuts *her* off from the careful and tearful seeking for some place of repentance.

Newman and his followers tried afterwards in their own way, and not wholly without a certain kind and measure of success, to revive our Church. This movement had about it much of the old ultramontane madness, which showed itself by many, and they the most logical of them, rushing down that steep place, and being lost in the abysmal superstition. Nay, the same virus works still in the "Anglican" blood, in that so many hold to the fetish, which, as that singular man himself told me, was the heart of the Romish system. These remain where they are, only because they think they have discovered that an "Anglican" Rome is preferable to an Italian. But before the Church made this frantic effort to come back to her sacerdotal activities, the people, as I have said, had come to the rescue, and reformed, so far as they then could, the Christianity of England.

Thus it is from the people, we see, that amidst all their other and more questionable movements, these great and holy Revolutions also take their rise. The vile ingredients of a nation float up into frothy plutocracy, into dangerous prosperity, into imposing hierarchies; or else stagnate, and diffuse some festering form of social miasma. But the best hope of Christianity still lies mainly below the surface, and lives in the ever rising phases of the infinite resources of the multitude. As a tradesman looks for his profits, not to his few wealthy and fickle customers, but, as any shopkeeper will tell you, to the gathered half-pence of the market-day, so the muckle fortunes of Christendom will always come from the multitudinous mickles of the children of the people.

The Church however of late years has not, thank God, been idle. She has rubbed her eyes and looked about her. She has learned the wisdom to watch how the people rouse each other. Plans which before she haughtily regarded as the vulgar modes of an uncultivated dissent, and the mere "madness of the people," she very sensibly herself begins to adopt. I do not know that they have actually brought the sinners to "the penitent bench," but, like the Primitive Methodists, they have in the very Metropolis gone down in their surplices among the seats of those whom their preaching had excited, and asked in whispers "if they had got it," or have used words to the same effect; and they have adopted the very name of the "Class Meeting." All this has been on the right track; but it is late, if not too late, for the Church's credit; nor has it been done on the scale which popular need had arisen to demand.

And now the self-same spirit which has thus moved even the stiffer and more formal tempers of Churchmen, and which long ago, between the days of Wesley and Newman, had moved the spirits of Simeon and his good old Evangelists—antipathy to whom gave in fact its main impetus to that Romano-Tractarian revival—this spirit, stealing a march upon the slow-going Establishment, has beyond all assignable bounds seized, as we cannot but hear and see, upon the spirit of the population. We note that a new spring-tide of Grace has risen to the flood, and is sweeping over all precedented and recognised channels. It covers all the old landmarks like an inundation, and is refreshing with the noise of its waters the farthest creeks of the haunts of the people. They call it "The Salvation Army"; nor ever certainly was the Church of Christ—perhaps even in Apostolic times—in a spiritual sense more militant.

Huxley, you may remember, thought, and for what I know has reason still to think, that he found in the deep seas a reservoir of vitality, which he called Bathybius, or life in the depth, ever ready to rise beneath the fructifying sunlight, and to break up into all forms of being—of plant, animal, and man. Whether his rival scientists were correct in their surmise that what he thought he had found was but some residuary effect of alcohol, I know not, nor here very profoundly care—except that I should be sorry to find that so beautiful an illustration of the facts of humanity had proved unfounded. At any rate, whether the illustration be fallacious or not, this illustrandum no less holds true; namely, that in the deep sea of this ever-multiplying Humanity there is an infinite resource of the best vitality. The Personal Source of all life generates it there; and He in His hour is sure to bring it to the surface. This is necessary by that law of change and growth with which His indwelling Spirit vivifies the whole body of Being.

Let me here pause and ask—is not this a notable lesson to all Churches? The Church, we see, in all its national forms, must once and for ever forego the narrow notion that the origination and initiation of the ministry of the Spirit, Who proceeds from the Father and the Son, rests wholly with herself. I am afraid our venerable Establishment fancied herself sitting in Christendom as sole mistress of the situation; when, lo and behold, up comes before her eyes from the streets and alleys, the lanes and slums of the nation, a force of spiritual protoplasm which must make her perceive that, for the time at least, though she harbour the most kindly feeling for the movement, she is, in point of fact, "nowhere" in respect to it. She feels, nor that without a somewhat comic consternation, that this force gets the whip-hand of her, takes the reins out of her hands, and takes the wind out of her sails. See how the people arise and assert their right to the Spirit of Jesus—and that, I repeat, wholly apart from any agency of the authorised and ancient Priest. While the old Romish Church is battling with the newer Churches; while the parties within our own Church, whatever good they also may be doing, are bickering with one another about antique rites and ceremonial modes of posture and costume, these woe-begone wretches, these abandoned drunkards start up by thousands, find to their ecstatic delight that they also are each one of them children of the King, and vindicate to themselves each his personal Priesthood. Every one of them turns, as if by a flash of miracle, into a minister and an evangelist. The Lord again gives the word, and great is the multitude of the preachers. We may repeat with the Apostle of Pentecost—for I see that only the other day there were in some theatre or public hall another 3,000 on their knees, many of whom perhaps had never prayed before—we may quote with St. Peter the words of the prophet Joel. Mr. or Mrs. Booth, or anybody else, is at liberty to stand up with all the "successors of the Apostles," and use St. Peter's very words—nay our own beloved Bishop of Chichester charmed many of us at the Conference by much the same language, when he gave the key-note to the splendid address of Mr. Hubbard and to the just and noble sentiments of Canon Awdry, Principal of our Theological College. What did Mr. Hubbard utter but the same words, or words to the same purport, as those used first by Joel and then by Peter? "Ye men of England, and all ye that gather to the Conference at Horsham, be this known unto you and give ear unto my words. For these are not fanatics, as ye suppose; but this is that which hath been spoken by the prophet Joel—

'And it shall be in the last days, saith God,
I will pour forth my spirit upon all flesh:
And your sons and your daughters shall prophesy,
And your young men shall see visions,
And your old men shall dream dreams.
Yea upon my servants and my handmaidens in those days
Will I pour forth my Spirit, and they shall prophecy.
* * * * * *
And it shall be, that whosoever shall call on
The Name of the Lord shall be saved.'"

Thus we see the unlimited, illimitable Spirit of the Omnipotent and Universal Father is taking this matter of Salvation into His own hands. How should the Spirit of the Life-Source be bound by all our cautious routine and by modes of procedure palpably and confessedly antiquated? And, I am sure few of us, if any—though some by their temper at the Conference might seem to say so—can be so unobservant, so narrow, so churlish, so unimaginative, so like the dog in the manger, as to stand aloof, sulk in their dark Church corners, and be chagrined if they find that by any means, however unorthodox, the souls of these poor unreached countrymen of ours are calling upon the name of the Lord and being saved? Would you have these helpless people die under "regular practice" or in utter neglect of all remedial measures, rather than be saved by physicians of

The Spirit, who prove themselves gifted with this rare insight, this new power to heal? God forbid that such should be the creeping meanness of any ministers of Religion. If our venerable Church of England is anything, she at least is lady-like; and would it, I ask, be gracious, would it betoken good manners, if she were to deny to this movement of Salvation that consideration which is its due? The least methinks we should do, if we cannot for one reason or another take part in it, is, like Manoah and his wife, to stand by and prayerfully watch how wondrously some angel of the Lord is working, "confounding our ignorance and amazing indeed our very faculties of eyes and ears."

Yet it were surely not well for us merely to stand by. Are we so muddy-mettled, so unpregnant of our Cause and theirs, that we are to peak like John-a-dreams and that we can say nothing to cheer on these poor soldiers of our King—upon whose property and most dear life such foul defeats are being made in the masses of our population? We must do more than stand and look on with our hands in the pocket of our cassocks—if, that is to say, we would not forego, and turn traitors to, the very principles of our Master. With all these impotent and diseased folk standing on the edge of this new Bethesda, shall we not be in a false and most inhumane position if we also, in our own way, do not spring forward while the water is being stirred, and help some of them to go down into it? No doubt we must always feel somewhat abashed, pained, humiliated, and generally uncomfortable, to think that this boiling-well of wholesale conversion did not bubble up through our own good old Church spring. But let us be glad that as yet it is all on our own premises. Let us thankfully apply what Christ said on this head. Let us remember and take note that "other sheep He has," though at present not all of this His "Anglican" fold. I verily believe there are some good easy souls who fancy that the Church to which they belong is the only footpath to Heaven, and that in Heaven all the Saints will have used, and with slight variations will for ever use, the Church of England formularies and the Liturgy of the Act of Uniformity.

The attitude of the Church should be, as it commends itself to me, to say with open heart to God, while thankfully watching these diversities of His operations, " Here am I also : send me." " Bless me, even me also, oh my Father : bless me and my ministry with this new power of turning souls from darkness to light, from the power of Satan unto Thee."

As the Persian proverb says—
> All skirts extended of thy mantle hold
> When angel hands from Heaven are scattering gold.

While the people are holding wide their laps for it, let our Church also be God's almoners in this largess of blessing. Indeed it was evident that this was the feeling and spirit of the leaders of our Sussex Conference. The whole of a morning's sitting was devoted to this inspiriting topic. You, my Lord Bishop, in your address at the outset, urged the subject upon us with the most affectionate solemnity. Mr. Hubbard, with unanswerable force, took up the pleading. Canon Awdry covered the only ground of objection by his wise and well-put reminder that " *Vulgarity is not Sin ;* " and the interest excited was so great that the branches of the discussion ran over the wall, and reached up to the last hour of our meeting—hardly leaving time " to give " Mr. Mundella " his due."

At the same time I own it is a most delicate and difficult question, how a Church like ours can best fulfil at a crisis like this functions which are obviously her own.

With the due retention of her great and rightful reverence, her ancestral dignity, and her calm and orderly culture, it is not to be expected, and the good taste of those gentlemen who at present are her Bishops and ministers would not allow, that with crozier and mitre, pastoral staff and cassock, our Church should plunge headfirst and rush pell-mell into this Carnival of Conversion. Is it not her very function to school ignorance, to curb excesses, to tame what is wild, and " to make mild a rugged people and subdue them to the useful and the good"? Whereto, we may ask, serves Culture but to confront, if need be, the visage of fanaticism? And yet I know full well this congenital temper of hers is sure and certain to bring down upon her the heavy and, I trust upon the whole, unjust charge of carnality, of lack of spirituality, and of lukewarmness in the great Cause, which, God knows, we have at heart.

The other day an "evangelist," as he styled himself, called upon me as Vicar, and asked me to lend my sanction to his preaching in my parish. I conversed with him for three hours, and, though I found that he was disposed to work on different lines from mine, yet, having given him certain due cautions and received assurances of his consent to my obvious caveats and restrictions, I told him he might try and gain a hearing on a Thursday night in my licensed Cottage-Church—a building in which the people of that hamlet take a singular delight and a pardonable pride, and whither they crowd to hear our Church of England gospel—a building which you, my Lord, having robed (but not, that I remember, having at the moment found occasion to refresh) yourself at the Royal Oak hard by, my young friend bearing your pastoral staff, opened for me with your blessing, and an address which won all hearts. At the close of the Sunday evening service this evangelist rose, and, without (as he afterwards assured me) meaning any offence at all, he managed in one sentence to rouse the whole rustic assembly to indignation. "Come on Thursday," he said, "you will have something very different from what you are accustomed to: we'll soon fill this old barn." This was in the presence of my excellent and earnest lay-reader, licensed by the Bishop, to whom the poor folk had lately given a sweet and kindly testimonial and £10 worth of valuable books of divinity. The consequence was that the good farmer who acts as Churchwarden, and to whom this loose evangelist had not told that he had my permission, summarily ordered our large-hearted Congregational Board-School Mistress, (who brings all her children to my Sunday-School to teach them the Church-Catechism, and who was now seated at the harmonium) to play up and stop his harangue. Next morning I was informed by two members of my Parochial Council of what had passed. There was no course left for me but to withdraw from this hot-headed, but no doubt excellent "evangelist" the permission which I had felt I could not but grant. I believed the man to be capable of turning souls from the power of Satan unto God ; but, as I told him, he had here cut the ground from under his feet. He took the matter fairly well, and made his explanations ; but with sad deliberation he felt bound by his conscience to inform me that I showed " an absence of the Holy Ghost." He did not charge me, which I would sadly have confessed, with sad shortcomings, but he denied point blank my having part or lot in the matter ; and with *plusquam*-Papal authority he questioned my having any mission from that Divine Person by Whom I believed, and still believe myself called to the sacred ministry of The Word. Well, I thanked him, without any touch of irony, for his candour, and told him it would interest, and possibly benefit me much, if he would point out to me the "grave errors" which he said he had discovered in me, and that, when he had done this by letter, I should be pleased, after self-examination had, to speak with him again. I mention this incident to show how this rising spirit of independent evangelisation—this guerrilla warfare of fiery voluntaries—(though it is fair to say that this man did not work with the " Salvation Army ") must almost necessarily clash with the ordered ways of such a Church as ours. The "dancing dervish" (not that I call this good man by that name) will doubtless find his counterpart even in Christianity, as indeed the history of Religion has shown. And there will always be those earnest and even useful men, who will, as a matter of course, scorn and outlaw the measured tread of perhaps a too sober-suited wisdom.

But are these honest folk, amidst their toil and moil, to be denied the liberty of breaking into such merriment as gracious Heaven may mercifully provide for them? Are the visages of Churchmen to cream and mantle in their presence like a standing pond? Are we to blacken these newborn souls, and, with the Pharisees, to say "these men speak blasphemy," if we see them, now that their back is lightened of its life-long load—I do not say *dancing* like the sweet Psalmist-King before their new-found Ark (for never do *they* so far forget themselves!)—but if we see them, forgetting their sorrows, burst into such "original poetry" as suits them? It is a matter of profound regret that a noble and venerable Lord, eminent hitherto for his piety, has lately used this heavy word "blasphemy" of those who mean to speak no hurt. *Vix datur hæc venia antiquitati.*

It is bad enough if at the dinner-tables of "society" a certain crabbed and unnatural reserve ousts by common consent topics of the most sublime and stirring interest. I remember Lord Radstock, a man instinct with the divine life—who goes about like his Master, doing good—telling me with infinite gusto, how that once at such a lively reunion there befel in the general hubbub of common talk, a chance pause, which rendered audible from the lips of a sweet-souled lady sitting by his side, the Name of JESUS. He narrates how the Name fell like a bomb-shell into that party. Host and hostess, Statesmen, and even dignitaries of the Church looked nervously this way and that, and never was harmless bread so crumbled by disconcerted fingers. What! Is the worldling, making merry with his friends, to be allowed to vent forth at will his rollicking jests, and, thumping among his imperilled glasses, to vindicate, half-drunken with wine wherein is excess, the agreeableness of some questionable boon-companion and reiterate to nausea his intention of not retiring till the dawn? And yet, I ask, are these good folk, when filled with the genuine spirit of the Pauline brand, to have no way allowed to *them* of letting off their hilarity? Do we suppose that the Hallelujah lads and Hosanna lasses of Jerusalem, when they marched that day with the youthful Sovereign of their hearts, moving all the city, and especially vexing the local-boardsmen by destroying the foliage of the palm-trees, do we imagine that they were all so highly proper, so very refined, and so exceedingly reverential in the exuberance of their delight? They that use only delicate expressions have their own swept and garnished drawing-rooms; but how can we expect the denizens of the court-yard and the slum to make the melody of their heart in the strains of the Court and after the fashion of Eaton-square? "Leave them alone"—says CHRIST. If these hold their peace, the very paving-stones will find tongues. If we are so extreme to mark what is done, or said, or sung amiss, how many of our Church hymns—apart, I mean, from their hazy doggrel—shall be found to hold water? Was not the first Litany of the Church " a popular supplication, sung or shouted, not "within the walls of any consecrated building, but by "wild excited multitudes, following in long files, through "street and field, over hill and valley, as if to bid Nature "join in the depth of their contrition?" Let me pursue the language of the historian, who being dead yet speaketh. The late Dean of Westminster, in his last and, as I think, his most striking book called "Christian Institutions" [page 235] writes as follows:—

" It is well to remember that the goodness of a thing de-
"pends not on its outward form, but on its inward spirit. The
" very word ' Litany ' in its first origin, included long processions,
" marches to and fro, cries and screams, which have now disap-
" peared almost everywhere from public devotions, even in the
" Roman Catholic Church. Those who established it would not
" have imagined that a Litany without these accompaniments would
" have any efficacy whatever. We know that the accompaniments

"were mere accidents and that the substance has continued. What "has happened with the Litany has occurred again and again with "every part of our ecclesiastical system. Always the form and the "letter are perishing; always there will be some who think that "the form and the letter are the thing itself. Generally in the "Christian Church there is enough vitality to keep the spirit, "though the form is changed; generally, we trust, as in the Litany, "so elsewhere, there will be found men wise enough and bold "enough to retain the good and throw off the bad in all the various "forms of our religious and ecclesiastical life."

Yea, even though adult and ordered communities have discarded some of those tokens of undue excitement and spiritual ectasy which our friends of the Salvation Army will soon learn to abandon, yet throughout our own formularies, as in the "Te Deum" and "Benedicite," the keynote remains of much celestial jocundity; and it is plain that our glorias, our Hosannas, and our Hallelujahs were not meant by the pious minds who left them with us to be muttered with doleful visage and monotonous drawl, but rather to be uttered so as to rend the heaven with jubilation.

As for the *humour* of these enthusiastic souls, is it not a part of their new life? Why should they not enjoy to the full this great and almost sole reason left them for joy—persons who for the most part were in this life of all men the most miserable, till this bright and balmy effulgence broke upon them from above? Their hearts before knew their own bitterness, and let strangers to their new joy take heed how they intermeddle with it. Why not, at least, leave them with their great military metaphor to turn it about and play with it as they please? This high and quaint humour is in point of fact the most wholesome sign about the movement. Let Church and State be thankful that they are no longer, as their spiritual ancestors were, grim iconoclasts humming their surly hymns, and let us be content that the only antiquities they wish to break down are the strongholds of Satan in the hearts of our people. Those souls alone can in fact rightly afford to be merry, who also know how to be

wise unto Salvation. Have not the holiest men found a
buoyant satisfaction in venting their humour, sometimes
in the very moment of death? May not humour serve
as the panacea of the worst ills, the correction of the
most dangerous follies, and the transfiguring garb of the
best emotions? If we only cultivated more humour—
of course good humour—in the way of looking at things,
do you think these inanities and insanities over which
now we have to wail in Church and State, would stand
against it for a generation? This *Erinys* which haunts
us now, making wise men weep, would soon hurry from
our precincts. Is not humour one of the most divine
and saving elements in our existence? Is it not a faculty
of which most of us—I can speak for one—peculiarly
admire and envy the happy possessor? And surely our
Conference of Chichester, so long as we have among us
our pious and genial Dean—(genial, except, I regret to
say, sometimes with his pen, and sometimes when
speaking on such topics as these) ought we not to be the
last body in the world to object to throwing a spice of
humour into solemnities? When he himself was urging
with masterly force the importance of the holy function
of the lay-agent, who would have been willing to miss the
inimitable and inevitable —I had almost said histrionic
—gesture with which he expressed his horror at the smell
of boot-leather from under the sideboard of the clerical
secretary of some Shoe-Club? These touches, I venture
to affirm, were quite the last portions of those speeches of
our good Dean, which, while he spoke on the Salvation
Army, we would willingly have spared. We should
think it very hard if Mr. Booth had cavilled at those
outbreaks of humour, as being out of place in that discussion—solemn as it was—in the presence of our
Ordinary, who, if I mistake not, himself cared not to
conceal his smile. We cannot afford to be too hard on
the "Army," if in those Feasts of Booths they break
out into these sallies of religious hilarity. Nay, if it
comes to that, when we examine closely, and without

the prejudice of habit, the language of the *dolce Maestro* Himself, do we not find it redolent of pleasantry? *Sed hæc hactenus.*—Let us be content to note with interest the manner of our awakened people, and not hurt their poor souls and "hunt them to make them fly" by bearing down upon them too hardly with our ancestral propriety. The "Hallelujah lass" was in point of fact the very handmaid that Joel had in his mind, and Peter before his eyes at Pentecost, with the Spirit poured out upon her. Let it suffice that they do not *mean* to be blasphemous.

Still, however all this may be, here is this great movement to be dealt with; and, like some ill-broken and mettlesome leader in the hands of a driver unaccustomed to his team, the question turns round and stares us in the face. If our self-consciousness makes cowards of Churchmen, and if we allow our dignified countenances to be sicklied o'er by the pale cast of over-long reflection, why then in the Church's hands this enterprise of great pith and moment will turn its current awry from us, and for us will lose the name of action. Nothing, I grant, can require more prayerful wisdom and more careful thought. But one thing is certain—that hesitation will be as fatal to us as a declension of the combat. The battle is the Lord's, and in His name, with all our Christian armour on, we must descend into the arena. We need not in all things go with them, lest we be partakers of their mistakes. But how can we set ourselves against them? We must take heed "lest haply we be found fighting against God!" There *are* however movements of Christian energy, which are *not* those of the dervish, and there are modes of spreading the Redeemer's kingdom, which are *not* those of the fanatic. Such modes we must discover and adopt forthwith. And it is a comfort to remember that the English are after all a sane people; and that therefore, as all undue excitement dies down, and when these wild commotions, this "eager" on the river of popular Christianity has run its course and begun to subside, they will thankfully allow their own Church, which in some respects is the sanest there is, to help them to come to GOD through CHRIST by any channels which her gravity and common sense will shew to be navigable.

One of the most palpable modes is Lay Agency, of which so much was said at the Conference, both in the direction of Parochial Councils and by the employment in Church ministrations of authorised persons other than the Clergy. As there are some who for various reasons have gone, and perhaps still go, into Holy Orders without being specially fitted for it, so it is very clear that there are many, who, being specially fitted for it, yet, for reasons equally various, do not go into Holy Orders. The main principle of the Christian life is to push the Kingdom. The main sign of vitality is to desire to do this by all and any practicable means. Every man who has life in himself is naturally constrained by the Love of CHRIST to bring others to a "knowledge of the truth." The reserve of that man who declined to save another from drowning because he had not been introduced to him, is unknown to the genuine Christian. Like that river-weed introduced a few years ago from America, which, propagating itself by the life which every joint supplies, has began to choke the river-system of England, so, with rapidity no less astonishing, the Christian life, breaking off at each joint, multiplies itself in an untold ratio. Nothing has ministered more to dissent, and made, if I may so say, more dissenting ministers than this law of the new nature. Freedom naturally gives energetic Christian people scope for speaking forth those glorious truths of the inner life which they have seen and heard. The Church, if she would work out her splendid chances of doing her proper work, must go and do likewise. The common people not only hear CHRIST gladly, but *speak* Him gladly; and surely we should gladly further their doing so. The country is now, as we see, full of these irregular forces of the best type of life. Dry bones are happily beginning again to revive in almost every valley and village, town and city. As in the vision of the prophet, do we not see them starting up into armed hosts, and turning to flight the armies of the aliens?

But there is an idea abroad—not, alas, wholly without foundation—that our beloved and ancient Church is stagnant, effete, incapable of revivification, a dumb old institution, and in many parts still sleeping, lying down, loving to slumber.

I went to the house of an elderly female not long ago, and opened fire by saying in the most suave and winning manner of which I was master, "I hope you find a comfortable seat in Church, Mrs. Richards, where you can hear me well?" She bridled up and said with a magnificent *hauteur* "Church! why, bless the Lord, I was 'brought out' 30 years ago, come Whitsuntide." I fear that venerable lady spoke the language of many multitudes. The contrast between their view of conversion and ours is at present like that between light and darkness. While *we* are apt to regard the making our neighbours into good Churchmen as the bringing them out of darkness into light, *they* are also too apt to regard the leaving of the Church and joining the ranks of some form of dissent as a coming into light out of darkness! Too many of the more serious of our fellow countrymen, I fear, regard awakening, conversion, and all vitality as a thing quite out of the question within what they call the cold shade of our precincts. Now it is plain that, if our Church cares, or means, to survive, the people must be disabused of this disastrous misconception. We must go out into the highways, streets and lanes, and not be too nice how we compel them to come in. It is our function and our mission, and in doing so we must obtain all the help we can. This cannot be done only by the clergy, nor can they be much helped merely by men who are simply endowed with a dull respectability, **and** who do it solely for a livelihood. The labourer is of course worthy of his hire, and this must in each case be settled justly and to mutual and common satisfaction; but the main point is that every man who is to sow the good seed of the Kingdom must first have some of it in his own heart—else how can he effectually sow it? There happily *are* such persons, and there are plenty of them, and they grow under culture, both spiritually and numerically—persons, both men and women, who have not only the spirit of power and a sound mind, but who have the spirit of a glowing and all-embracing love. They must not be persons who cannot speak; rather they must be men and women who *cannot but* speak the blessed things they know. And here let me add, that it gave me no little surprise to find that no one reminded the Conference, while upon the subject of lay-agency, that our Bishop has a special Form of Service (of which I have myself experienced the advantage), for the ordering and licensing of lay-agents.

It has been said most truly, but said, I fear, not wholly with the right *animus*, that the Church is not congregational, but parochial. And this, if it means anything, means that the clergy and people must in every way and in diversities of operations *work together*. The *Parochial* idea is in fact the only mean between the *sacerdotal* and the *communistic*. If you wish to make proper use of lay-agency, it must be done by a co-agency which must be parochial.

Let me on this head quote the sentiments of a statesman, the brilliancy and utility of whose past career is but the promise of a still more splendid and useful future and whose pronounced attachment to our National Church is in these days a matter for profound congratulation. Speaking at Rugby on November 29th, 1881, Mr. Goschen said:—

"There is one form of possible local activity which I fear is "utopian, but which, if practicable, would be a great civilising "influence. The workhouse is not the only building in the "parish. There is another public building, not the refuge of "despair, but the sanctuary of holy hopes, the building round

" which cluster memories of the most sacred moments of family
" life—the Parish Church. Would that more power could be
" given to Parishioners to associate themselves with the manage-
" ment of the Church, which, whatever the definition of the law
" may be, is after all *their* Church! Would that *the laity might be*
" *given some voice in parish business connected with the church, its*
" *services, and its charitable work!* The despotic sway of the
" parish incumbent is opposed to the whole spirit of the age. It
" is, in my judgment, dangerous to the interests of the Church.
" But *a distinct and visible connexion of the national lay element*
" *with the local management of the Church would strengthen the*
" *foundations of religion, soften sectarian distinctions, and open up*
" *a fresh and most ennobling influence in local life.*"

It is only by the lively, and growingly lively portion of our laity working with us, that the Church can, I will not say counteract—GOD forbid—but by co-operation turn into national channels that spiritual life which already is welling forth in other directions; and this for her own sake as well as for the sake of the nation.

Mr. Hubbard, in soothing the fears of those who were for drawing alarming pictures of what this Salvation Army might drift into, said very wisely "we need not trouble ourselves about its future." By this he doubtless meant, that, if we for our parts deal rightly with its present, its morrow will take thought for the things of itself. But, by a parity of reasoning, that thoughtful speaker would agree with me, and in fact himself also implied, that in the alternative case, in the case of our *not* dealing wisely with its present phase, there *is very great ground* for our being "troubled about its future." Our beloved National Church is beset—within perhaps even more than without—by bitter and unrelenting enemies, who wish it not so much to be sensibly reformed as to be nationally destroyed. We have good and ample proof that the serious and religious spirits of existing Nonconformity are disposed to break off from these, and to say "Destroy it *not*, for a blessing is in it." But the Liberation Society, which methinks had been better called the Vivisection Society—for never was there contemplated so gross and grievous an act of vivisection as that which would cut the spirit out of the body politic—has for its one cry "Down with it, down with it, even to the ground." These men, both in the length and breadth of the country, and in the House of Representatives, hate and dread nothing so much as to note among Churchmen any of the vitality and reality of reformation. The coming conflict will be so mortal that we shall not be able to cope with the Enemy, unless we throw aside every weight and the sins which most easily beset Establishments. We must shame the adversaries by abjuring every blame which attaches to us, and we must strengthen our alliances with all that is sound and healthy, holy and vigorous in the manhood and womanhood of the Nation. We might perhaps hope to grapple successfully with bodies of men whom the candour of public opinion would perceive to be but reckless and Godless gangs of political freebooters; but if these are, for totally different reasons, joined in the conflict by a contingent who have, or who might fairly be thought to have, divine right on their side, then it is only too clear that the day will be lost to us, for the battle will not then wholly be the LORD's—and the LORD's side is in the long run of course certain to win. Here is a vast body, an "army" of persons who take for their oriflamme to-day the word "Salvation." Their motto is not "dissent," but "consent":—"Let all who name the name of CHRIST depart from iniquity. Save yourselves from this untoward generation; save yourselves from drink, from lust, from filth, from degradation, from all manner of vice and every form of sin. Let JESUS bring you out of your misery into the embrace of your Heavenly Father." "We beseech you"—say they to those whom *we* have failed to reach—the rough, ribald, and lawless population—to those who are the worst difficulty alike of the Church and of the State—"we beseech you," say they, "in CHRIST's Name, be ye reconciled unto GOD." Why, is not to do this thing the very work and mission of our own National Church?

Is the Church of the Nation to taboo and outlaw from her sympathy such missioners of national blessing? Are we to stand trifling, and picking and choosing, and raving at those whom the Spirit of GOD Himself has beyond doubt chosen for His instruments? Are *we*, because of any formal differences in their operations, and because we have been too stupid and slow-hearted to understand modes of popular conversion, with which others have been long familiar—are we at this juncture "to stand at gaze like Joshua's moon in Ajalon," and, instead of bidding them with all our hearts " GOD speed," disclaim or damn with faint praises their magnificent crusade? Our late Archbishop, to whom our Bishop so feelingly referred, and one of whose last acts was to send them help and lend them his name, with our Bishop himself in his grave and fatherly monitions, have set us a far nobler example.

But if we *do* take the contrary part, now let me advertise to you what will come to pass—for here is one reason among many why in the out-look we may well "trouble ourselves about their future." Remember that this Salvation Army is also an Army of Voters. "General Booth," an ominous name, will, when the question, which is now rapidly gathering head, breaks out anew—that question which I have called the vivisection of the Church from the State—be General at the Pollingbooth. Which side is he to take *then?* Ask yourselves that. If we ignore his "Army"—much more if we oppose them—if thus we take the part of those powers of evil which they oppose—if we stand by the side of the national drunkard, the national libertine, the national blasphemer, in reviling those who would turn them to GOD—what reason can we show why they should not then side with the Vivisectionist? Why should not "General Booth" say when that day comes "Your old Church has proved itself rotten at the core—cut it down, why cumbereth it the ground?" You refused to come in the day of *our* battle to the help of the LORD against the mighty—can you expect us to side with you in *your* battle-day? While *we* jeoparded all our fortunes in the high-places of the field, why abodest *thou*, oh Church of the nation, in the sheepfold, listening to the bleating of thy priests? Our evangelists came and fought, kings and priests unto GOD, fought against the forces of the English heathen in the highways and in the theatres, by the waters of Thames and Tyne, of Avon and of Severn. Our river of Salvation was sweeping heathenism away, that ancient river, our river of Salvation. Why did you leave us to tread down their strength alone? Curse ye the Church of the nation (the General may be apt to say), curse ye bitterly the priests thereof, because they came not to the help of the LORD, to the help of the LORD against the mighty."

Thus, we see, this question of how we are to deal with this "Salvation Army" becomes a very practical one, and may *indeed* give us "trouble about their future."

The great question of the Rules of Procedure has been before the nation. What is to be the rule of *their* procedure? If we do not take good heed and be reconciled to them, whiles we are in the way with them, (the Church of England *reconciled* to those who are for saving England!) it is very plain that they and their representatives, soon to be redistributed and largely enfranchised, will step in by the side of the Spirit of Devastation; and then it will be by no bare majority, but by a very overwhelming majority, that they will overwhelm the Church—nay, stop as obstructives the mouths of her advocates—of men who never should have been *their* adversaries. The venerable Mother-Church will thus fall—e'en at the base of Bradlaugh's statua—fall by the wounds of those who had sought earnestly to be her friends.

My Lord Bishop, Lords and brethren of the Conference, let it not be so. Let us on every ground, on grounds of that public Christian honesty which is always, and here obviously, the best policy, welcome their co-operation—nay, co-operate with them so far as we fairly and safely can; so that, in the great battle-day which is coming, this sister Army may come up and help the cause of our Church, which should be the constant cause of the best blessings to the people. Let General Booth— for when I speak of that one man, I speak, remember, of a man whose voice carries with it a multitudinous mandate—let the good "General" be able to say, now and always, " My heart is towards the Governors of our Christian Israel, towards the Archbishops and Bishops and ministers of the Church, that offered themselves willingly among the people." Then there will be mighty reason for Great Britain, sitting under her historic oak-tree, to exclaim " Bless ye the LORD."

One last word. There are two great waves now rolling to meet each other at the Harbour-mouth of the Haven where we would be. There is the wave of Atheism —practical Atheism—for it will now more clearly be seen who serveth the LORD and who serveth Him not. There is no longer any halting between two opinions. That is *one* terrible oncoming wave. The other is this divine wave of popular conversion. This Church of ours will fare ill, if her Ark, declining to be carried on with this wave of GOD, be tossed in hopeless wreck on the meeting crests of these deadly opposites. The only course for those who stand at her helm, is to make common cause with all those who name in sincerity of love the name of the LORD JESUS. For love of the brethren is after all the true test of our love of the Master; and those who lay the working of the Spirit of GOD to the power of the Evil One and to mere Fanaticism, are in the fair way for falling into that sin which cannot be forgiven, either in this world, or in that which is to come.

If my unspoken speech, for which I crave all needful indulgence, has, for unavoidable reasons, come late, it is not too late for its object, and it cannot at least be said to lack the merit of deliberation.

EDUCATION AND PERMISSIVE BILLS.

(PART OF A PROLOGUE TO PENNY-READINGS.)

* * * * * * *

Now, while the preacher cries, and cries what's true:
"In all we seek we seek not yours but you,"
We, friends, who bring you to these school-room doors,
Must frankly own we seek not you, but yours!
We have our "little winning ways" to win ye;
We do not hunt you up to get your guinea;
But, penny-wise, we draw you by good sense
To get your pound's worth while you pay your pence;—
Tho' not a few, I'm glad to see, are willing
To pay our Penny Readings with "the splendid shilling."

Forster, Right Honourable W. E.,
Has sent a little Bill to you and me:
Says he—"To argue further profits nought,
"I tell you, these small fry must all be taught.
"Lest Tom become a rake, and Jack a fool,
"And Sall a slut,—they *must* be sent to school.
"These are the future salmon of the state:
"Teach 'em to climb without or with a Rate;
"Send 'em where'er you list, but mark me still,
"If you won't send 'em somewhere, Forster will."
So, willy-nilly, as we must befriend 'em,
We must provide big rooms to which to send 'em;
But all this outlay how can *we* afford?
Bored we might be by Schools with that School Board.

Yet schools are moral sewers, to deliver
Folly and vice to Time's all-sweeping river;
Drainage, or Trainage, lo! our plight is such,
We must lay little out to save us much.
'Tis thus by these few pence you save the State—
And, what of course is more, you save the Rate!

All said and done, 'tis so we best forestall
The sore temptations that beset us all;
The reason why men topple into crime
Is that they know so ill to spend their time;
But if from tender years and early youth
We learn the sacred secrets of the Truth,
And grow to use the powers kind Heaven hath
    given,
We come to know how time is spent in Heaven.

I'm not so sure I don't in part agree
With that pert epigram of Pat. Magee,
Who says 'tis better to be drunk and free
Than make the one a slave to two in three.
'Tis after all a question of degree:
I hold a fraction drunk and wholly free
Better than barley-water slavery;
And then, to draw it mild, in every troth, ⎫
We Britons are, no doubt, uncommon loth ⎬
To bid that long farewell to barley-broth! ⎭
Indeed I think I safely may foretell
We *shall* be long in bidding that farewell.
In fact, before two parts their beer will part with,
They'll have to be three parts in beer to start with!

Then if two-thirds, by just assembling here,
Can rob poor Littlehampton of its beer,
We soon may find we're in a precious mess,
For there are divers kinds of drunkenness.
Permissive Bills are simple and come pat—
Permissive first of this, and then of that.

Suppose two-thirds get Church-drunk, they may say,
"Pull down Sam Morley's schism-shop o'er the way!"
Or Chapel-drunk, and filled with that sweet wine
Of Knight, or some less tolerant divine,
May call a meeting and decide in turn
How brightly *someone's* new green stole would burn!—
In short, two-thirds might venture pretty larks;
Great fires, we know, are kindled oft by Sparks.
What if my friend and neighbour, Mr. Town,
With those neat tracts should turn us upside-down?
Old England he might here to-night condemn
To-morrow to be New Caphoozalem!
Nay, more, two-thirds might some fine morn agree
To make you all walk the Broad road with me,
And think, good folk, how monstrous that would be!
Why, you would fairly have to do—guess what—
To live with both eyes open on the spot!

But yet—Heaven help us!—what were Freedom worth?
A drunken England were but hell on earth;
Teetotallers, and such, we fairly warn,
Before they put the hay upon his horn,
John Bull is thick with old John Barleycorn;
But if John Barley make John Bull run mad,
Some remedy must speedily be had.
Public and publicans can't both be winners—
(Which *are* but publicans, and which the sinners?)
Be saved by hook or crook of course we must,
Though toast-and-water lay our bit of dust.
· Stave cask, crack flask, smash measure and spill can—
Landlord and tapster—oust them to a man.

But yet, methinks, the remedy is here—
Not to go "rob a poor man of his beer,"
But do what Foster bids—and he's no fool—
Send little John and Jennie Bull to school.

But I must bid farewell, and hand you over
To "pastures new," where you'll be quite in clover;
So now, fair listeners, hearty thanks I pay
For having let poor Prologue say his say.

SEQUEL TO THE ABOVE.

And so you think my tone was somewhat freer
Than suited men who wisely war with beer?—
Let's have a little further talk, good brother,
For surely you and I can meet each other.

Show me the man who, having once been cursed
By quenching virtue while he kindled thirst,
Now rubs his eyes to find the good of life,
And fights with that old drink-god to the knife:
Who in his own best cause his soul engages—
Wages a war that wars no more with wages:
Who, to cure crooks of many a blundering day
Now bends his stick awhile the other way;
And lest again he sink into the sot
Hates the mad foam that crowns the pewter pot:—
There is a man whose stern resolve shall take
From both my hearty hands the friendly shake;
From me that man all honour shall command—
I'll run and stand before him hat in hand.
Blest be that beverage from the crystal well
Whose every draught can wean his soul from hell;

Blest be the pence, the shilling, and the pound,
Saved as the days and weeks and months go round;
For now in shop, in mart, in street, in field,
He knows what pleasure life's best cup can yield,
And has for beastly bout and revel wild,
Smiles of a well-pleased wife, and merry laugh of child.

And, since the Doctor says some water here
Has in it nastier things by far than beer,
I'll do what Local-Boardsman can t' ensure ⎫
That you shall drink at least your *water* pure, ⎬
And not be pledged to drain the public sewer. ⎭

Me it delights, I own, to lip the foam
That flows from Him who brings my children home;
Or now from cheerful labour to unbend
And clink the glass with some familiar friend;
Or, faint from work, with Timothy to take
A little Sherry " for my stomach's sake."
Nor grudge, kind sir, to me that simple charm
Of dewy cups that never did me harm :
Be frank and give me credit—for 'tis true,
That blesses me which only curses you.

You own that gin has jaded all your frame,
Faded your flower of health, disgraced your name,
And, robbing you at last of self-control,
Has done organic damage to your soul.
Well, such you were, you're not ashamed to show it;
And the best thing about you is—*you know it*.
⎧ But, picked a month ago i' the public way,
⎨ Locked up by 'bobby', fifteen 'bob' to pay—
⎩ Are *you* the man to be our judge to-day?
⎧ Are you, good soul, fresh floundering from your mire,
⎨ —From which Heaven help you is our first desire—
⎩ Are you to Heaven's own function to aspire?

Shall you, so ill-behaved at life's good feast,
Scarce washed, arrange what's good for man or beast?
And sot turned censor,—lest the Town turn sot
Dictate what drinks are wholesome, which are not?
{ Nay, friend, tis well you put yourself to school;
{ But, lest another way you play the fool,
{ Just keep your breath your own weak broth to cool!

It may be *we* shall find, as years go on,
Temptations rise where now, thank God, are none:
For safe it is that you, and I, and all,
Hoping to stand, be heedful lest we fall :—
I—who but lately wrote on Freedom's part, }
And now take up once more my pen and chart }
Lest things said freely hurt one sober heart— }
I may be drawn or driven—which Heaven forbid—
To find no pleasure where I do and did;
I might be dragged to drug with gin my care
Rather than work it off by doing prayer—
Well, if indeed I find it come to that,
O'er my blear eyes I'll slouch my battered hat,
I'll take a leaf from Father Matthew's book,
With horror on the smallest beer I'll look;
We'll try whose parable shall then avail
To rail more bitterly on bitter ale :—
With you, Good Templars, then I'll beg to dwell,
And fill with you my flagon from the well.

If, turning tables, you, good sir, should find
Pure water wash you to a purer mind;
If, when you've found the fumes of malt depart
And leave you certain master of your heart;
If, under your own figtree and your vine,
With Cana's Guest, you're not afraid of wine,
Why then, dear friend, how happy I should be
To see you come and hob-a-nob with me.
Till then, may Heaven help us both along—
You to come right, and me to keep from wrong.

I said just now there's one to whom I'd stand—
Begging to do him service, hat in hand.
But there's another, nobler yet than he—
And many such in our good town there be.
Tis he, who, master of his own desire,
From grace to grace climbs higher yet and higher;
Who, though himself he 'likes his drop o' beer,'
Waives for some weaker sake his proper cheer;
And, lest he make his brother to offend,
Vows tea and ginger-pop till time shall end;
Who has a law to live by, and obeys it,
Nor yet upon his neighbour's conscience lays it:—
To him I'll doff—my hat?—aye do off two—
Yea, six—had I as many as a Jew!

Thus if two-thirds in any given place
Rise to the selfsame eminence of grace,
That were but doing on the social scale
What your one Martyr does with his own ale;
Bending too far for the liberty of State
In hopes one day to make us all walk straight:
Well:—if old England *must* go mad without it,
God's will be done—and let us set about it.

Nov. 14, 1872.

FUNERAL ORATION ON PROFESSOR GEORGE LONG.

ON Thursday, August 14th, 1879, at the Cemetery of Chichester, were interred the mortal remains of Professor George Long. Among the mourners Cambridge was represented by Canon Swainson, the newly appointed Lady Margaret Professor of Divinity.

The ceremony, in compliance with the last request of the departed, was performed in consecrated ground by the Rev. William B. Philpot, M.A., Oxon., Vicar of South Bersted, a neighbour and friend of his latest years. At the close that minister spoke words to the following effect :—

"I know that in England, on such occasions as this, public feeling is mostly silent, and none the less deep for that. Yet it seems natural that something should be said when so notable a man as George Long is carried to his grave. We have given him that general requeim of his Church which we are wont to say over any of our Christian babes; but I have craved leave of his family to say a few words with a more special bearing.

"Born with this most cultured of the centuries, this man became fellow-labourer with some of the greatest and best of its spirits. It were idle to dwell here and now upon those early honours, which, so far as they are merely earthly, vanish away. On this head, suffice it to say that, having taught himself Greek, he was yet elected, with Thomas, afterwards Lord Macaulay, to the highest Greek and Latin scholarship in the University of Cambridge : that he became First Chancellor's

Medallist, and at once received Fellowship at one of the first Colleges in the world, the College of the Holy Trinity. Of work, however, I *may* speak; for work is divine; and into that he plunged forthwith, and worked to the last, and his works remain. America soon called him over to be Professor in Virginia. When called in due course to the English Bar, he so mastered the principles of Law, especially of that Roman Law which forms the basis of civilisation, that the Benchers of the Middle Temple made him their Lecturer on Jurisprudence.

" In these days we have become familiar with fuller modes of popular culture; but let us do all honour to those who first put us upon these more excellent ways. Having lent a busy brain and active hand to those early popular periodicals which used to instruct and interest our boyhood, he became the main Editor of that *Bibliotheca Classica*, to which the best and brightest youths of England owe—and long will owe—their best classical knowledge, and much that they themselves may achieve of fame. The late Emperor Napoleon owned his obligation to Professor Long for the light which he had thrown on the doings and writings of Cæsar.

" But though Roman Law was the subject which he himself felt that he had mastered most, it was in the charms of divine Philosophy that he found his last and best delight. How beautifully has he rendered in our mother-tongue the splendid common sense of the slave Epictetus, and the wisdom of the Emperor Marcus Aurelius. To our lost friend, if ever to any man, his philosophy was practical. In those last months of unusual pain he said he could now understand better than before what the Stoics meant, for that he himself was developing powers of endurance which he had little imagined that he possessed.

"And this leads me, lastly, to say of George Long that which it best becomes a minister of Christ to say here. For have I not learned from him the best lesson which any of us can learn in life? Have I not witnessed how truly he could echo his Saviour's words—'Thy will be done'? Have I not seen how all his philosophy kept flowering into absolute resignation to the disposal of his Father and his God? While he experienced all that dutiful pleasure in raking together and cradling for the use of the modern world those golden grains of the old philosophies, I can testify that he called no man Master upon earth.

"Moved with the childlike simplicity with which I saw him turning in his agony to the bosom of his God, I felt—and I feel— profoundly thankful to witness in these days that unshaken faith with which this wise thinker could, amidst all its mystery, embrace the blessed hope of *immortality*. Under the stress of this emotion, and feeling how truly the words were suited to his state, I once repeated to him those words of Jesus—'Verily, I say unto you, Except ye be converted, and become as little children, ye shall not enter into the kingdom of Heaven.' 'That,' he said in his simple, childlike way, 'that is a good word.'

"How tender was he in spirit! His voice would tremble with grateful emotion, and his eyes would overflow with tears, when he said to me, not once but often, that it was to him an idea wholly new that there could be on earth so great a blessing as a nurse. And these kindly women told me this morning that in all his pains no pain troubled him so much as the trouble which he thought he was giving to them. Well, these I maintain are the last and best blooms of all philosophy which is worthy of the name.

"How many talents did he thus put out to how many exchangers! May we not humbly trust that he now hears the great 'Well done?' Though merit, as we know, lives but from man to man, and not from man to God, yet we cannot doubt that such a spirit as George Long's has gone to that world where merit will not pass, as it does too often in this world, inadequately rewarded.

"We may rely upon it, that he who said nothing without point and did nothing without meaning, meant what he said and meant what he did, when he made it his last wish that a minister of Christ should lay his body to rest with the rites of his country's Church.

"So let us leave his head upon its lap of earth, and his spirit with God who gave it!"

An *arbor vitæ* stands by his grave. Of this the speaker, after his last words, plucked a spray, and cast it among the crosses and wreaths of flowers with which the affection of friends had covered the bright oaken coffin, which bore on its brass plate the name and the dates.

The family afterwards thanked the speaker, and the Lady Margaret Professor of Divinity told him he was glad that he had said what he had said.

PART OF A DISCOURSE ON THE OCCASION OF THE DEATH OF THE EARL OF BEACONSFIELD.

OUR Church and our State, so far as they can be spoken of apart, are happily still so held together—much as we speak of our soul and body being held together—that as Churchmen we are moved when a Statesman dies. Indeed may we not say that he who has been the First Servant of our Crown, has been for that time, aye and also afterwards, a main power, under God and the Queen, in our Church? We your Christian ministers are, as you know, all instituted to our sacred cures by our Bishops; but he who nominates and appoints all our Bishops and Archbishops is that Prime Minister of the day, whom the nation agrees to follow as its leader.—Let me ask, in passing, if you think it wise that the people should allow the Liberation Society to induce them to throw this splendid patronage into the sea? Do you think it likely? Not if they know it; but they do not know what they are being cajoled into doing.—To take an example near home of what I was saying about the intimate relation between Church and State, the Primate who sends many of us clergy into these parts (and the Vicar of Bersted among the rest) was himself sent into his place by the late Premier, —late also in the sad sense that now he is with us no more. I have said enough to show you, should any question it, that when so great a Statesman and so powerful a Churchman passes away, it is not out of place to mark the occasion here.

By stem and birth a Jew, the departed Earl of

Beaconsfield was baptised a Christian, and that Christian Faith he maintained through all the strange vicissitudes and all the Imperial and literary labours of his life. And if you hear what the minister of his own parish says, you will learn that in his private life and in his well-loved village home, where he best was known, this was most to be observed. The Semitic or Hebrew race, the children of the faithful Abraham, whom the Scriptures called "the Friend of God," is as I have often reminded you, the highest joint in the stalk of the Human Plant, and thus in the whole range of visible Being. It was, and could have been, from none other than this stem of Jesse that, in the line of nature and in accordance with the sure word of prophecy, there rose to bloom the Man Christ Jesus, the New Man, the last Type, the ultimate Species of Man, the consummation of God's design for Being, the demand and satisfaction of Divine Humanity—in a word the fulness of the Godhead so far as the Personal Father can ever show Himself forth in Form. It is by the spiritual seeds shed from this ripened Personal Flower that not only the Jewish race, whom He called "His own," but all our races, East and West, North and South, may hope to be restored and renewed and made partakers of His divine nature. I have said this in order to remind you that a genuine Jew—and no families are kept so pure in race as the Abrahamic—is naturally of a type to take the lead. This doubtless is sufficient to account, beyond all individual and incidental causes, for that mysterious and easy power, evinced in so many remarkable instances, in all ranges of gifts, at which men of lower type are wont to gaze up with open mouth, but which they fail to comprehend. You may find this powerfully set forth in "Coningsby" and other works, for Benjamin Disraeli was loyal to his lofty line and not ungrateful to the Providence that made him a Jew. To this original advantage were super-added in his case, in degrees that corresponded thereto, many special talents. These he "put to the exchangers"—with what signal effect we know. Our daily papers with astonishing rapidity, and many of them with admirable fidelity, have put us in possession of the main incidents and doings of his wonderful career.

But what seems to me to be most significant is *the line which he chose for himself*, no less than the steady purpose with which he drew it out to the period of his triumph. I do not mean only his determination, by God's blessing, to be a Prime Minister, but to be a Conservative Prime Minister. I am not speaking in this place and at this time in any party sense, but simply drawing a lesson from a biographical fact. For might it not have been expected that a spirit so rare, so daring, so gifted, and so brilliant, would rather have chosen—especially at the outset and in the heyday and impetuosity of youth—that more tempting region of politics to which naturally belong the ideas of novelty and change? The eccentric, rather than the concentric, would seem to have proffered the larger and more welcome scope for the magical play of such an ardent genius. You would have thought that such a temper would rather have taken a delight to call up spirits from the vasty deep of democratic possibilities, than to ally himself with those elements of the State which active thinkers of shallow perception were wont to stigmatise as tardy and outworn. Flights into the dark would have seemed to offer to a singularly meteoric mind the better background whereon, had his ambition been only selfish, to "stick" more "fiery off." But you observe that, of those two forces—one away from, the other towards the safe centre—which in due equipoise preserve a State in its orbit of duty and progress, this great and wise man selected, not that which would carry a nationality off into blind space, heaven knows whither, but rather that which holds men to the known principles of the venerable and storied Past. He made it his object, not to dissipate but to consolidate, not to pander to, but to refine and educate popular sentiment. He used his insight and employed his gifts, not to the wild uses to which an imagination like his might so readily have lured him, but to help those masses of the people—in whom the more timid and less able of his party commonly supposed that there were to be found merely the elements of discontent and revolution—to feel that to them also belong not only a Future but a Past. Thus he taught them to cherish the institutions which they inherit, and showed them that their true greatness and their hope of orderly power lies in following the lines laid down for us by our fathers—a lesson which, pray God, they may for ever remember.

Was it not a touching sign of this, that there gathered in those last memorable days to enquire for his failing health, not only the Queen, the Prince and the Princess, not only the Court and the potentates and the ambassadors of every foreign land, not only his old rivals and political opponents—with an exemplary generosity which makes us think it a pity that in the arena of politics all men should not be animated when they are all alive and well with sentiments more akin to those which so laudably affect them towards one another when they come to die—not only, I say, were the thresholds of the dying statesman thronged by these; but there came day by day, in their humble attire, with their tools in their hands, countless numbers of his brother workmen of England, proving how truly and how deeply they also felt him to be their friend.

Well, he has left us more lessons to ponder and to practise than I can go through to you here and now. Who knoweth the things of a man, much less of so unusual a man, save the spirit of the man within him? That is a wide and somewhat ungraceful field which is chosen for themselves by such critics as choose to imagine, out of their own morbid consciences, another man's motives of conduct; nor are those likely to arrive at the truest and wisest decisions, who set themselves to canvass conduct of which they themselves have first imagined the motives. It were better to ponder the language of facts. And are there not facts enough in the life of the late Earl of Beaconsfield to furnish the English people with food for reflection, if we dwell only upon his vigour, his perseverance, his even temper, his cheerful heart, and the crown of success to which he was led from first to last by an ambition which upon the whole was a right one?

As to his last days, we have been told everything, to the minutest detail, of the changes of his body and the movements of his mind. The lightning was never impressed to a more kindly task than when it flashed to the extremities of the planet his slightest alterations from head to foot. It would no doubt have been agreeable, and useful in a high degree to the cause of the Master, had custom allowed his church minister to do as we gladly do when our villagers pass away, and to inform, in this case, the listening world of his experience of the "Peace which passeth understanding," or of any triumphant utterances of his hope and faith. But suffice it to say that, interesting as this would have been to millions of his fellow mortals, this is not at present the habit by the death-beds of the great. Let us respect, as far as we can, this curious and half-educated reserve, which will probably give place, as our Saviour comes to be better understood and more freely confessed. So let us thankfully gather that, in so duty-doing and laborious a nature, in a spirit which fought so manfully against the infirmities of age and the trials of illness, all his patience, obedience, resignation and unselfishness—in keeping with what we know of his private life and his pure affections—sprang from no other root but from its natural and best root, I mean from his Faith as a Christian. The character certainly of the men whom he appointed, with a pleasure which he immortalises in one of the few personal confessions in his last book, to the highest work in our Church, shows, if there were nothing else to show it, that he had at heart the advance of the Kingdom of his Saviour, who, having redeemed us all with His most precious bood, is his Eternal Judge and ours.

SOME REFLECTIONS AT ELECTION TIME.

TO men whose earnest convictions override party considerations; whose open eyes desire above all things what light they can gather, break from what side it may; who cherish above all things the right to exercise independently a judgment which they have learned to enlighten rationally—it is a matter of deep interest, not without its side of melancholy amusement, to watch what is passing below in the arena of party politics. This is the more marked when through the length and breadth of the land there is that "post-haste and romage" which accompany preparation for the battle-day.

Through all the woof of our politics does there not run confessedly the warp of farce? When power was avowedly Imperial there was indeed a philosophy about it, and a palpable *rationale*. When it was possible for a bluff Harry, in the people's name and for the people's sake—as they and their wrongs were indubitably and simultaneously represented to him by his kneeling Queen—to give orders there and then to Wolsey to cancel his income-tax, why then Government was at once Imperial and intelligible. No man in his senses can now regard England as represented. We have at present but the rudimentary organs of representation. "Representative Hare" is achieving his end, but is at the pace of the Tortoise. The philosophy, that is the reason of the case, is yet but on paper and between the boards of his masterly book. In fact, were the representation to become numerically equitable before the Prime Minister shall dine again with the Lord Mayor, there would remain a thousand considerations which must still leave hugger-mugger for the order of the day. Could we find in each constituency on the average a hundred minds of even fair political culture, the judgment of these, to whichever side they might incline, would obviously outweigh in value whole polling-booths of others. But who would ever even attempt to strike a balance between so-much clod and so-much culture? The thing never can be done; partly because culture must retain so much that is cloddish, and cloddishness so much that in the original make of man is more solid and valuable than it can be made by any " management " that our present civilisation can top-dress it with. The two terms are incommensurate. No sliding-scale can adjust the voting-capacity with the number of voters. We might as well attempt to reduce a bag of groats to its equivalent in ether.

To say that culture makes up its lack of numbers by its preponderate influence with tongue and pen, must always be on the roughest estimate. Indeed, the estimate would be too rough to be of much practical utility, even if the mental capacity of enfranchised masses were to be schooled and boarded up to the sorry mark of comprehending the mere argumentations of statecraft. Such a result moreover would be the work of many generations, even if the elements of true Political Economy were to be made a necessary element in the training of all our future citizens. Any attempt to introduce this element, which must seem to all to be so reasonable, is open to a jealousy, corresponding to that which prevents the most cherished truths of the highest life from being taught in childhood, from a dread lest any favour be given to this or that *mode* of a Christianity which, in one mode or another, a vast majority of the parents of England piously admit and thankfully would bequeath. So the cultivation of the truths of state-life, with the truths of the spiritual life, are, by this unreason of political combatants, left mainly to chance influences and random formation, in minds wholly unprepared to understand their gist and bearing;—a jealousy which pushes still further off the hour when England can feel that she is in any just sense represented.

But to the independent politician, when he surveys the seething of this *olla podrida* of political feeling, the most quaint, queer, and comic touch of all is *this*—that each party propagates the idea that, whatever our inherited or our habitual politics may be, it is an intrinsic virtue to be *staunch!* The state of politics, and politics in the State, being however such as we have shown—can anything be more transparent than the fact that to propagate and inculcate such an opinion of staunchness to party only betrays a fear lest any gleam of light from the other side should break in upon those parts of it which are dark? Having got the pig in the pen, of course the drivers must take care lest any more lively-minded voter jumps over the hurdle. To tell me that it is a virtue in me to be staunch—what is it but to tell me that I am too ignorant to be trusted, too dull to be judicious, too brutal to be allowed to think?

Every orator, long-winded or short, habitually and very reasonably seeks to convert whole masses of blind and hereditary electors into deserters and turncoats; though that is the very temper which, in addressing his own adherents, he has just reprehended as renegade and stigmatised as vicious. Thus, while everybody struggles to convince everybody else, everybody makes it a political vice to be open to conviction! This, in the words of the poet, puzzles us quite. In fact, of what profit is it that these angels of the State at a certain season, notably before an election, step down to trouble the stagnant pool of politics, if it forms part of their counsels to the halt, maimed and impotent folk, who are waiting for the moving of the water, to lie still where they are? So manifestly is "staunchness" in politics another name for an admission of impotence and a resolution to make no move to mend it.

If every man, whether Liberal or Conservative, —though, we confess, our own politics, while all along in due degree partaking of both, are English before they are either one or the other—if each of us is to hold it to be a virtue to stick like a pin-patch to the side, which in a wholly different state of things, was that of his venerable and conscientious grandmother, why then it is the most prolific families who are to govern us ; fertility is to be the sole rule of progress ; and elections are to be decided by the Registrar-General.

From all of which it is plain that those whom each party brands as turncoats, are, in fact, the men who at each juncture are left to turn the helm of the State, and to determine the changes of Government. Such an honourable and momentous part is that which is always and only chosen by the men of Independence.

There *is* a staunchness indeed which is a public virtue ; the staunchness of loyalty and of adhesion to eternal principle, a staunch preference to such common sense and such cool, unbiassed judgment as we can gain to guide us at all turns and all times, especially at such a crisis as that of an election. This means a love for a fair field with no slavish favour. It means the unmasking of all shows and the maintenance of whatever may seem to us, and is admitted by the best, to be eternally true—unbeguiled by the temptations of any passing interest. While paying all due regard to the past which we thankfully inherit, so as never to see without indignant remonstrance the Constitution of our country, and her best Institutions, bedraggled in the mire at the heels of demagogues, let us remember that we belong to a Mother-Age which is expected to hand down to posterity an England, not worse, but far better than we found her. And herein we gather no little comfort from the reflection, that *as Great Britain has lived to be what she is out of what she was, so, out of what she is there is a still greater hope of what she will be.* But we must all do our several parts to make her and to leave her a yet Greater Britain.

www.ingramcontent.com/pod-product-compliance
Lightning Source LLC
Chambersburg PA
CBHW031850220426
43663CB00006B/570